D1570839

FINAL
FRIDAYS

FINAL
FRIDAYS

ESSAYS, LECTURES, TRIBUTES & OTHER
NONFICTION, 1995–

JOHN BARTH

COUNTERPOINT
BERKELEY

Library of Congress Cataloging-in-Publication Data is available.

ISBN: 978-1-58243-756-9

Cover design by Charles Brock
Interior design by meganjonesdesign.com

Printed in the United States of America

COUNTERPOINT
1919 Fifth Street
Berkeley, CA 94710
www.counterpointpress.com

Distributed by Publishers Group West

10 9 8 7 6 5 4 3 2 1

For Shelly

CONTENTS

II.
TRIBUTES
AND MEMORIA

ACKNOWLEDGMENTS

MOST OF THE pieces here collected have been published separately, in slightly different form. The author gratefully acknowledges the following sources: *The New York Times Magazine* for "Keats's Fears, Etc."; *The Wilson Quarterly* for "The State of the Art"; Dalkey Archive Press for the forewords to *LETTERS* and *Sabbatical*; Anchor Books for "'In the Beginning'"; U. Michigan Press for "Further Questions?"; Story Press for "Incremental Perturbation"; *Context* for "'The Parallels!'"; U. Mississippi Press for "My Faulkner"; U. de León for "¿Cien Años de Qué?"; *Journal of Experimental Fiction* for "The End of the Word as We've Known It?"; Hartford *Courant* for "The Place of 'Place' in Fiction"; Albuquerque *Tribune* for "Liberal Education: The Tragic View"; Einaudi for "The Relevance of Irrelevance: Writing American"; *Poets & Writers Magazine* for "'All Trees Are Oak Trees . . . : Introductions to Literature'"; *Writers Digest Press* for "The Inkstained Thumb"; *Tin City* for "Future Imperfect"; Sarabande Books for "I."; The *Believer* for "'In the Beginning, Once Upon a Time, It Was a Dark and Stormy Night'"; Signet Classics (Penguin Group USA) for "The Morning After"; *The Atlantic* for "Do I Repeat Myself?"; *Granta* for "The End?"; Random House for "Introduction to *Not-Knowing*"; *New York Times Book Review* for "The Passion Artist"; U. Delaware Press for "The Accidental Mentor"; *Review of Contemporary Fiction* for "'As Sinuous and Tough as Ivy'"; *American Scholar* for "The Judge's Jokes."

FINAL
FRIDAYS

FOREWORD:
To the Hyphen, and Beyond

I N 1984, HAVING reached age four-and-fifty and published eight volumes of fiction, I assembled a collection of essays, lectures, and other nonfiction pieces under the title *The Friday Book*.[1] It was so called, its preface explained, because 1) at that time and for years thereafter, my wife and I, teachers both, routinely met our classes from Mondays through Thursdays and then shifted from Baltimore across Chesapeake Bay for long weekends and summer vacations at our Eastern Shore retreat near the old colonial customs port of Chestertown, Maryland; and 2) being prevailingly a novelist by temperament, with the habit of scratching away at some extended prose fiction on those weekday mornings before my afternoon sessions with undergraduate and graduate-student apprentices in the Johns Hopkins Writing Seminars, I found it a refreshing change of pace as well as a logistical convenience not to haul the accumulating notes, drafts, and research materials for whatever novel was in the works back and forth across the Bay, and instead to dedicate those Friday work-mornings to the muse of nonfiction. The practice soon became so established that I found myself inclined to it more often than not on school-vacation Fridays as well, when Logistical Convenience was no longer a factor. A sort of *Shabbat*-respite, it was, from the

1

invention of characters, scenes, and plot-developments for novels, novellas, and short stories: one that, however—unlike the Jewish or Christian Sabbaths—could readily be shifted to a different day if the demands of some fiction-in-progress (or travel commitment, or whatever) took precedence. Contrariwise, I might declare some Tuesday or Saturday to be a "Friday" if some lecture- or essay-draft needed extra attention as its deadline approached.

Thus *The Friday Book*.

Three novels and 520 Fridays later, I had accumulated a second volumesworth of such pieces: *Further Fridays: Essays, Lectures, and Other Nonfiction, 1984–1994*.[2] By then five-and-*sixty*, I retired from 40-plus labor-intensive but enormously rewarding years of teaching, as did my wife from her less lengthy but even more intensive pedagogical career. We continued, however—and, as of this writing, continue to continue—our weekday work-morning routines: me seeing what my primary and secondary muses will come up with next, she serving as my indispensable Primary Editor, General Manager of our household, and what in French resort hotels is called *Le Planning*: the arranger and scheduler-in-chief of our appointments and errands, chores and pleasures.

Et voilà: After not another ten this time, but some fifteen years-worth of further Fridays since *Further Fridays*, having delivered myself of six more volumes of fiction, I find as I approach age 80 that I've accumulated enough nonfiction-pieces for yet a third collection: not *1995–2005*, in tidy sequence with its predecessors, but *1995–*.

AND I PAUSE at that hyphen, which *gives* one pause, like those cemetery headstones bearing a deceased spouse's birth- and death-dates and the bereft survivor's birthdate followed by hyphen and blank marble awaiting gravure. (Remember the awkward situation of some such pre-planners at the turn of the millennium, who had engraved their headstones *1910–19__*, say, and finding themselves still breathing air and taking nourishment in c.e. 2000, were obliged to have their grave-markers replaced or re-engraved? Given the ever-increasing longevity of dwellers in our planet's better-off precincts, best to end with the hyphen, even in a new century.) Just as my waiting grave's marker, if there were one, would read *1930–* , I'm dating these Friday-pieces *1995–* ; and I call their assemblage *Final Fridays* on the same actuarial grounds that lead me to regard my eighties as my Final Decade.

"You should live so long!" some friend or family member might well tease. Given my thus-far-uncommonly-good health, and barring accident or general catastrophe, I just might, guys[3]—and even longer, though I've no desire to unless this book's dedicatee is with me and we're still enjoying life more than not. A fair-fortuned life it's been: If we know some more-blessed ones, we know ever so many less. Among its blessings, in my case, has been the pleasure of imagining, languaging, and publishing all those stories and essays—the latter mainly, though by no means exclusively, on the reading and writing of fiction. The ones in *The Friday Book* and *Further Fridays* were ordered chronologically by date of first publication; in the present volume they're ordered likewise, but within two groups: pieces about "Reading, Writing, and the State of the Art," and then "Tributes and Memoria" to sundry literary comrades, colleagues, and other navigation stars.

I CONCLUDE THIS Foreword on the final Friday of the fifth month of the ninth year (or tenth, depending on one's counting-system) of the 21st century of the Common Era, having published yet another story-book[4] and preparing to review and revise these accumulated nonfiction pieces over the next many "Fridays"—some of them Mondays, Tuesdays, Wednesdays, Thursdays, perhaps even the odd Saturday or Sunday—while awaiting re-inspiration[5] by my Muse-in-Chief. I do not know now in what year these *Final Fridays* will appear in print ("The world should last so long!" I hear again that Yiddish-inflected Voice Off, probably the Muse's, simultaneously hoping, half-doubting, teasing, and counter-*verhexing*). Nor do I promise that there'll be no further Friday-pieces thereafter from this pen: At my age and stage, one presumes neither way. But in the not-unimaginable event that the world, my muse, and I all manage to persist, I intend to leave open in this collection's subtitle that space beyond the hyphen.

—LANGFORD CREEK, MARYLAND: FRIDAY, MAY 29, 2009

I.
ON READING,
WRITING, AND
THE STATE
OF THE ART

Keats's Fears, Etc.

An extended reflection on Getting Older, first published in *The New York Times Magazine* for a 1997 issue on "The Age Boom," when its author was a mere and still-frisky 67-year old. . . .

AMBIVALENT RITE OF authorial passage! Just the day before yesterday, one was gratified to be listed among the Literary Upstarts to Keep an Eye On; today one's sentiments are solicited under the aspect of Storyteller Emeritus, Still-Functioning Codger Novelist, Superannuated Scheherazade.

Well, it happens. In the foreshortened busy interval between that Day Before Yesterday and this Today, one's fortune has been neither to autodestruct nor to be by the world destroyed; to sire and raise a family, among other adventures; and with the muse's connivance to perpetrate some 5,000 pages worth of fiction[1]—this while one's life (which is *not* a story) exfoliated in accordance with its own, imperfectly comprehended principles. Like one's biological children, those book-bound pages, once launched and independent, have made their way as chance and their merits would have it: praised here, trashed there, attended and ignored, but somehow (knock on wood) surviving, persisting, even modestly thriving unto the present hour, their expiration-dates bidding fitly to extend beyond that of their author.

"What a long, strange road it's been!" used to exclaim the Grateful Dead's (late) Jerry Garcia. Even for the least programmatically colorful of us, quite so. I could tell you a story. . . .

But one's calling is invention, not confession, and the subject in hand is neither Yesterday nor the Day Before, but Tomorrow, as seen from the presumable vantage-point of a fairly high-mileage Today.

Tomorrow and tomorrow: On average and on paper, one has more of those in prospect these days than folks did formerly. At age 67, Yours Truly is on the one hand 95 percent through the "biblical" threescore-and-ten, while only 56 percent through the 120-year span alloted us mortals in Genesis 6:3 and reneged on ever since, but latterly affirmed by some gerontologists to be the inherent design-life of *Homo sapiens sapiens*. More probably—after jiggering my American generation's actuarial averages upward for my skin color, downward for my gender, and upward thrice again for (knock on wood) my rude good health, the longevity of my parents, and a blessed remarriage—I can with luck anticipate perhaps 20 more years of breathing air, with most of my faculties more or less though ever less and less intact through much of that period, and always allowing for the circumstance that the world might end (one's own world, anyhow) before this sentence does, or the one to follow.

20 years more: That many? That few? One feels a proper twinge of that *echt*-20th-century emotion, Survivor's Guilt: Donald Barthelme, Italo Calvino, Raymond Carver—splendid writers cut off in the full fruition of their gifts at a younger age than one's present, their voices stilled for keeps while one's own yarns on. One recalls John Keats's famous fears (well justified, in the event) that he might cease to be before his pen had gleaned his teeming brain; likewise the writerly counterfears (let's not name names) that one might go

on being and being and being *after* one's pen, et cetera, silenced not by death or devastation but by mere bare-cupboardhood. One takes courage from the exemplary counter-instances, e.g., of Arthur Miller, just past 80 and evidently going strong[2]; of even-older-at-the-time Thomas Mann, bringing off as his final novel the high-spirited elaboration of his early short story *Felix Krull*—a stunt about which I could write a whole praising page but won't, here; of even-older-yet Sophocles, closing out at age 90 his Theban trilogy with the magnificent *Oedipus at Colonus*.

And having thus twinged, thus recalled, and thus taken courage, one draws yet another deep bonus breath—refills one's trusty fountain pen, boots up one's trusty word processor, whatever—and like the afore-invoked Scheherazade (perhaps for not-dissimilar reasons) deftly segues into the one about . . .

Et cetera.

The State of the Art

When this essay was first-drafted back in 1994 (too late for inclusion in the *Further Fridays* collection), subsequently delivered at the Woodrow Wilson Center in Washington, D.C., as part of their lecture series "Novelists on Literature," and first published in the *Wilson Quarterly*,[1] "electronic literature"—fiction to be read and in many cases interacted with on a computer—was still a novelty. 15 years later, as I pen this head-note, it remains, if no longer a novelty, still an oddity, enjoyed by a comparitively small audience. My interest in it back then was mainly dutiful: a checking out of the edges of my medium's envelope for my fiction-writing coachees' benefit and my possible own: I even agreed to be listed on the advisory board of the newly-formed Electronic Literature Organization (ELO), just to stay abreast of things. Some of its members' productions I've found impressive, literarily as well as technically. I remain, however, a bookperson, for whom the computer is a workshop-tool: useful indeed for revising, editing, and printing out my fountain-penned first drafts, for sending and receiving e-mail, and occasionally for Googling some item on the Web (my wife, the house WebMeister, uses its vast resources for everything from trip-planning to recipe-checking), but not a source of sedentary entertainment or aesthetic engagement. For those, in our leisure hours, we turn to music (mostly on CDs, although I still enjoy playing Renaissance and Baroque recorder-duets now that my jazz-drumming decades are behind me), to a nightcap hour of television (mostly movies on DVD rather than network or cable shows)—and above all to the printed, usually book-bound, page, long may it endure: not "virtual reality," but deliciously virtual virtuality (see below).

T HE ART WHOSE state I mean to review here is that of the novel in particular; the art more generally of printed fiction, especially in the USA; and the art most generally of fictional narrative in whatever medium—again, especially in this country, where certain aspects of the scene are changing more rapidly, for better or worse, than they seem to me to be changing elsewhere.

By way of beginning, I submit the following gleanings from my recent and by no means systematic reading on the subject. Readers unfamiliar with some of the names I'm about to drop should not feel particularly left out; I'm unfamiliar with many of them too, and once I've dropped them, I intend to drop them.

"We are [in] . . . the late age of print," declares the hypertextualist Michael Joyce in the *American Book Review*, "a transitional time when the book as we know it gives way to writing the mind in lightforms." (By "lightforms" Mr. Joyce means reading and writing on computer screens; more on "hypertext" presently.)

A writer named Mark Amerika (too good to be true), again in the *American Book Review*, declares, "The zine scene is alive and well. . . . Offhand, I can think of a dozen zines that are doing wonderful stuff: *Further State(s) of the Art, Puck, Sensitive Skin, Red Tape, Taproot Reviews, Dissonance, Boing Boing, Frighten the Horses, Central Park, Nobodaddies, Science Fiction Eye, MAXIMUMROCKNROLL*, just to name the first dozen that come to my mind." (Those are not the first dozen that come to *my* mind, but let that go.) And one Mr. Lance Olsen, likewise in the *ABR*, in an essay entitled "Death-metal Technomutant Morphing," declares, "Me, I'm going down reading Mark Leyner and Jean Baudrillard simultaneously, a copy of *Wired* in my lap, hypertext by Carolyn Guyer on the computer screen, television turned to MTV, windows wide open, . . . my fire-retardant corrosion-resistant nickel-base alloy robo-enhanced methyl isocyanate flamethrower exploding, while I listen to Sonic Youth's *Dirty* turned up real, REAL loud."

I confess to being addicted to such catalogues of Where It's At: catalogues with which the *American Book Review* particularly abounds. Here is another from the same lively source, by one Martin Sheter, in an essay called "Writing As Incorrectness":

> *And then there's what I call the "third rail": the remarkable*
> *. . . resurgence of all sorts of creativity going on in the nineties, right under the nose of all these [American academics]—*
> *people ranging the spectrum from Hakim Bey, Fact-Sheet*
> *5, R U Sirius, ACT-UP graphicists, feminist collaborators,*
> *black and Native American oralists, and shock performance*
> *theoreticians, all the way to . . . MTV's "Liquid Television,"*
> *the San Francisco "transgressive" school, Brown-University-*
> *sponsored "unspeakable practices," various cyberpunk and*
> *slipstream fictionalists . . . (no doubt I've left out quite a*
> *bit here).*

Perhaps he has; but the aforecited essay by Mr. Mark Amerika goes far to fill in any gaps in Mr. Sheter's checklist of the contemporary Action. I quote again from Mr. Amerika:

all kinds of viral shit festering there, not the least of which
would include dissident comix, wigged out zines, electronic
journals, quick-time hypermedia CD-ROMs, a voluminous
melange of hardcore industrial grunge post-everything mu-
sic, the Internet, surfpunk technical journals, interactive
cable TV, . . . hypertext novels, . . . single-user films, gen-
derfuck performance art spectacles . . . teenage mutant ninja
gangsters, C-Span . . . feminist deconstruction . . . the list
goes on.

And on and on and on: avant-pop, splatterpunk, cybersex—you
name it, if you can, or make it up if you can't. Indeed, it's tempting
to imagine that the pugnacious contributors to the *ABR* invent these
wonderful catalogues as they go along; but I am assured by my more
with-it informants—if scarcely reassured—that the items, however
ephemeral, are for real.

If among the intentions of such in-your-face lists is to make us
dinosaurs from "the late age of print" feel our dinosaurity, then they
quite succeed. I confess to being out of the loop of contemporary
American letters in their most aggressively avant-pop aspect. I cannot sing along with the "voluminous melange of hardcore industrial
grunge post-everythings"; I cannot line-dance with the cybersexual
splatterpunk avant-poppers. And while I do not revel in my end-
of-the-century troglodytehood, I'm inclined to shrug my shoulders
at it. I scan the *American Book Review* with considerable interest
and amusement, likewise some of those "wigged-out zines" when
my former students publish in them and kindly send me copies; I
maintain a benevolent curiosity about hypertext (of which more presently) out of my long-standing interest in the nonlinear aspects of life

and of literature. But the American perodicals that I actually subscribe to and thoroughly *read* are the *New York Review of Books*,
Harper's, the *Sciences* (the journal[2] of the New York Academy of
Sciences, which my wife and I enjoy as much for its art as for its
articles), and *Scientific American*—the latter two partly as a source
of fictive metaphors. Also *Sail* magazine, but never mind that, and
Modern Maturity, the journal of the American Association of Retired
Persons, which subscribes to me more than I to it; I look through it,
but I don't inhale. The current American fiction that I most relished
while preparing these remarks happens to have been John Updike's
latest collection of short stories, *The Afterlife*, and William H. Gass's
monumental novel *The Tunnel*—two comparably masterful though
radically different works of literary art from "the late age of print."
They make me pleased to have lived before the transition from "the
book as we know it" to the "writing [of] the mind in lightforms" is
complete.

Let me say at once, however, that I do not doubt the reality of
that transition. Granted that a few writers still compose on the typewriter, even on *manual* typewriters: Saul Bellow says that he uses
two, one for fiction and the other for nonfiction; my Johns Hopkins
colleague Stephen Dixon worries that his prolific fiction-writing career will crash when he can no longer find anybody to service his
brace of Hermes manual portables, or to supply ribbons for them.
A very few of us, believe it or not, still prefer to draw out our first-
draft sentences the even older-fashioned way, with fountain pen on
paper.[3] Despite these exceptions, however, most of my comrades in
arms and all of my recent students compose their fiction on word
processors, and of the few of us who don't, most (myself included)
depend absolutely on our computers for editing and revision, whether

we do that on hard-copy print-outs or directly onscreen.[4] Our publishers now routinely expect the finished product on disk or e-mail attachment as well as on paper, and the hottest, thorniest issue these days in the *Authors Guild Bulletin* (another "zine" that subscribes to me) is the protection of its members' electronic rights in our book and magazine contracts, as more and more of our originally printed publication goes online one way or another down the road, and our control of copyright tends to evaporate in cyberspace. Although I might disagree with Mr. Michael Joyce about the implications of his proposition, I quite concur with the proposition itself: that we are indeed in "the late age of print," not only as a means of producing and publishing literature, but, importantly, as a means of *reading* it. One New York playwright recently described all of us authors-for-print as "roadkill on the information superhighway." He may be right.

To afford some perspective on this "transitional time," I want to back up a bit now: first just a few years back, then a few decades back, if not farther yet, always keeping a navigator's eye on where we are and where we seem to be going, literature-wise, as we briefly retrace where we've been (this is the *Sail* magazine approach to navigating the State of the Art).

A MERE 15 years ago, in 1981, we received at the Johns Hopkins Writing Seminars our very first word-processored manuscript in an application to our graduate program in fiction-writing. Although the piece itself was unremarkable, I was impressed by its virtually published look; it was, in fact, an early specimen of "desktop publishing." Remembering how instructively chastened I myself had been in the early 1950s to see my own apprentice efforts first set in official, impersonal print in a student magazine—which seemed to me to make strikingly manifest both their small strengths and their large shortcomings—I imagined that this newfangled mode of manuscript-production might afford our apprentice writers some measure of the critical detachment that print confers. The farther their words were removed from longhand, I reasoned, and even from homely old-fashioned typescript, the more objectively the apprentice authors would be able to assess them.

And so I showed the handsome specimen to our visiting fiction coach that year (Leonard Michaels) and expressed my pedagogical sentiments: wave of the future, et cetera. Michaels took one suspicious look at the justified right-hand margins, the crisp print, and handsome typefaces, and said, "This is terrible! They're going to think the stuff is finished, and it only *looks* that way!"

He was right, of course. Indeed, I came to repeat this anecdote annually to each new crop of my graduate-student apprentices by way of cautioning them *against* fancy presentations of what is, after all, still work in process. No desktop publishing, please, I advise them: Just give us and your future editors tidy, well-copyedited pages, remarkable only for their author's brilliance, and let's leave publishing to the publishers.

That was in 1981. Thirteen years later, in 1994, we had our first ambassador from the vertiginous realm of Hypertext, a.k.a. "e-fiction": interactive computer-fiction in which the "author" designs a matrix of "lexias" through which the "reader" navigates with clicks of the mouse or the keyboard, perhaps entering or exiting the narrative at any of many available doors and steering the plot along any of many optional way points.

The seminal work on the medium itself (*Hypertext*, authored by George Landow of Brown University, but published by our Johns

Hopkins Press in 1992) declares hypertext to be the third great technological advance in the art of writing, after the development of the alphabet and the invention of movable type. Some curmudgeons have grumbled that the whole thing is more hype than text, but my comrade Robert Coover, also at Brown, has become so involved in the medium that his official academic title these days is Professor of Electronic Fiction. In 1993, Coover published two landmark frontpage essays on the subject in the *New York Times Book Review*, one called, provocatively, "The End of Books?" (it's important to hear that question mark at the end of his title), and the other called "Hypertext: Novels for the Computer."

I INVITE ANY innocents still unfamiliar with hypertext to imagine a "text" (the word is already in quotes, the signal or symptom of virtuality), every word of which—at least many a key word of which—is a window or point of entry into a network of associated "texts" (or graphics, music, statistics, spoken language, whatever a computer can reproduce), these several networks themselves interconnected and infinitely modifiable—or *virtually* infinitely so—by "readers" who can enter the "story" at any point, trace any of a zillion paths through its associated networks, perhaps add or subtract material and modify the linkages as they please, and then exit at any point, in the process having been virtual co-authors or co-editors as well as "readers" of their virtual text. That's hypertext.

The quick brown fox jumps over the lazy dog. Imagine a "loaded" display of that innocent proposition on your computer screen, such that "clicking" on any item in it opens a window menu of associations available for exploring, from the relative nimbleness of temperate-zone quadrupeds, through the history of fox hunting and its representation in painting, music, and literature, to soundtracks of hounds in full cry (with or without expert commentary) and disquisitions on animal rights—and every one of those associated "lexias" similarly loaded, another ring of keys with which one may open yet further doors, and on and on and on—no two routes through the maze ever likely to be the same, and every venturer thereinto not only a Theseus but a Daedalus, remodeling the labyrinth at will en route through it. That's hypertext, more or less, and as a potential medium of art it both intrigues and disquiets me. If the prophets of the *American Book Review*, not to mention the *New York Times Book Review*, are correct, as no doubt they are, we'll be hearing more and more about it as our weary century expires (it has already made the cover of *Time*). Indeed, a recent number of the *Authors Guild Bulletin* (Winter 1995), along with its now-standard cautionary piece on "Fair Use in the Electronic Age," included its first-ever mention of hypertextual narrative: "Electronic Fiction," by Sarah Smith (subtitled "The State of the Art"). An articulate practitioner of and apologist for her medium, Smith quotes a fellow hypertextualist's decription of their art as "designing golf courses with holes that can be played in any order by players with greater or lesser degrees of skill and commitment." I like that metaphor—although I modestly submit that "ski slopes" would be an even better one, since, unlike golf courses, they have no prearranged sequence to be ignored or altered.

Back to my story. We welcomed our young graduate-student pioneer, Ho Lin—who had already worked with Coover and Landow in Brown University's vigorous hypertext program—into our Hopkins Seminars, as did our university library into the organizing of its burgeoning CD-ROM operation: a genial and knowledgeable harbinger, I reckoned, of things inevitably to come. Fortunately for us, who had neither equipment nor expertise nor, for that matter, sufficient departmental enthusiasm to deal with this novel medium—it turned out that Mr. Lin's Hopkins project was a straightforward, engaging, traditionally linear print-novel ("p-fiction," I guess we have to call it now) about young Chinese-Americans dreaming of Hong Kong and heisting computer chips to get there. At my urging, however, he obligingly arranged "e-fiction" demonstrations for us at the university's computing facility, and we did a certain amount of disk-and-software swapping.

Now, I'm a book-person myself, but I try to keep an open mind and a mindful eye on the parameters of the medium. I had already read Coover, Landow, and others on the subject of hypertext; if I were 25 instead of 65-plus, I daresay that I would be vigorously exploring its possibilities for my fictive purposes. I rather expected our roomful of talented Hopkins apprentices—who, after all, grew up with desktop computers—to take to hypertext fiction like grade-schoolers to Nintendo. Has it not been the job, after all, of each new artistic generation since the advent of Romanticism to render its senior mentors gently obsolete (what one sociologist has called "filiarchy," the rule of the young over their elders, and what others might call "parricide")? To my surprise, however, I found that I was doing the prodding—"Better expose yourselves to the virus, if only to build up your antibodies," et cetera—and that they, for the most part, were taking the skeptical Leonard Michaels role. Reading and writing literature in the normal way, most of them felt, is interactivity enough; when we're being writers, we'll plot the course for you; when we're being readers, leave us alone and steer the boat yourself. My feelings exactly—more or less exactly, anyhow—but I confess that it was a touch dismaying to hear them voiced by young apprentices.

In any case, their sentiments are sound, I believe, if unadventurous. Note that their reservations were not to the tiresome business (as many of us find it) of reading for pleasure off a video display terminal rather than curled in a comfortable chair; we agreed that by this century's turn, the hardware for hypertexts will likely be as portable and maybe even no harder on the eyes than that jim-dandy item of low-energy, high-density information technology, the printed book. Nor had they anything against hypertext as a high-tech mode of reference browsing. What they objected to, and in this I'm much more with them than not, was mucking around with the traditional job-descriptions of Author and Reader. "You don't like the restaurant? Then dine elsewhere—but stay out of my kitchen while I'm cooking for you, please, and I'll return the favor." (You ought, however, to *try* the hypertextual broccoli before making up your mind.)

I mention these two instances, from fifteen and two years ago, as straws in the potentially much bigger wind of Electronic Virtual Reality, which I won't attempt to consider more than briefly here. My point is that although a few of us still prefer to compose our sentences in longhand before turning them into pixels on a computer monitor en route to their returning into print on a page, and a few more prefer still to eschew computers altogether, the super-convenient word-processor has become, in only a dozen-plus years, the production mode of choice for most writers of most kinds of writing, whether or not it affects the quality of the product. Interactive computer fiction (especially as it comes to include whole repertories of graphic, cinematic, and auditory effects) is too fascinating not to become yet another competitor for audience attention, but one doubts that it will have nearly the market-share effect on "straight" fiction-reading that movies and television—and, more recently, surfing the Internet—have had already. Those of us who still read literature for pleasure at all (no more than 10 percent of the adult U.S. population, says the *New York Times*) are likely to go on preferring, most of the time, the customary division of labor between Teller and Told. The Authors Guild's justified concern with the protection of authorial electronic rights down the Infobahn is more commercial than aesthetic: a concern more about copyright than about readership. E-fiction versus p-fiction is apples versus oranges, really. In the case of either of those versus Electronic Virtual Reality, however, the difference is so enormous as to be a matter not of apples and oranges but rather of lotuses and rhinoceri, or perhaps hawks and handsaws.

MORE PRECISELY, IT is the difference between virtual reality, which deals in *real virtualities*, and the purely virtual virtuality of literary texts, especially printed texts. The sights and sounds and feels of EVR, from pilot-training flight simulators to the wraparound fantasy-worlds of high-tech amusement parks, are literal physical sensations generated by artificial stimuli. The printed page, on the other hand—except for illustrated texts and things like scratch-and-sniff kiddie books—is strictly anesthetic, however incidentally appealing to the eye and hand may be its typeface, paper stock, and binding. Even in the greatest, most spirit-stirring novels there are no literal sights/sounds/feels/tastes/smells, only their names, artfully invoked in silent language. The virtual worlds of literature are unencumbered by literality. It is both their great limitation and their indispensable virtue that their virtuality is virtual; that they exist not in our nerve-endings but in the pure hyperspace of our imaginations.

I will make my way back shortly to that distinction between the hyperspace of hypertext (not to mention the cyberspace of virtual reality) and the "meditative space" afforded by the silent, privileged transactions of the human mind and spirit with the fixed, anesthetic medium of the printed page. Before I do, though, I want to back off again, this time by 30 years or so, to explain why the electronic-fiction and virtual-reality phenomena give me a strong but rather comforting sense of déjà vu. In the late 1960s I was living in Buffalo, New York, at the very edge of our troubled republic, and teaching at the state university there while the USA appeared to be more or less auto-destructing. I vividly recall flying cross-country on a lecture tour in 1968, just after Dr. Martin Luther King's assassination, and seeing the smoke of protest rise from one burning American inner city after another, sea to smoke-obscured sea, as in a World War II newsreel; frequently the campuses that I visited, like the one that I came home to, were occupied either by Vietnam-war-protesting students and faculty members or by tear-gas-firing riot police and National Guardsmen. I quite remember one of my graduate students, late in the war—when the exasperated riot police moved in on us for the how-manyeth time with their gas grenades—sniffing the campus air calmly and observing, like a wine-connoisseur, "Pepper-gas, Berkeley, '66 or '67." All about the city, between campus strikes and trashings, pop art was popping, happenings were happening, street theater and new electronic music were ubiquitous, young American men were fleeing across the Peace Bridge to seek refuge in Canada from the draft—and back across the polluted Niagara River from Toronto came the siren-song of Professor Marshall MacLuhan, author of *The Gutenberg Galaxy*, that the medium is the message, and that we "print-oriented bastards" had better *get* the message that the electronic global village had rendered our hopelessly linear medium obsolete.

It was in this apocalyptic, Death-of-the-Novel, death-of-the-print-medium ambience that in 1968 I published a book called *Lost in the Funhouse: Fiction for Print, Tape, Live Voice*. Its title says it all, or enough anyhow for my purpose in these pages. My own attitude was that, whether or not the world ends, if enough thoughtful, intelligent people *suspect* that it's ending, then that shared apprehension becomes a significant cultural-historical datum, which an artist in any medium, even poor old print, might well take note of and even turn to good account. The threat to p-fiction back then was not hypertext and EVR; we didn't yet even have desktop personal computers. It was movies and television: the movies increasingly since the end of WWI, television increasingly since the end of WWII. The "Death of the Novel" was one of the classical riffs of Modernism, that regnant aesthetic of the first half of the 20th century. The semioticist Robert Scholes quotes a mid-1960s colleague's description of the novel as "a moderately interesting historical phenomenon, of no present importance," and I remember my Buffalo colleague Leslie Fiedler's[5] predicting at about the same time that if there's any future for narrative at all, it's up there on the big screen, not down here on the page (this was before VCRs and DVDs, when people still went out to the movies). Indeed, one of Fiedler's later books is titled *What Was Literature?*—the same Modernist riff, rescored for full orchestra.

But I also remember a little book from that period by Ron Sukenick, founding editor of the *American Book Review*, teasingly titled *The Death of the Novel and Other Stories*; and I myself used to like to say that inasmuch as I hadn't been born in time to write the *first* novel, maybe it would be fun to write the last one. In short, one didn't have to be a weatherman back then to see which way the wind was blowing.

The point I want to make is that a number of the talented graduate-student apprentice writers in my workshop back in those years seriously wondered whether to abandon the sinking ship of print while they could and get themselves a movie camera instead. It seemed to them quixotic, at best, to be apprentices in a very possibly moribund medium, and although I reminded them that *Quixote* is just about where we came in, that 1968 workshop turned itself into a seminar on Alternatives to the Line and the Page. The room was alive with pop-up fictions, three-dimensional fictions done on Buckminster Fuller polyhedrons, serial fictions on scraps of paper like fortune-cookie fortunes, shaken up in a cereal box (appropriately), poured out into a cereal bowl, and read serially as the members of the group passed the bowl.[6] At one defining moment that year, we received a solicitation from a professional avant-garde anthologist (Richard Kostelanetz) who was assembling a collection to be called *Untried Forms in Fiction*, and who was offering to pay his contributors by the page. My young pioneers were appalled: "By the *page*? Where has this guy *been*?"

BUT—AND HERE IS the moral of this tale—a number of us, myself included, learned from all this experimentation two lessons that I regard as equally important. The first was that the medium of print is, indeed, almost inescapably linear—*this* word and then *this* and then *this*; this line after that, this page after the one before it (what Sven Birkerts has called "the missionary position of reading")—whereas a very great deal of our experience of life is decidedly *not* linear: We think and perceive and intuit in buzzes and flashes and gestalts; we act in a context of vertiginous simultaneity; we see and hear and smell and touch and taste often in combination, whereas print, as

I've mentioned, is a peculiarly *anesthetic* medium of art, the only one
I know of that (except for such aforementioned incidental pleasures
as handsome typefaces and bindings) appeals directly to none of the
physical senses. Linearity and anestheticity: two tremendous limitations indeed of the medium of print.

However—Lesson Two—what a few of us, at least, came to appreciate is that to be linear is not necessarily to be obsolete, much
less wicked. We live and think and perceive and act in time, and time
implies sequence, and sequence is what gives rise to narrative. *This*
happened and then *that* and then *that*, and if we want to recount
what happened, to share it with others and even with ourselves, we
have to proceed in narrative sequence: the story of our day, the stories
of our lives. Those stories are linear, even when their subject is often
not; they remain linear even when the order of narration is dischro-
nological. And for those aspects of our experience of life that happen
to be of a linear character, the medium of print may be a uniquely
appropriate vehicle of rendition.

IN SHORT, THERE are lots of things you can do with a camera that
you can't do on the printed page, but there are also important things
that you can do on the printed page that can't be done with a camera.
Most important among these, obviously, is the rendering of *sensibility*, as apart from sensation itself. Fiction can't give us the sights,
sounds, feels, and smells themselves—language itself cannot, except
for occasional onomatopoeic suggestion—but fiction is uniquely
privileged to tell us what things look/taste/sound/feel/smell *like*, to
particular human sensibilities in particular situations. Aristotle declares that the subject of literature is "the human experience of life,
its happiness and its misery." I would add that the true subject of

printed lit is the human *experiencing* of that experience: not sensation, but the *registering* of sensation in language; the typically interior, unphotographable universe of perceiving, feeling, and reflecting,
as well as the visible manifestations of those feelings and perceptions.
(Compare the sensuousness of Diane Ackerman's *Natural History
of the Senses* [the book] with the surprising aridity of its PBS-TV
version.)

Forget for a moment television, movies, stage plays, and virtual-
reality devices. Why can hypertext narrative, for example, not do all
that I've just been praising print for doing, since its medium remains
(mainly) "written" words? Well, it can, to some extent, and the proponents of electronic fiction incline to declare further that their medium "sets us free from the domination of reader by writer, from the
traditional concepts of beginning and middle and end, and of fixed,
permanent texts"—from, in Coover's own words, "the tyranny of
the line," not to mention the traditional concepts of copyright versus public domain. But what's typically missing from e-fiction, precisely, are good old linearity and those traditional job-descriptions of
Author and Reader, which at least some of us find to be not oppres-
sive or tyrannical at all. On the contrary.[7]

It is in this connection that the aforementioned critic Sven
Birkerts (in *The Gutenberg Elegies*, his lament for the passing of
the Age of Print) speaks of "meditative space." Interactivity can be
fun; improvisation and collaboration can be fun; freedom is jolly.
But there are dominations that one may freely enjoy without being
at all masochistic, and among those, for many of us, is the willing,
provisional, and temporary surrender of our noisy little egos to great
artistry: a surrender which, so far from diminishing, quite enlarges
us. As my Hopkins coachees pointed out, reading a splendid writer,

or even just a very entertaining writer, is not a particularly passive business. An accomplished artist is giving us his or her best shots, in what she or he regards as their most effective sequence—of words, of actions, of foreshadowings and plot-twists and insights and carefully prepared dramatic moments. It's up to us to respond to those best shots with our minds and hearts and spirits and our accumulated experience of life and of art—and that's interaction aplenty, for some of us, without our presuming to grab the steering wheel and diddle the driver's itinerary. The kind of reading I've just described requires not only meditative space but, as Birkerts observes, a sense that the text before us is not a provisional *version*, up for grabs, the way texts in the cyberspace of a computer memory always are, but rather the author's very best: what he or she is ready to be judged by for keeps.

THE UBIQUITOUS APOCALYPTICISM of the High Sixties turns out to have marked, in the aesthetic sphere, the wind-up not of printed literature or even of the novel, quite, but of High Modernism, for better or worse, as a "cultural dominant." Here in America, the writers who perhaps commanded the most critical respect back then were the likes of Saul Bellow, Norman Mailer, William Styron, and young John Updike; to some of us literary deckhands, however, those indisputably talented writers seemed of less impressive stature than the preceding generation of Faulkner, Fitzgerald, Hemingway, and Gertrude Stein—not to mention Joyce, Kafka, Mann, and Proust. My own living navigation stars and ship's officers in those days were Samuel Beckett, Jorge Luis Borges, and Vladimir Nabokov, joined presently by Italo Calvino and Gabriel García Márquez. Although the vessel didn't have a name yet—Ihab Hassan's *Dismemberment*

of Orpheus: Toward a Postmodern Aesthetic wasn't published until
the early 1970s—a number of us felt that we were working something out that would honor the high artistic standards and radical
innovations of our great Modernist predecessors while maintaining
a degree of skepticism and modest irony with respect to their heroic
ambition. (What self-respecting Postmodernist would presume, like
Joyce's Stephen Dedalus, to "forge in the smithy of [his] soul the un-
created conscience of [his] race"?). If they were the century's Homers
and Virgils, we would endeavor to be its Catulluses and Ovids and
Petroniuses—an honorable aspiration.

All of that was, by now, a generation ago. Given that the icono-
clastic, filiocratic spirit of 19th-century Romanticism has persisted
right through our own time, it was to be expected that the second
generation of (lower-case) postmodern culture would look to distance itself from its immediate forebears; that impulse is as American
as . . . Immanuel Kant and Friedrich von Schlegel? I don't know
how much and how consciously it has impelled younger writers in
the ever-more-beleaguered medium of American trade p-fiction; I
do suspect it to be among the impulses behind the phenomenon of
e-fiction.

And that is quite all right: "Let a thousand flowers blossom,"
et cetera. If the edifice of printed lit is tottering, long may it totter,
like the Pisan campanile, and become all the more appealing in its
totterment. If we are in the late-Cretaceous era of print, and if e-
fiction turns out to be the asteroid whose impact spells our doom
"in lightforms" (which I doubt), let us take comfort in the reflection
that the great dinosaurs not only hung in there for another million
years or two before realizing that their time was up, but in a few
instances attained their most ultrasaurian proportions even as those

newly evolving mammalian critters scampered between their tremendous feet—and occasionally got squashed flat. It was the same with
cathedrals and square-riggers and zeppelins and ocean liners. *Que
será será*, but not always in a hurry.

Someone might assert that the sentiments I've expressed here are
an example of what the aforementioned e-fictionist Michael Joyce has
wittily called "modality envy." So be it, if so it be, although I believe
"modality curiosity" to be a more accurate characterization: Mine is
the ongoing curiosity of a Postmodern Romantic Formalist about the
state of the art, as well as about the state of such new and, after all,
essentially different arts as I believe e-fiction to be—in case there's
something there that a writer like myself might make use of in my
venerable medium.

THIS JUST IN from *Scientific American*, one of those "wigged-out
zines" to which I subscribe: It appears that we late-Cretaceous p-
fictionists may have an unappreciated edge in the evolutionary competition down the road. Give us acid-free paper, a source of light,
and familiarity with our language, and we are in business for the long
haul. Digitalized information, on the other hand (including e-fiction),
turns out to be only theoretically invulnerable to the ravages of time;
the alarming fact is that the physical media on which it is stored, not
to mention the software and hardware required to get at it, are far
from eternal, either as items in themselves or as modes of access. Jeff
Rothenberg, a senior computer scientist at the RAND Corporation,
declares (in print) that "the contents of most digital media evaporate
long before words written on high-quality paper. They often become
unusably obsolete even sooner, as media are superseded by new, in-
compatible formats (how many readers remember eight-inch floppy

disks?). It is only slightly facetious to say that digital information lasts forever—or five years, whichever comes first."

Good luck, electronic fictioneers: Golf courses and ski slopes last longer than that; may the products of your lively medium fare as well.

Two More Forewords

"Two more" in two senses: 1) This essay-collection has been fore-worded already; and 2) its forerunner, *Further Fridays*, included a section called "Four Forewords"—to my first five published nov-els, on the occasion of their later reissue as trade paperbacks by Doubleday's Anchor Press.[1]

T IME WAS WHEN the publishers of good-quality books with less than best-seller appeal could hope at least to break even by keeping such works in print and selling a modest number of copies per year over an extended period, meanwhile deducting for tax pur-poses the cost of warehousing the unsold copies. The U.S. Supreme Court's unfortunate "Thor Tool Company" ruling in 1979[2] declared that practice illegal, with the unhappy result that in America nowa-days, a book either makes its publisher a profit in a hurry or is fed to the shredder—just as, in commercial television, a high-quality drama series may be canned because its audience, while sizeable, is less so than that of some competing network's offering: bad news for the culture in both cases. Periodic attempts by such organizations as the Authors Guild and PEN (Poets, Essayists, and Novelists) to over-turn that infelicitous court ruling have thus far been unsuccessful; until they succeed, if ever, the slack has been taken up somewhat

by university presses and others outside the "trade," where volumes of poetry, essays, and good-but-non-"commercial" fiction
may find sanctuary, and by the larger houses' "trade paperback"
lines: Doubleday's Anchor Press, Random House's Vintage Books,
Houghton Mifflin's Mariner Books, et cetera.

A number of my own past productions have had the good fortune
to lead second lives in such editions, for which their new publisher
often requests a foreword. Hence the "Four Forewords" aforementioned, and hence the two here following: one to the large and complex novel *LETTERS*, first published by Putnam in 1979; the other
to the smaller, more straightforward *Sabbatical: A Romance*, from
the same publisher three years later. Neither novel was a commercial
success; happily for their author, both were subsequently reissued (in
1994 and 1996, respectively) by the University of Illinois' excellent
Dalkey Archive Press, to continue their trickle of annual sales. After
all, one reminds oneself, long-haul trickles can have large effects: e.g.,
the Chesapeake Bay and its tidal tributary outside my workroom
window, both formed in part by the eons-long trickles of the last Ice
Age's retreating glaciers. . . .

LETTERS

"Another interminable masterpiece," my comrade-in-arms William
H. Gass has called the novel here prefaced. I like that.

"Irritating and magnificent," says the critic Zack Bowen of the
story's ground-plan and overall conceit.[3] I like that, too.

Gore Vidal, on the other hand (Or was it Tom Wolfe? One of
those knee-cappers, anyhow, who write so entertainingly on other
matters but often get literature all wrong), in a general diatribe against
fictive Fabulism, Postmodernism, you name it, has declared that the

movement "culminates in John Barth's novel *LETTERS*, which even its author admits is unreadable."

Author admitteth no such thing. Author happeneth to believe the novel enormously readable, as well as enormous in other respects. Complex? Well, yes. Complicated? For sure. Designed and constructed with a certain rigor? You bet: As in pro football and the knitting of argyle socks, rigor in novel-writing is the zest of complexity; the aim is to bring it off with brio, panache, even grace—"passionate virtuosity," I've heard it called—never dropping the ball or a stitch. Not for every taste, no doubt; but in the author's opinion (15 years now after the novel's first publication) there is in *LETTERS* sufficient humor, range of passions, historical seriousness, and bravura theater to make it a rousing read *despite* its elegant construction, if "despite" is how it need be.

But let's hope it needn't.

HERE'S HOW THE thing came to be written:

- Although its action takes place through seven months of 1969 (seven years before the U.S. Bicentennial, which some Americans at the decade's turn, myself included, were beginning to note the approach of), it was in 1973 that the novel itself moved from accumulated project-notes to the front burner of my concerns. That's the year when the American 1960s really ended: with the Israeli/Egyptian Yom Kippur War and the consequent Arab oil embargo; with the humiliating wind-down of our Vietnamese misadventure, which had fueled and focused countercultural protest; with the leveling off and subsequent erosion of

U.S. economic prosperity, which had grown with all but uninterrupted vigor through the generation since Pearl Harbor—an erosion that, for the Baby Boomers at least, continues yet. Not a bad benchmark, in short, '73, for the beginning of the end of "the American Century," as under the Nixon/Kissinger administration the nation ground un-enthusiastically toward its 200th birthday—an event that I'd had my eye on, novel-wise, for some while already. This for the reason that

• I myself had passed Dante's *mezzo del cammin di nostra vita* and begun the second half of my projectible life-span, actuarially and otherwise. A 20-year first marriage had ended in divorce, and at age 40 I had married again (the second union, as of this writing, happily older than its pre-decessor and going for the distance). In those first 20 years of adulthood I had sired and co-parented three children, and by 1973 was managing them through college. I had contrived to ascend the American academic ladder from teaching-assistantship to endowed-professorship while at the same time writing and publishing my first half-dozen volumes of fiction, and my literary offspring had earned some degree of critical notice—sometimes hedged, like the quotes above. Indeed, the first and fifth of them had been bridesmaid finalists for the National Book Award in fic-tion, and the sixth a bigamous bride: A divided jury named *Chimera* co-winner of the 1973 prize.

- All things considered, a not-inappropriate time to take stock, as the USA was warming up to do—perhaps via a Bicentennial novel that would concern itself with (and be the first fruit of) second halves and "second revolutions," in my country's history[4] as well as in my personal and professional life. What I aimed to do—when by 1973 those aims had clarified themselves—was write a seventh novel that would address these bicentenary, second-revolutionary themes and at the same time be a sequel to all six of its forerunners, carrying representative characters from each into the second cycles of their several stories—without, however, requiring that its readers be familiar with those earlier works.

- Moreover, two decades of reading, writing, and teaching literature had bemused me with the three main senses of our English word *letters*, to wit:

  1. Alphabetical characters, those 26 atoms that in their infinite supply and innumerable but finite recombinations comprise the written universe.

  2. Epistolary missives, that homely but splendid technology of human telecommunication in the 18th and 19th centuries especially—the golden era of general bourgeois literacy and, not coincidentally, of the novel as a popular medium of art and entertainment. The English novel, in particular, had from the first an almost proto-Postmodern awareness of itself as words on paper, a document imitating other sorts of documents, especially

letters; even where its form was not epistolary, its plot often turned on letters mislaid, misdelivered, misread or miswritten, intercepted or purloined. By 1973, telephony had all but supplanted the writing of personal letters, as film- and television-watching had all but supplanted novel-reading—Adieu, dear media! Such later technologies as e-mail lack the distinctive element of individual penmanship (I kiss your handwriting, love, in lieu of your dear hand); even telefaxed longhand isn't *her* ink, on *her* personal stationery, a souvenir of herself. . . . And

3. the third sense of "letters," Literature: dear dwindling diversion, sometimes made of letters made of letters by men and women of letters, its measureless inventory of passions, situations, speculations, flights of fancy, heartbreaks/ha-ha's/ho-hums all ultimately reducible to a couple-dozen squiggles of ink on paper.

"Work all of this in," I instructed my muse, "in a certain arrangement of eighty-eight epistles from seven correspondents over seven months of the seventh year before Seventeen Seventy-Six's two hundredth anniversary—and have the thing ready for publication by that date, okay?"

She obliged, except in that final particular. "I'm not a demand feeder," she reminded me, and took her own sweet time lactating *LETTERS*: seven years, appropriately, from the first work-notes to the novel's first publication in 1979, by when the Bicentennial was yesterday's newspaper and an even meaner decade waited in the wings. Six books later, as in 1994 I write this foreword letter by letter (never since unaware, at least subliminally, of every l, e, t, t, e, r, & s I scrawl), *LETTERS* is the fit midpoint of my bibliography, perhaps of the road of my life as well.

I like that, and am gratified to see the old girl here second-cycled into print.

SABBATICAL

Sabbatical: A Romance, written between 1978 and 1981 after my seven-year involvement with the novel *LETTERS*, was indeed a sabbatical from that extended, intricated labor. The project's original working title was *Sex Education and Sabbatical*; I had in mind an odd Siamese twin of a book comprising a fantastical playscript (about a postmodern romance between a skeptical spermatozoon and a comparably wary ovum) followed by a realistic novel involving a middle-aged male *Homo sapiens*, recently retired from the CIA, and his somewhat younger professorial wife, newly pregnant with, perhaps, the consummation of that playscript romance—which she may decide to abort. For better or worse, as happens with a fair percentage of twin pregnancies, the weaker sibling expired *in utero* (to be resurrected, more or less, in *The Tidewater Tales: A Novel* [1987]). The survivor is the work in hand, narrated from a viewpoint that I believe myself to have invented: the first-person-duple voice of a well-coupled couple.

The story was suggested by the curious death in Chesapeake Bay, my home waters, of one Mr. John Arthur Paisley, an early-retired high-ranking operative of the U.S. Central Intelligence Agency who, in late September 1978, disappeared from his sloop *Brillig* during an overnight solo cruise in fair weather on this normally tranquil estuary. The unmanned sloop was found aground soon after, all sails set, lunch half prepared in the galley, no sign of foul play, et cetera; the body of its owner/skipper, levitated by the gases of decomposition, surfaced a week later, 40-odd pounds of scuba-weights belted to the waist, a 9mm bullet hole behind the left ear. In those halcyon Cold War years of CIA/KGB huggermugger, when such more or less deranged intelligence chiefs as the Soviet Union's Lavrenti Beria and the USA's James Jesus Angleton saw or suspected moles within moles within moles, "the Paisley case" received much local and some national and international attention, duly echoed in the novel. Had the fellow been done in by the KGB because he had discovered their Mole in our agency? By the CIA because he *was* the Mole? By one or the other because he was only apparently retired from counterintelligence work in order to scan covertly from his sailboat the high-tech snooping gear suspected to be concealed by the Soviets in their U.S. embassy vacation compound, just across the wide and placid Chester River from where I write these words? Et cetera. A few less intrigue-driven souls, myself among them, imagined that the chap had simply done himself in, for whatever complex of personal reasons and despite certain odd details and spookish unresolved questions (see novel)—but by the end of the American 1970s one had learned that paranoia concerning the counterintelligence establishments was often outstripped both by paranoia *within* those establishments and by the facts, when and if they emerged.

INDEED, MY U.S.-HISTORY homework through that decade for the *LETTERS* novel, together with our war in Vietnam, cost me considerable innocence concerning the morality of our national past and present, especially with respect to foreign policy and to such agencies as J. Edgar Hoover's FBI and Allen Dulles's CIA, whose clandestine, not infrequently illegal operations I found to be rich in precedent all the way back to George Washington's administration. Given our political geography, a fair amount of that activity turns out to have taken place in and around my tidal birthwaters (see novels).

During the long course of writing *LETTERS*, I happened to move with my new bride back to those birthwaters after a 20-year absence, to teach at Johns Hopkins, my alma mater, and to begin for the first time ardently exploring, in our cruising sailboat, the great estuarine system that I had grown up on, in, and around. It was sobering, in those high-tension times, to see the red hammer-and-sickle banner flying above the aforementioned Soviet embassy retreat across the river, and to note on our charts (abounding in Danger Zones and Prohibited Areas) the 80-plus Pentagon facilities scattered about this fragile tidewaterland—including the Pentagon itself, the U.S. Naval Academy, and the Edgewood Arsenal's chemical and biological weapons development facilities, not to mention several CIA "safe houses" and the headquarters of the Agency proper. Sobering too to sail past the odd nuclear missile submarine off Annapolis, packing firepower enough to wreck a continent, and to know that among one's fellow pleasure-sailors and anchorage-mates would be a certain number of federal employees including the occasional admiral, active or retired, taking a busman's holiday, and the occasional Agency spook, ditto, perhaps ditto. And sobering finally to be cruising the pleasant waters that a British task force had invaded during the War of 1812, burning Washington, bombarding Fort McHenry in Baltimore Harbor, and inspiring our national anthem—waters increasingly stressed by agricultural run-off ever since the first European settlers cleared the forests to farm "sot-weed" in the 17th century; by military dumping and residential development through the 20th; and by history, more or less, over that whole span.

Sabbatical glances at all that, perhaps even attempts here and there to stare it down, but it's really only marginally about the Wonderlandish machinations of the CIA/KGB and the American heritages represented (in the novel) by Francis Scott Key and Edgar Allan Poe. First and finally, the story is what its subtitle declares it to be: a romance, in the several senses of that term.

> *—Postscript, possibly evidencing that truth is more Postmodern than fiction:*
>
> *After* Sabbatical's *first publication in 1982, I learned from certain ex-colleagues of his and readers of mine that the unhappy Mr. Paisley had toward the end grown fond of declaring that "in life, as on the highway, fifty-five is enough" (his age at death). Moreover—and more poignantly, soberingly, vertiginously—I was informed by his son that the late Agency operative had been a fan of my novels, especially* The Floating Opera *and* The Sot-Weed Factor—*which it pleases me to imagine his having enjoyed in happier times as he and Brillig sailed the Chesapeake.*
>
> *R.I.P., sir: Having surfaced in* Sabbatical *as in the Bay (and resurfaced in this novel's successor,* The Tidewater Tales*), you shall not float through my fiction again.*

"In the Beginning": The Big Bang, the Anthropic Principle, and the Jesus Paradox

Turning now to a bit of proto-Postmodernism: Though far from being a Biblical scholar myself, I was successfully tempted by the bona fide Biblicist David Rosenberg to contribute the following essay on Genesis and Matthew to his anthology *Communion*[1]—having perused which, the distinguished journalist Bill Moyers persuaded me in 1996 to take part in one episode of his 10-part PBS series *Genesis*:[2] a lively round-table conversation with Moyers; the novelists Rebecca Goldstein, Mary Gordon, Oscar Hijuelos, Charles Johnson, and Faye Kellerman; and the theologian Burton Visotzky, on the subject of "The First Murder," Cain's offing of his brother Abel in Genesis 4. Whereafter I happily retired from amateur scriptural exegesis.

1.

Bereshith—in Hebrew, the first word of the first verse of the first chapter of the first book of the Bible—says it more aptly than does the usual English translation, "In the beginning." Both expressions are adverbial, and their sense is inarguably the same: *Bereshith* means, indeed, "in the beginning,"[3] its first syllable corresponding to the English preposition. But if, as John's subsequent gospel affirms (1:1),

43

"In the beginning was the word," then any form-conscious writer
of a creation-story will prefer that beginning word to be the word
Beginning. The text of Genesis (called, in Hebrew, *Bereshith*), especially its opening chapters, is virtually proto-Postmodernist in its
deployment of what art critics call "significant form"—the form a
metaphor for the content, or form and content reciprocally emblem-
atical—and the original Hebrew begins the story best: *beginningly*.[4]

In the "Near Eastern" stacks of my university's library, once the
distinguished haunt of William Foxwell Albright's Oriental Seminary,
there is half an alcove of scholarly commentary, in a babel of languages,
on the text of Genesis; enough to frighten any self-respecting fictionist
back to his/her trade. Of all this (except for Sacks's excellent treatise aforenoted) I remain programmatically innocent. No professional
storyteller, however, especially of the Postmodernist or Romantic-
Formalist persuasion, can fail on rereading this seminal narrative to
be struck by two circumstances, no doubt commonplaces among Bible
scholars: 1) that the structure of Genesis, particularly of its opening
chapter, is self-reflexive, self-similar, even self-demonstrative; and 2)
that its narrative procedure echoes, prefigures, or metaphorizes some
aspects of current cosmogonical theory.

- Taking, like an artless translator, second things first: As
  everybody knows, according to the generally accepted Big
  Bang hypothesis (as opposed to various currently-disfavored
  "steady state" hypotheses), our physical universe in one
  sense came into existence "all at once"—at the moment
  dubbed by astrophysicists "Planck Time" (10^{-43} seconds
  after T-Zero), prior to which the concept *time* is virtually as
  unintelligible as are physical processes at the infinitely high

temperature of the original "naked singularity." Exquisite scientific reasoning from known physical laws and processes has made possible a remarkably precise scenario/timetable for the universe's subsequent expansion and differentiation, through its radical metamorphoses in later fractions of that first second,[5] to the formation of galaxies and solar systems over subsequent billions of years and the evolution of life on Earth—including, if not culminating, in the day-before-yesterday development of human consciousness and intelligences capable of such rigorous formulations as the Big Bang hypothesis in all its scientific/mathematical splendor. In two other senses, however, the astrophysical creation-story ongoes still:

- The observable universe continues the "creative" expansion and exfoliation more or less implicit in its first instant (in the language of complexity physics, or chaos theory, its processes are "sensitively dependent on initial conditions," more particularly on certain aboriginal inhomogeneities crucial to the uneven distribution of matter into galactic clusters, superclusters, and superclusteral "superstrings")—a continuation whose own continuation apparently depends on the as-yet-imprecisely-known amount and distribution of "dark matter" out there. Moreover,

- The intelligence capable of observing, experimenting, reasoning, theorizing, and reporting on these astrophysical matters likewise continues to evolve, refine itself, and

build upon its accumulated knowledge, toward the point
where the question of the universe's ultimate denouement
(infinite expansion, apocalyptic Big Crunch, whatever)
will in all likelihood prove answerable, perhaps also the
question whether the extraordinary intelligence that can
conceive and successfully address such questions is confined to a few *Homo sapiens* on planet Earth or is after all
less parochial than that.

In the astrophysical beginning, in short, were the seeds of several
beginnings-within-beginnings: the beginning of spacetime, the beginning of matter, of radiant energy, and of galaxy formation, down
(or up) to the beginnings of life, of human consciousness, of rational
inquiry, of scientific reasoning and experiment, and of contemporary
cosmological speculation capable even of some empirical verification
of these several beginnings.

Analogously, Genesis 1:1—"In the beginning, God created
heaven and earth"[6]—in one sense says it all. And then the next four
verses (i.e., Day One: the creation of light, its division from darkness,
their naming as Day and Night, and, coincidentally, the initiation
of time) sort of say it all again; and then the remaining 26 verses of
Chapter One (the ensuing five days of creation, echoing on a larger
scale and with more particulars the first five verses, themselves an
expansion of 1:1) sort of say it all *again*. Whereafter, Chapter Two
(following God's three-verse rest on Day Seven) proceeds to say it all
yet again—"This is the generations of the sky and the earth in their
creation on the day in which God made the earth and the sky," et
cetera—replaying the same creation-riffs in so different a key that
some scholars take it to be another tune altogether (Sacks, pp. 18 ff.).

In either case, what's undeniable is that each successive expansion *is* an expansion, both in textual space, like the universe's expansion of physical space (not, strictly speaking, *in* physical space, since at any moment its expanding space is all the space there is), and also in particularity, differentiation, multiplicity. From mere sky and earth in 1:1, we have evolved by 2:23 a cosmos replete with heavenly bodies in motion, speciated life on Earth, and sexually differentiated human beings endowed with language and intelligence, though not yet with upper-case Knowledge and its attendant hazards.

The rest, as they say, is history:[7] the rest of Genesis (creation + fall, flood, and bondage); the rest of the Pentateuch (Genesis + Exodus through Deuteronomy); the rest of the Hebrew bible (Pentateuch + prophets and "writings"); the rest of the canonical Christian Bible (Hebrew Bible + New Testament)—all implicit in the beginning, *bereshith*. Indeed, one might call the opening verse of Genesis the macrobang from which evolve not only the Jewish and Christian sacred texts but the centuries of commentary thereupon: an evolution no more "finished" than that of the physical universe, as biblical scholarship and archaeology expand our knowledge and understanding of the texts. Witness, for example, the recent scholarly catfights over publication of the Dead Sea Scrolls, and the expectable deluge of associated books and papers now that the text is readily available.

As a creator myself, of word-worlds, I'm admiringly envious— not so much of the universe's genesis, which is beyond my agnostic ken, as of Genesis's genesis; less of divine Creation than of this art-fully created creation-story.

DID I EVER actually *believe* any of it? The six-day cosmogony, Adam and Eve and the serpent, and for that matter the text as God's

word and the a priori existence of its divine author? In the sluggishly
Christian but essentially secular household of my small-town boyhood, one dutifully attended the neighborhood Methodist Sunday
school as a child and then, as an adolescent, the Friday-evening
Junior Christian Endeavor, as well as "joining church" round about
puberty-time. I did all that in the same mainly unprotesting spirit in
which I attended Cambridge (Maryland) public schools: It was what
one did. But the air of our house, while not openly skeptical, was in
no way suffused with religious belief: God, the afterlife, the authority
of biblical texts—such matters never entered our table talk. The first
time I heard the Genesis story questioned on scientific grounds (God
knows where, in that venue), whatever notional assent I'd given it as
a literal account slipped lightly away forever, as did by high-school
days any notion of its divine authorship. Later, in university years
and the beginnings of my own authorhood, I would come to appreciate metaphor and to respect the power and profundity of great
myths, the biblical creation-myth included—but that's another story.

As for the one told in the book of Genesis: Bravo! What a splendid beginning!

2.

For believing Christians, Act Two of the creation-drama is mankind's
vicarious redemption by the Messiah from man's original sin and fall
from grace in Act One.[8] I shall now audaciously rush in where no an-
gel would presume to tread and draw another analogy with contemporary theoretical physics, as I understand that vertiginous discipline.

Werner Heisenberg's celebrated Uncertainty Principle and Erwin
Schrödinger's quantum-mechanical wave-function equations, taken
together, declare in effect that the position of an electron, say, is

"merely" a field of probabilities until we observe it, whereupon its "wave function collapses" and it may be said to *have* a position. Extrapolating from these axioms of quantum physics, some later theoreticians have maintained that in a sense, at least, such observation may be said to be not only uninnocent (i.e., not non-disturbing) but downright causative: We didn't observe Electron X to be at Point A because that happens to be where it was; that's where it was *because we made the observation*, prior to which its position was no one particular point but a probability-field. On the microlevels of particle physics and the macrolevels of astrophysics, such counterintuitive *bizarries* are in rigorous conformity with empirical observation; quantum physics has been an extraordinarily successful scientific theory, with formidable predictive power. The Anthropic Principle, which comes in several flavors,[9] carries these extrapolations to startling lengths: Had our universe not happened to develop precisely within a number of very critical parameters (as could just as possibly and much more probably have been the case), there would have been no evolution of planetary systems, of life, and of intelligences capable of measuring (never "innocently") and theorizing upon those critical parameters. Depending on whether you take your Anthropic Principle in its diluted or its industrial-strength versions, the universe may thus be said to have evolved precisely such that astrophysicists can exist to understand its evolution, or it may be said to exist as we observe it to exist at least in part because we make those (never non-disturbing) observations. As John Wheeler succinctly puts it, "The observer is as essential to the creation of the universe as the universe is to the creation of the observer."

Without rigorous amplification, at least, this smacks of teleology, not to say tautology, as even some proponents of the principle agree

(Wheeler declares that he wholeheartedly believes in his Participatory Anthropic Principle "every February 29th"). It also echoes, in my ears anyhow, the "Christian-dramatic" view that the universe was created as the theater of mankind's fall and messianic redemption. On this view, while the Old Testament implies and validates the New, the New reciprocally completes and validates the Old (more to come on this reciprocity). Every playwright and novel-plotter knows that while the events of Act Two will appear to the audience/reader to have been necessitated by the events of Act One, it is reciprocally true that the events of Act One may be said to have been necessitated by the requirements of Act Two. To Chekhov's aforenoted injunction I would add that many a scriptwriter has been obliged to go back and hang a pistol on the wall in the story's beginning because it turns out to be needed for firing at or near the story's end.[10] Do physicists observe the universe to be such-and-so because its evolution has narrowly permitted the existence of physicists, or vice-versa? Was the Messiah's coming necessary because of Original Sin, or was Original Sin (in Catholic tradition, *felix culpa*, Man's "happy fault") necessary for the Messiah's coming?

Either way, it all begins in the beginning, dramaturgically speaking, prefigured in Adam and Eve's tasting the forbidden fruit of knowledge—including self-knowledge, the original causative, uninnocent observation:

> *And the eyes of them both were opened, and they knew that*
>
> *they were naked; and they sewed fig leaves together, and made*
>
> *themselves girdles. . . .*

And they likewise stitched together, in their subsequent/consequent generations, everything from scripture and scriptural commentary to quantum physics and the Anthropic Principle—all implicit, though not predictable, *bereshith*.

NOT PREDICTABLE? So says chaos theory about the exfoliation of any complex system, such as the weather or the evolution of life on earth, "sensitively dependent on initial conditions"—small differences among which (Eve eats the apple; Eve doesn't eat the apple; Eve eats, but Adam doesn't; they both do) rather quickly generate large differences in outcome.[11] But such paradoxes of postlapsarian self-consciousness as the Anthropic Principle permit us to muse on some other modes of "reciprocal validation," which I'll approach via a brief detour from scriptural into secular literary classics.

Virgil's *Aenead* is more aware of itself as a monumental epic poem than are its great predecessors and models, Homer's *Iliad* and *Odyssey*. Just as the poem's story-line traces the triumphant Roman empire back to wandering refugees from fallen Troy (and thus settles historical scores with Homer's Greeks), so the Roman poet programmatically combines in Aeneas's adventures an Odyssey and an Iliad, respectfully going one-on-one with the master, so to speak, in episode after episode, as if to say "Anything you Greeks did, we Romans can imitate, equal, and perhaps exceed." Politically and militarily there are winners and losers in such competitions; in art, one does better to speak not of victors and vanquished but of inspiration and reciprocal enrichment. Readers who know both Homer and Virgil find their enjoyment of each enhanced by its prefiguration or reorchestration of the other. Whether or not, as Jorge Luis Borges declares, "Every great writer creates his own precursors" (a sort of literary Anthropic

Principle), great artists unquestionably enrich and revalidate their precursors, as well as conversely.[12]

In analogous wise, the Christian New Testament is much aware of itself—or at least its compilers and commentators have been thus aware of it—as following, perhaps as "completing," the Hebrew Bible. To this lay and respectfully agnostic reader, that awareness is most intriguing in what I think of as the Jesus Paradox. Indeed, at a point some decades past in my novelizing career, this paradox virtually possessed my imagination, although I came to it not from any particular preoccupation with the Bible but via a more general preoccupation with the myth of the wandering hero—Joseph Campbell's "hero with a thousand faces"—as it appears in virtually all ages and cultures. The résumés of such mythic figures are famously similar: Lord Raglan's early study *The Hero* lists 22 items more or less common to their CVs, from "(1) The hero's mother is a royal virgin," to "(22) He has one or more holy sepulchres," and proceeds to measure against this template a fair assortment of candidates, from Oedipus to Robin Hood, giving each a score.

Fascinated, in the 1960s, with three novels under my authorial belt, I set myself the following thought-experiment: Imagine a candidate for or aspirant to mythic-herohood who happens to *know the script*, so to speak, as Virgil knew Homer's epics and as Dante knew both Virgil's and Homer's, and who takes it as his project to attain mythic-herohood by following that script to the letter: by repeating or imitating in detail the curriculum vitae or typical career-moves of his eminent predecessors. Those precursors, let us imagine, unselfconsciously did what they did, as we imagine the bardic Homer unselfconsciously composing, evolving, or refining his brace of epics; our man, however, does what he does *because he knows that that's*

what mythic heroes do. He is, in a word, uninnocent. I then imagined (and got gratifying fictive mileage from) two exemplary, perhaps
cautionary, case studies: the minor Greek mythic hero Bellerophon
and the tragicomic protagonist of my novel-then-in-progress, *Giles
Goat-Boy.*

In Case 1, per my reorchestration of the myth, Perseus's envious cousin Bellerophon conscientiously and meticulously imitates
the pattern of mythic-herohood as embodied by his celebrated relative and becomes, not the mythic hero he aspires to be, but a perfect
imitation of a mythic hero, which is of course not the same thing at
all. He has completed the curricular requirements, as it were, but
that circumstance no more makes him a bona fide mythic hero than
completing the requirements for an M.A. makes one a true master
of the arts. Similarly (to reapproach our subject), one might imagine a David Koresh or Jim Jones who takes himself to be not only
divinely inspired but in some sense the son of God, and who also
happens to know the Old Testament prophecies; in order to validate himself as the Messiah, he sees to it that whatever that script
calls for—"whatever the part requires," as proverbial starlets say—
he does, perhaps including even death by immolation or poisoned
Kool-Aid. He has followed, more or less to the letter, the messianic
curriculum, but. . . .

Case 2 is altogether more problematical and interesting: Suppose
our candidate to be not merely an aspiring mythic hero or one more
entertainer of messianic delusions, but a bona fide young Aeneas or,
in fact, the long-prophesied Messiah. He understands what he must
do[13]—here is the monster to be slain, as aforewarned; here is the
prophesied kingdom to be established or reclaimed; here approaches
the foretold dark consummation, et cetera—and he does it, not in

this case because that is what aspiring mythic heroes or messiahs are expected to do in order to qualify, but because he is in very truth a mythic hero or the Messiah. In short, while the template or the prophecies validate him, he likewise validates them. To get right down to it: Among Jesus's contemporaries, the fellow's claim to messiahship might be buttressed by his doing what Isaiah and company predicted that the Messiah will do; to believing Christians, however, it is at least equally Isaiah's claim to prophethood that is buttressed by Jesus's fulfillment of the prophecies.

That reciprocal or coaxial validation—for Christians, the very crux (pardon the metaphor) of that between the Old and New Testaments—is the paradox of the Jesus Paradox, to which I shall return after pointing out that its secular analog applies not only to "later-arriving" mythic figures like Bellerophon and Aeneas but to later authors like Virgil, not to mention us Postmodernists. As afore-suggested, by writing an *Aenead* that combines an *Odyssey* with an *Iliad*, Virgil gives the impression of wanting to outdo the Homer of whom he is the self-conscious heir and to whom his Latin epic is also a homage, just as Augustan Rome is at once the cultural heir and the political master of classical Greece. You want to be a great epic poet? Here are your models. Virgil follows them—programmatically but not slavishly—and because he happens to *be* a great epic poet, his *Aenead* turns out to be not a monumental Case-1 imitation of the great model, but a great epic poem. Thirteen centuries later, Dante compounds the stunt, taking as his literal and figurative guide not "unselfconscious" Homer but self-conscious (and Homer-conscious) Virgil, and not only scripts *himself* into the wandering-hero role but orchestrates his own welcome, as afore-footnoted, into the company of the immortals—in a Limbo, moreover, where they must ineluctably remain, but from which he will proceed through Purgatory to Paradise. Talk about chutzpah! Happening to *be* a great poet, however, Dante brings the thing off—and we now return to the Jesus Paradox.

Of the gospeleers, the most "Virgilian" in this respect is Matthew, in whose account of Jesus's career just about *everything* goes literally by the book:

- The Annunciation (1:22, 23): "All this took place to fulfill what the Lord had spoken by the prophet: 'Behold, a virgin shall conceive [et cetera].'"[14]

- The family's flight into Egypt (2:15): "This was to fulfill what the Lord had spoken of by the prophet, 'Out of Egypt have I called my son.'"

- Their subsequent residency in Nazareth (2:23): "And [Joseph] went and dwelt in a city called Nazareth, that what was spoken by the prophet might be fulfilled, 'He shall be called a Nazarene.'"

- Jesus's later move to Galilee (4:12–14): ". . . he withdrew into Galilee . . . that what was spoken by the prophet Isaiah might be fulfilled. . . ."

- His "confidential" healing of the sick and the lame (12:15–21): ". . . many followed him, and he healed them all, and ordered them not to make him known. This was to fulfill what was spoken by the prophet Isaiah: '[The Messiah] will not wrangle or cry aloud, nor will anyone hear his voice in the streets. . . .'"

And so on and on. It is from the master himself, one guesses, that the apostle borrows this operative formulation: from Jesus's flat-out declaration in the Sermon on the Mount, as Matthew reports it (5:17)—"'. . . I have come not to abolish [the law and the prophets] but to fulfill them'"—to his reminding those of his followers indignant to the point of violence at his arrest and impending judgment (26:53, 54): "'Do you think that I cannot appeal to my Father, and he will at once send me more than twelve legions of angels? But how then should the scriptures be fulfilled, that [what's about to happen] must be so?'" For this reader, the climactic such moment comes at the Last Supper, when, facing the prospect of his "death foretold," Jesus declares (25:24), "The Son of man goes as it is written of him." Even nonbelievers may feel a *frisson* at that remark: the hero's calm acceptance of his hard fate. He has, in effect, no choice: If upon his agonized later prayer the bitter cup really *were* rescripted to pass from him, then either he or the sacred original script would be falsified.

Self-conscious, uninnocent mythic herohood; historically aware and prescient messiahship—they are not callings for the faint of heart.

In real, non-scripted life, of course, the distinction between Case-1 and Case-2 heroes and saviors is often notoriously less clear, at least as perceivable from "outside," than it is in these thought experiments.[15] God knows whether the Nazarene from Galilee was the Messiah, although every Christian ipso facto believes him to have been, and it is only on the hypothesis of his *having* been that the Jesus Paradox is energized. He knows by heart the excruciating script; per the poignant paradox, however, he isn't *acting*, but reciprocally validating to the end what has validated him—from the beginning.

How It Was, Maybe: A Novelist Looks Back on Life in Early-Colonial Virginia and Maryland

This address, on a subject about which I'm a bit more knowl-edgeable (or once was, anyhow) than about Biblical texts, was delivered at the Williamsburg Institute's 50th Annual Forum, in Colonial Williamsburg, Virginia, in February 1998—a novel and rather challenging lecture-venue for me, but an attractive one. I include it here with a tip of the hat to the endlessly resourceful, somewhat protean Captain John Smith on the 300th anniversary of his first exploratory cruises from Jamestown to the head of Chesapeake Bay.

THE OPERATIVE WORDS in my title, as I trust you'll have no-ticed already, are the words "maybe" and "novelist." They are intended not quite to *disqualify* me from addressing an audience of professional and amateur specialists on the subject of colonial life hereabouts, but to disclaim any particular authority in the matter—in short, to cover my butt. By trade and by temperament I am in fact not any sort of historian or antiquarian, but a novelist and short-story-writer, a fictioneer—a professional liar, we might as well say, of whom the most one can reasonably demand is that his fabrications be of professional quality. I'll do my best.

What's worse, I'm not even a historical novelist, properly speaking. The straightforward historical novel—Margaret Mitchell's *Gone With the Wind*, Nordhoff and Hall's *Mutiny on the Bounty*, James Michener's *Chesapeake*—is a category of fiction that makes me just a tad uneasy,[1] even though I've much enjoyed such exceptional specimens as Robert Graves's Roman-Imperial epic *I, Claudius*. Of my dozen-plus published books, only one and a half have anything at all to do with colonial Virginia and Maryland, and the one called *The Sot-Weed Factor*—which very much *does* have to do with life in early-colonial Tidewaterland—was written between 1956 and 1960, when its author was not yet thirty years old. I wasn't exactly a greenhorn back then in the medium of fiction (my first two novels had been published already), but I was an entire novice in the area of historical fiction and its attendant research. It's gratifying to me that this many years after its initial appearance, the *Sot-Weed* novel remains in print. The flip side of that gratification, however, is that its author is still sometimes mistaken for an authority on matters of regional history, when in fact what I'll be looking back on here is not only Life in Early-Colonial Et Cetera but my researches into that subject four decades ago.

Just recently, for example, I got a call from a bona fide colonial historian at work on a study of William Claiborne's 17th-century Virginian trading post on Kent Island, in the upper Chesapeake: a famous thorn in the side of Lord Baltimore's first Maryland settlers. She had noticed, this historian told me, that in my *Sot-Weed Factor* novel Lord Baltimore refers to that rogue Virginian as "Black Bill Claiborne"; her question was whether I could vouch for the use of

"Bill" as a nickname for William in the 17th century. Heck no, I was obliged to tell her: Back when I was up to my earlobes in the documents of our colonial history, I might have confirmed or disconfirmed that usage with some confidence, but that time itself was history now. I then offered her my guess that although "Will" was unquestionably the most common nickname for William back then, if I chose to have Lord Baltimore say "Bill," it was quite possible that I had seen that sobriquet deployed in some colonial document or other. But I reminded her, as I now remind you-all, of Aristotle's famous distinction between History and Poetry—between how things were and how things *might have been*, or let's say between verity and verisimilitude—and further, that while my memory is that in that novel I tried to stay rigorously close to the facts of colonial life and language where such rigor was appropriate, it was not at all impossible that the muse of Poetry rather than that of History dictated "Black Bill Claiborne," as a denunciation more euphonious than "Black *Will* Claiborne." ("Wicked Will," I guess I could've called the fellow, if "Bill" is in fact an anachronism—but then "Wicked Will" sounds too much like that night-calling bird, doesn't it. . . .)

You see how we storytellers operate: Truth, yes—but not always truth to the historical data. And how do historians operate? Well, my caller dropped me a note somewhere later to thank me for my assistance and to announce her intention of staying with "Bill," despite my warning, on the strength of *The Sot-Weed Factor*'s "general historical authenticity." It makes a person wonder.

Is THAT THE end of my disclaimer? Not quite, for it needs to be pointed out that except for *Sot-Weed*'s "true story of Captain John Smith and Pocahontas"[2]—which a Richmond book-reviewer back in 1960 found so scandalous that he seriously wondered whether present-day Virginians who claim descent from Chief Powhatan's daughter mightn't find my version legally actionable—except for that interpolated story-within-the-story, the novel deals almost exclusively with life in late-17th/early-18th century *Maryland* rather than Virginia, and as everyone here knows, "the fruitful sisters Leah and Rachel" (as John Hammond called the two colonies in his promotional tract of 1656) were different siblings indeed. To the Native Americans of Chesapeake country who were busily being displaced, it may well be that one boatload of paleface imperialists seemed much like another; but by the end of the 17th century the third and fourth generation of mainly Anglican colonial Virginians were a relatively established and even somewhat civilized operation, at least in the Old Dominion's tidewater areas. Catholic-refugee colonial Maryland, by contrast—R.C. in its origins, I mean, although its policy of religious tolerance soon enough led to the displacement of Catholic by Protestant regnancy and the attendant shift of the colony's capital from St. Mary's City to Annapolis in 1695—was a generation behind and in my (amateur) opinion still comparatively raw at the century's end. Fourteen years ago, on the occasion of Maryland's 350th birthday, I spoke about this difference in a little commemorative piece for the Baltimore *Sun*'s Sunday magazine, from which I'll quote a few paragraphs here by way of approaching our subject:

> *When Lord Baltimore's expeditionary vessels Arke and Dove entered Chesapeake Bay 350 years ago [1634], their passengers and crew did not discover Maryland. The place was already here. The main features of its present topography—the ocean barrier islands, the flat eastern peninsula*

with its southern marshes, the piedmont country rolling
west to the mountains, and at the heart of it all the great bay
with its intricate estuaries and tributaries—these had been
pretty much in place since the latest glaciers leaked away
10,000 years before. Various "Indians" had settled in over
the last millennium or two and, like Adam in the Garden,
had given names to the things around them. In our ears
now, those names are both a litany and an elegy: opossum,
raccoon, tomahawk, tobacco; also Chesapeake, Choptank,
Patapsco, Piankatank, Sassafras, Susquehannah, and the
rest. . . . These musical Algonquian names are about all
that remains to us of the people who lived here many times
longer than our comparatively short but enormously consequential residency. From time to time the aboriginals hassled
one another; the northern Susquehannocks were regarded
by their tidewater neighbors as particularly pushy, as are
some out-of-state weekend watermen by today's locals. But
rearranging the landscape on any very significant scale was
both against their principles and beyond their technology.

Other settlers before Lord Baltimore's, however, had already made a fair start on that. A quarter-century before Arke
and Dove raised the Virginia Capes, Captain John Smith's
Anglican crowd had reconnoitered the upper Bay from their
Jamestown base. The official reason for that cruise from the
James River all the way up to the Susquehannah and back—
two cruises, actually, in the summer of 1608—was explora-
tion: the Northwest Passage and all that. But the skipper
famously notes that the gentlemen who comprised his crew

*were a bunch of layabouts and troublemakers; he wanted
to get them out of town and keep them busy. Cruising the
Bay is good for that; my wife and I have occasionally taken
houseguests out on the water for somewhat similar reasons.
"A surpassing clumsie daye of Sayling," Captain John ex-
asperates to his log-book at one point; we too, with novice
crew-members aboard, have known a few of those. By 1634
the trees of tidewater Virginia were fast being cleared for
agriculture, its aboriginals were more or less in hand, and its
soil was being leached of nutrients by commercial tobacco-
farming and permitted to silt the pristine creeks and coves.
Nothing large-scale yet, but a beginning.*

*On the other hand, illicit interstate commerce, so to
speak, was already a growing enterprise. The forcible take-
over of William ['Black Bill'] Claiborne's prosperous but
not quite legitimate Kent Island trading post would be
Maryland's military-naval debut; it accounts for the care-
ful wording of a prominent historical marker on Route 50
just across the Chesapeake Bay Bridge from Annapolis: The
first English settlement within Maryland happens to have
been a settlement of Virginians, not of Marylanders. Their
expulsion was the overture to a veritable floating opera of
waterborne friction between the Old Line State and the Old
Dominion that ongoes yet; as recently as 1984 [the year I
wrote this paragraph] the Virginia crabbers were complain-
ing that the Maryland crabbers were checking into motels
on the lower Eastern Shore, crabbing right around the clock
in Virginia waters, cutting loose the Virginians' pots, and*

*"hot-sheeting" the motels into the bargain by paying one tab
and sleeping in shifts. . . .*

*My point is that the seeds of such prickly nettles had
already sprouted when the first Marylanders arrived to cul-
tivate their garden. Even the African slave business was fifteen years old already; by 1634 it was a going concern, and
by century's end a growth industry, like computer software
nowadays. In short, what Lord Baltimore's "boat people"
accomplished—that band of more or less intrepid, more or
less Roman Catholic adventurers, self-exiles, and politico-
religious refugees from a now-and-then anti-papist homeland—was not the discovery of Maryland, but its invention,
followed by its appropriation (expropriation where necessary), and as quickly as possible thereafter by its busy "development." That is to say, by the exploitation of its abundant and scarcely scratched natural resources for their own
and their patron's benefit and—the expedition's chaplains
being Jesuits—"for the greater glory of God."*

Amen, and end of quotation. My point *here* is that in the extent
of that "development," by the century's turn the Virginians remained
substantially ahead of the Marylanders, for good and for ill. I venture
to say that while the serial misadventures of Ebenezer Cooke's original sot-weed factor (of whom more presently) could perhaps have be-
fallen him in colonial Virginia, their comic plausibility is strengthened
by their happening in colonial Maryland.

WHAT WERE THOSE misadventures, and what do they tell us about
life back then and there? Knowledgeable as you-all are, I'm not

going to assume that every single one of you has read and retained
in memory the 600-plus pages of my *Sot-Weed Factor* novel or even
the couple-dozen pages of the original Eben Cooke's satiric poem
of 1708—which, by the way, I warmly recommend. Let me briefly
summarize the situation of both, and then I'll get on with our subject.

No need to explain here the terms *sot-weed* and *factor*—although
some readers are surprised to learn that those terms don't refer to an
element in a situation, like the "fudge factor" in statistical analysis or
the notorious "sleaze factor" in some national political conventions.
Wholesale tobacco agents who traded English manufactured goods
for hogsheads of tobacco from the plantations of tidewater Virginia
and Maryland were a feature of everyday life here in the colonial
period, and they supplied both the title and the luckless hero of one
of the very first American literary satires: Ebenezer Cooke's fierce
and funny antidote to the promotional puffs that characterized most
other contemporary writing about life in colonial Tidewaterland: the
Edenic landscape, the noble savages and honest tradespeople, the civilized gentry on their elegant and hospitable plantations. . . . All true
enough of colonial Virginia, maybe; but when Cooke's anonymous
first-person narrator, a young Englishman down on his luck, arrives
in this fabled New World to try his hand at sot-weed factoring, he
finds tidewater Maryland to be an uncouth, pestilential place where
the natives stink of bear grease;[3] the colonials are drunken, brawling,
illiterate sharpsters whose hospitality is not to be trusted; the women
are bawds and fishwives; and the courts of law are prevailingly cor-
rupt. Among other misfortunes, the poor greenhorn is robbed of his
clothes, treed by hound dogs, plagued by mosquitoes and by the "sea-
soning" fever so often fatal to new arrivals, and ultimately cheated
out of his stock in trade. A ruined man, he takes ship homeward

from what he calls "that Shore where no good Sense is found, / But Conversation's lost, and Manners drown'd," and the poem closes with his malediction:

May Wrath divine . . . lay these Regions wast
Where no Man's faithful, nor a Woman chast!

So much for everyday life in early-colonial Maryland. Cooke's poem is of course a satire, programmatically hyperbolical for comic effect like most satires; and it is to be noted that unlike its antihero, the poem's author (about whom not a great deal is known) evidently chose to live out his life over here instead of back in London, where the first edition of the poem was published.[4] But like any good satire, Cooke's "Sot-Weed Factor" overstates for corrective purposes what our sense of reality tells us must have been overstatements in the other direction by the existing literature, which has the air of a sales prospectus. In any case, having been born and raised on the Choptank River just a few miles upstream from Cooks Point (named for Ebenezer's father, who established a seat there in the 1660s), I knew the name and the geography long before I knew anything of its history. During my student days at Johns Hopkins I came across the *Sot-Weed Factor* poem in Roy Harvey Pearce's 1950 anthology of colonial American writing, and later in my literary apprenticeship it occurred to me to imagine a novel premised on the notion that Cooke's poem was more or less autobiographical: the misadventures of a programmatically innocent aspiring *writer*, precociously commissioned by Lord Baltimore to go sing the praises of life in early colonial Maryland—"the Graciousness of Maryland's Inhabitants, Their Good Breeding and Excellent Dwelling-places, the Majesty of Her Laws, the Comfort of Her Inns & Ordinaries, &t &t"—in a word, a

Marylandiad. In my version, Cooke's misdirections and innocent pre-
tensions cost him not only his goods but the family estate. While then
regaining that lost estate at the sacrifice of his ever more technical innocence, he also learns the hard way some facts of literary life; under
all his rhetorical posturing and attitudinizing he finds an authentic
voice and discovers his true subject matter and most congenial form.
In short, by writing not the fulsome *Marylandiad* commissioned by
his patron but the satirical *Sot-Weed Factor* instead, he manages to
become the writer that he had innocently presumed himself to be.

The same went, needless to say, for the author of the novel—
officially certified as a Master of Arts well before I had attained any
mastery of the art I aspired to. Even in 1956, with two novels under
my belt, I innocently presumed that since I had knocked them off in
about six months each, this larger and very different project might
take me as long as . . . two years, maybe? In fact it took four, and my
only subsequent venture into historical fiction, two decades later—a
huge, intricate novel called *LETTERS*, having to do with our War
of 1812—took *seven* years. Never again. It is one thing, I soon discovered, to decide to write a satirical 20th-century novel based on a
satirical early-18th-century poem about colonial America, and quite
another thing to learn enough about the facts of life back then to
bring the thing off. In a *comic* novel, obviously—especially in a satirical farce—one has more license for anachronism than one would have
in a straightforward historical novel or a period romance, such as
those I cited before. I remember a conversation with William Styron
back in 1965, in the course of which he mentioned to me that he was
at work on a "straight" novel about Nat Turner's Rebellion, and I
asked him how he planned to avoid nit-picking from experts on period detail. His working strategy, Styron told me, was systematically

to *avoid* such detail as far as possible and to concentrate instead on
the characters' psychology; *my* working strategy in *Sot-Weed* was to
invoke the Muse of Comedy rather than her grim-faced sister.

All the same, it seemed important to me to acquire a fair degree
of amateur expertise in three main areas—the history of the two colonies, the homely details of everyday life there (such as clothing, food
and drink, and what the poet Gerard Manley Hopkins called "all
trades, their gear and tackle and trim"), and the detailed flavor of
the colonists' written and spoken language, which also affords some
access to their thoughts and feelings. If I perpetrated anachronisms
of detail or language or psychology—and no doubt the novel has its
share of those—I wanted them insofar as I could manage to be *inten-
tional* anachronisms, not inadvertent ones. Even in satirical farce or
fantasy, one ought not ignorantly to put carburetors on fuel-injected
engines, for example, or have Charles Calvert call William Claiborne
"Black Bill" if that nickname hadn't yet come into use.

Back then I was living up in State College, Pennsylvania, on a
meager assistant professor's salary and had neither the funds nor the
leisure (nor for that matter the temperament) to make research expe-
ditions to St. Mary's and Jamestown, Annapolis and Williamsburg.
Other than such documents as Captain John Smith's *Generall
Historie*, William Byrd's *Secret Diary of the Dividing Line*, and above
all Ebenezer Cooke's *Sot-Weed Factor* poem, my primary resource
in this enterprise—and it turned out to be a splendid one—was the
multivolume *Archives of Maryland*, which I discovered in the stacks
of Penn State's Pattee Library and immersed myself in for the next
several years while drafting the novel. This formidable shelf of heavy
folio volumes comprises mainly transcripts of the proceedings of the
Governor's Council and the General Assembly of the province from

the time of its chartering up to the Revolution, but it also includes all sorts of depositions and complaints to the Provincial Court—an invaluable source for the names of everyday items, the kinds of hassles that folks were involved in, and the language they used to voice their grievances or defend their behavior. I wish I could give you pregnant examples, but at 40 years' distance I have forgotten what *frowes* and *inkles* are, and *suckets* and *pookes*, and how many *ells* make a *firkin*, although those magical terms still sing in my memory. I do recall being impressed with differences between the *English* English of the late-17th/early-18th century and the English of the American colonials at that time. The language of Captain John Smith, both in his own writings and in the documents that I ghost-wrote for him (such as his *Secret Historie of the Voiage up the Baie of Chesapeake*), has an Elizabethan flavor because Captain John was a bona fide Elizabethan; the language of Eben Cooke's *Sot-Weed Factor* a hundred years later, and of Maryland Provincial Court depositions taken at the time of its writing, remains more Elizabethan than Georgian, no doubt for the same reason that one still hears occasional Elizabethanisms in the speech of Tangier and Smith Island waterfolk: isolation from the evolving mother tongue. A few critics of my novel picked linguistic-historical nits: The verb *swive*, for example, meaning "copulate," which my characters employ with some frequency, is really more Chaucerian than early-18th-century, one such critic complained ("Thus swyvèd was that carpenteris wyf," Chaucer remarks in "The Miller's Tale"). True enough in merrie England, maybe, but we colonials were still a-swiving away and calling our pleasure by that name during the reigns of Queen Anne and George I. Call it cultural lag if you will; anachronism it is not. Thus swivèd was that particular book-reviewer, without his knowing it.

What else did I learn back then about everyday life hereabouts back *then* from my homework as a temporary amateur historian? What impressed me most, perhaps—and still does whenever my wife and I sail up the Potomac to St. Clements Island, where the *Arke* and the *Dove* first landed, or down-bay toward the James and Jamestown—is the dismaying *fragility* of those first English settlements, together with the formidable tenacity of the (surviving) settlers themselves: a tenacity in many cases born of desperation, to be sure, and of virtual lack of alternatives. Those little vessels and their meager provisions—meager even for those who could afford to bring with them the whole inventory recommended in Father Andrew White's 1634 *Relation of Maryland* (which inventory he lifted almost verbatim from John Smith's *Generall Historie*, and from which *I* lifted those aforementioned frowes and inkles and suckets and pookes)—so meager in the face of that green wilderness vaster by far than any of them could imagine, and their forsaken home so endlessly far behind! They were Robinson Crusoes, really, every one of them. We drop anchor and dinghy ashore; I try to imagine us landing not for a stroll and maybe a picnic and a swim, but *for keeps*, with fall and winter coming on, and the natives not necessarily delighted to see us laying claim to their turf, and everything to be done from scratch: shelters and defenses to be built, forests to be cleared and crops planted and clothing made and mended, teeth pulled and broken bones set and bread baked and babies delivered, not to mention courts and legislatures and such to be established. . . .

I shake my head. A catastrophe-in-the-making it undeniably was for the indigenous peoples and their cultures, this literal and figurative European infection; it was arguably a disaster-in-the-making for the natural environment, too—yet what a testament all the same to

the intrepidity of those men and women! A flick of the fingers, one
can't help feeling, would have been enough to push the whole fledgling operation back into the sea, for better or worse depending on
your perspective; yet not only did the surviving new arrivals hang in
there and quickly begin their fateful outspreading through the terri-
tory, but in no time at all they were hassling each other with their
left hands while scratching out niches for themselves in the wilderness with their right: Marylanders versus Virginians, papists versus
antipapists, neighbors versus neighbors, while rumors abounded that
the French and the Indians, or the Jesuits and who have you, were
conspiring up-country to sweep down and massacre all hands.

The first *murder* in colonial Maryland, for example, as I dimly
remember, occurred not long after Lord Baltimore's settlers stepped
ashore: Fellow killed his wife or vice-versa, I forget which or why.
No court to try the offender in; no law to sentence him under, come
to that; no jail to send him to—they're still unloading and unpack-
ing after months at sea, you know? And so with a figurative rap of
the gavel (I like to imagine this taking place right on the beach of
St. Clements Island, with the *Arke* and *Dove* still freshly anchored
offshore) the Governor's Council turns itself into a virtual legislature
and in effect affirms that murder is against the law in the Province of
Maryland; then turns itself into an inquest and takes depositions in
the case; then turns itself into a court of law, tries the defendant, finds
him guilty as charged (we'll assume it was the man; it usually is), and
sentences him to hang for his offense. Then, like mythical Proteus,
they turn themselves back into the Governor's Council and *commute
the sentence*, lest in all this more or less desperate improvisation there
have been some miscarriage of justice!

No doubt I'm improving this story a bit, but I swear I'm not making it up wholesale. The standard device of satire is supposed to be exaggeration, yet time and again I found myself having to *tone down* the historical facts of everyday life in the early colonies in order to make them plausible even in a satirical farce. Who would believe, for instance, that a boatload of mere rogues and renegades could sail up the river one fine afternoon while the provincial assembly was in session, bar the door of the assembly building with the members inside, and make off with the sterling silver Great Seal of Maryland? Well, something very like that happened—but at this remove, don't ask me for the details. "History," says Stephen Dedalus in James Joyce's *Portrait of the Artist as a Young Man*, "is a nightmare from which I am trying to awake." I, too, found it dreamish—more and more so as I left the history-textbooks and consulted the original documents— but I often woke up chuckling, and rolling my freshly-opened eyes.

In this vein, by way of conclusion I might as well confess— acknowledge, insist, whatever—that some of the farthest-out bits of everyday colonial life in my version of *The Sot-Weed Factor*—bits that nearly all reviewers took for granted had been invented out of the whole cloth—happen to be literal transcriptions of (reported) historical fact. The infamous eggplant-aphrodisiac recipe, for example, that I thoughtfully provided Captain John Smith with for his defloration of the impregnable Pocahontas, you will find in a work entitled *Untrodden Fields in Anthropology*, by one Dr. Jacobus X, privately printed by the American Anthropological Society in 1934 or thereabouts. Doctor X was a 19th-century French army surgeon and amateur anthropologist who, during his service in sundry outposts of empire, developed what you might call a Phallic Index for men of various ethnicities, and who collected from his native informants such esoterica as that inflammatory African eggplant concoction, whose ingredients, preparation, and *mode d'emploi* I faithfully plagiarized in the novel, although I cannot vouch for its efficacy.

It is also true, however—as the earlier-mentioned (now late) poet Robert Graves acknowledged about his novelistic forays into classical Roman history—that a fictionist, working by hunch and feel, may invent period tidbits that historians subsequently discover to be factual. That happened with certain details of Graves's *I, Claudius*, to the author's delight, and I've known the same pleasure, though not in *The Sot-Weed Factor*. In another novel of mine, having to do with everyday life not in colonial America but in the household of Sindbad the Sailor, I needed a medieval Arabic slang term for the female genitals. My usually reliable supplier of naughty medieval Arabic is Scheherazade, but it happens that while her *1001 Nights* abounds in slang terms for the male sexual equipment, I could find none for the female. Inasmuch as both Arabs and Persians of the period were intimate with the desert, I made an educated guess that the term *wahat*, one of several Arabic words meaning "oasis," might just serve my purpose, and so deployed it (the word *oasis* itself, you'll be excited to hear, is a Latin derivative from the same Egyptian root that *wahat* derives from; the two terms are etymological cousins). You will understand my subsequent joy upon reading an Arab-born British reviewer's sniffy observation (in the London *Times*, I believe it was), that while I had misspelled the Arabic slang term for the *male* sexual organ (I had not; it's a matter of transliteration and of dialect), I had got right the term for its female counterpart!

TWO CHEERS FOR the facts of history! say I, including the history of everyday life in early-colonial Maryland and Virginia. And *three* cheers for human narrative imagination, which ought properly to respect those facts, but which—when narrative push comes to dramaturgical shove—need not be bound by them like Jonathan Swift's Gulliver hog-tied by the Lilliputians. "Black Bill" Claiborne let it be: Damn the torpedoes, and on with the story!

Further Questions?

First delivered in the spring of 1998 as the University of Michigan's annual Hopwood Lecture (in conjunction with their awarding to some promising U.M. student the Hopwood Prize in creative writing), this essay was published later that year in the *Michigan Quarterly Review* and subsequently collected with sundry others in *The Writing Life: Hopwood Lectures, Fifth Series,*[1] edited and introduced by Nicholas Delbanco, himself an accomplished novelist and professor at the university.

H ENRY DAVID THOREAU begins one of his lectures by saying, "You have invited me; you have engaged to pay me; and I am determined that you shall *have* me, though I bore you beyond all precedent."

My resolve here is the same as Thoreau's. The better to implement it, I'm going to serve me up to you by asking myself and replying seriously to a number of altogether unexciting questions—the first of which, reasonably enough, is "Why bother to do that?"

Well: The fact is that like many another American writer in the second half of the 20th century, I served my literary apprenticeship not in expatriate cafés or Depression-era boxcars or on the assorted battlegrounds of any of our several wars, but for better or worse in undergraduate and then in graduate school—majoring in, of all things, *writing*. Ernest Hemingway would disapprove; likewise, no doubt, Charles Dickens, Honoré de Balzac, Mark Twain, and many another alumnus of the School of Hard Knocks. So did I, for that matter, now and then, for it was on such writers that I was raised. But except for a sculpting uncle of mine who attended the Maryland Institute's College of Art shortly before dying in the First World War,[2] I was the first of my immediate family ever to "go past high school," as people where I come from used to say (my older brother's educational trajectory was detoured by the *Second* World War), and on the whole I regard my apprenticeship in académe as both benevolent and beneficial indeed, although even at the time I understood that literature had managed nicely for several millennia without the benefit of creative-writing programs and would doubtless continue to struggle along if they should all disappear tomorrow. ("At the time" here means the late 1940s, when the then-new program at Johns Hopkins was only the second degree-granting writing program in our republic—second after Iowa's. At last count the number exceeded 400, I believe,[3] but I stand by my proposition.) I shall circle back, perhaps, to a hedged defense of this almost uniquely American, post-World War II phenomenon, the college creative-writing program, and of the concomitant phenomenon of poets and fictionists as professors. I bring the matter up now in order to launch the following reminiscence by way of reply to Question #1: "Why bother, et cetera?" It is an anecdote I've told elsewhere; kindly indulge its twice-telling:

My then-closest graduate-school-fellow-apprentice-writer-friend and I, as we were about to be duly diploma'd by our university as Masters of Arts, considered together one spring afternoon—no doubt over a couple of celebratory beers—what we might do to pay the rent until the golden shower of literary fame and fortune descended upon us like Zeus's stuff on Danae. Having had some school-vacation experience of such alternatives as factory-, sales-, and office work as well as manual labor, we agreed by passionate default that *college teaching* looked to be the least abusive of our available options and potentially the richest in free time for writing. It had not escaped our notice that doctors, lawyers, administrators, and businessfolk, for example, tend to get busier as their careers advance, whereas the workloads of university professors in the humanities appeared to us to get progressively lighter and more flexible as they ascend the academic ranks. Never mind whether this perception was correct; my buddy and I were persuaded enough thereby to decide to become writer/teachers: Writers in the University. Inasmuch as we ourselves had been blessed with splendid professors of a great many disciplines and were the opposite of cynical about the teaching half of our prospective double careers, our next consideration was how we might spend our classroom time most fruitfully for our students-to-be and ourselves. My friend—who had a stronger intellectual string to his bow than I and a more solid background in literature, history, and philosophy—decided that he would devote *his* academic life to the answering of rhetorical questions. Should some smart-ass future student of his happen to ask blithely, for example, "Who's to say, finally, Professor, what's Real and what isn't?" Ben vowed that he would tap himself on the chest, say "Check with me," and lead that student rigorously through the history of metaphysics, from the pre-Socratics up to the current semester.

And I? Well, the Answering of All Rhetorical Questions is no easy act to follow—Wouldn't you agree?—but it occurred to me to vow in my turn that I would spend *my* academic life saying over and over again All the Things That Go Without Saying; that (if I may paraphrase myself) I would stare first principles and basic distinctions out of countenance; face them down, for my students' benefit and my own, until they confessed new information. What is literature? What is fiction? What is a *story*?

And so for the next many years I did, and indeed continue still to do, although the dialogue is more often with myself these emeritus days than with students. And I hope to return to at least the last of those examples (What is a story?) later in this talk. So that's two things now to be perhaps returned to, the first being . . . I forget what, but trust that *it* will return to *me*. Meanwhile, having answered or at least responded to my opening question—"Why bother to attempt serious replies to banal questions?"—I now proceed to a few of those questions themselves.

MY GIFTED GRADUATE-SCHOOL pal, alas, died young, leaving many rhetorical questions still unanswered. In faithful pursuit of our jointly-declared program, however, I've been writing fiction as well as professing it ever since, and publishing it for 40-plus years or 5,000-plus pages, whichever is longer[4], and giving public readings from it, most often on college campuses, through at least 35 of those 40. More often than not, these reading-gigs include responding to questions from the audience afterward—something that for better or worse a writer doesn't normally get to do with his or her readers.

As you might imagine, over the semesters at least a few of those questions come to be fairly expectable and not inherently exciting— *Do you write your books with a pen or a pencil or what? Have any of your novels been made into movies? What effect, if any, has your university teaching had on your writing?* Whether or not such routine questions—and my earnest responses themto—are interesting, it *has* interested me to see both the questions and the replies evolve some- what over the decades. Taking them in order (I mean in order to get them out of our way):

1. The old question *Do you write with a pen or a pencil or a typewriter or what?* changed about a dozen years ago to *typewriter or PC?* (those were the innocent days when *PC* still meant "personal computer" instead of Political Correctness), and nowadays it seems to have become *desktop or laptop?*—as if that exhausts the imaginable options any more than does the classic "Your place or mine?" I have never understood the great pen-or-pencil question's point, so to speak, in either its low-tech or its higher-tech versions, but I'm impressed by its frequency. Is the asker an aspiring writer, I wonder, who imagines that a change of instruments might induce the muse to sing? Can she or he be thinking, "Since that guy uses Microsoft Word 5.0 on a Macintosh LCIII and his stuff gets published and even remains by and large in print, perhaps if *I* [et cetera] . . ." It's a magic syllogism. Even if the question's motive is less complimentary, its logic is no less fallacious: "Ah, so: He writes with a MontBlanc Meisterstück fountain pen. That explains the Germanic interminability of certain of his novels," et cetera.

No, no, no, dear interrogator: You must seek elsewhere the ex- planation of their Germanic *und so weiter.* What earthly difference can it make to the muses whether one composes one's sentences with a Cray mainframe supercomputer or with the big toe of one's left foot (like the cerebrally palsied Irish writer Shane Connaught) or with one's nose or with some other appendage of one's anatomy or for that matter of someone else's anatomy? It goes without saying—Does it not?—that those sentences are what they are, for better or worse, whatever the instrument of their setting down.

I do remember, however, once hearing the critic Hugh Kenner speak in an interesting way of how literature changed after the 19th century when it came to be composed on typewriters instead of penned, its alphabetical atoms no longer cursively linked within their verbal molecules (these metaphors are mine, not Professor Kenner's) but ineluctably and forever side-by-siding like wary subway passengers, and leached of individual calligraphy as well. When I objected that a few antediluvians, such as my Baltimore neighbor Anne Tyler and myself, still prefer the "muscular cursive" (Tyler's felicitous term) of longhand penmanship for first-drafting our prose, Kenner replied, "All the same, you grew up breathing the air of literature composed on the typewriter." Well, he had me there, sort of—except that the air that most oxygenated my particular apprenticeship was a fairly equal mix of high Modernism (presumably typewritten) and of quill-scrawled antiquity, with a healthy component of the oral tale-telling tradition as well. It is a mixture that I heartily recommend to apprentice writers: one foot in the high-tech topical here and now, one foot in narrative antiquity, and a third foot, if you can spare it, in the heroic middle distance.

My favorite response to the classic pen/pencil/PowerBook question, you'll be excited to hear, comes in fact from those older storytelling traditions. The enormous Sanskrit tale-cycle *Katha Sarit Sagara*, or *The Ocean of the Streams of Story*, was set down in the 10th or 11th century—with a quill pen, presumably—by the Kashmirian court poet Somadeva. Its ten large folio volumes pretend to be a radical *abridgment* of the surviving *one-seventh* of what has to have been in its original version the longest story ever told or written: the *Brihat Katha*, or Great Tale, first told by the god Shiva to his consort Parvati as a thank-you gift for a particularly divine session of lovemaking. By my calculations (based on what's conjectured about the Homeric oral tradition), it must have taken Shiva two and a half years to spin the thing out, while Parvati sat listening patiently on his lap—the primordial laptop, I suppose. No problem in their case, since the tale, the teller, and the told were all immortal. But when Shiva's Great Tale was first written down by the scribe Gunadhya (so our later writer Somadeva declares), its passage from the oral to the written medium required seven full years—which is just as well, inasmuch as the medium of transcription was the scribe's own blood.[5]

So it is, more or less, my friends, with all of us: a good case for writing short stories and lyric poems, perhaps, unless your blood-replacement capacity is that of an Anne Rice male-lead vampire. Just as Senator Daniel Patrick Moynihan suggested a few years ago that the efficient cause of American violence isn't guns but ammunition, so maybe the pen/pencil/PowerBook question ought to be *Skrip, Quink, ribbon, bubble-jet, or laser? Blood-group O, A, or B?* There is much more, by the way, to that exemplary *Kathapitha*, or Story of the Story, as Volume One of Somadeva's ten-volume abridgment of the surviving one-seventh of *The Ocean of the Streams of Story* is called. But I don't want to spoil the pleasure of your reading it for yourself.

Once upon a time a quarter-century ago, as I was driving the poet John Ashbery to his scheduled reading-plus-Q&A at Johns Hopkins, he wondered aloud to me what sort of questions he was likely to be asked. "The usual, no doubt," I assured him: "Like, *Do you write with a pen or a pencil?* Stuff like that." "Oh, I hope they ask *that* one," Ashbery said; "I *like* that one!"

Truth to tell, so do I. To get right down to it, breath-bated auditors, I write my fiction with a much-beloved old British Parker 51 fountain pen deployed in an even older three-ring looseleaf binder.[6] From there, at morning's end, the day's "muscular cursive" is Macintoshed for extensive editing and revision. And I compose my nonfiction, this lecture included, mainly on Fridays, with a MontBlanc Meisterstück 146 fountain pen bequeathed me by a beloved Spanish friend and critic[7] upon his untimely death from stomach cancer, he having chosen for his epitaph this line from a story of mine about a skeptical spermatozoon: "It is we spent old swimmers, disabused of every illusion, who are most vulnerable to dreams."[8] And I deploy that Meisterstück in an altogether different, history-free binder before Macintoshing, et cetera. Lately, however, I seem to have taken to non-ficting directly on the word-processor, without that cursive foreplay. Make of that datum what you will.

Q: *Have any of your novels been made into movies?*

A: I always used to answer No to that question, even when some film buff claimed to have seen *The End of the Road* back in the early 1970s, with Stacey Keach playing Jacob Horner, Harris Yulin as Joe Morgan, Dorothy Tristan as Rennie Morgan, and James Earl Jones as the capital-D Doctor. Despite my name in the credits and my modest payment for the film rights, I deny that that wretched flick has anything to do with my rigorous little 1958 novel of the same title and dramatis personae. (The movie critic John Simon declared at the time, correctly, that the principal difference between the novel and film versions of the story is that whereas my novel concludes with a harrowing abortion, the film is a harrowing abortion from start to finish.) But what was the question *for*?, I used to wonder, as I did with the pen-or-pencil one. I couldn't help translating it to mean "Reading's a drag, man, but I dig movies, so I'll maybe catch you out at the nabes and see if you're on my wavelength."

As you can tell from that vintage slang, the question as given is dated. Its current version would be "Are any of your novels available as videos?"⁹ The answer is still No, and I can't recommend the audiocassette versions, either. The updated question, I fear, has to be translated "Hauling out to the Cineplex has gotten to be almost as much of a bummer as reading books, but I do like to slug the old VCR if there's nothing on Cable."

What can a mere novelist say? Echoing Robert Frost's famous definition of poetry as "that which gets lost in translation," William H. Gass defines *story* as "that which is extracted from a novel to make a movie." I agree, I guess, although for me the element of story remains first among equals in the ingredients of fiction. But in a good novel (it goes without saying) the story is truly inseparable from the language it's told in and the voice that tells it. Movies are, literally, another story altogether, and videocassettes another story yet. As it happens, the best I can say even for a *good* movie-adaptation of a good novel—such as Anthony Minghella's film of Michael Ondaatje's *The English Patient* or Emma Thompson's screenplay for Jane Austen's *Sense and Sensibility*—is what Thomas Mann said about reading Shakespeare in German translation: "It's like taking a hundred thousand dollars from a millionaire," Mann declared: "He remains a very rich man."

It now appears evident that what movies and network television did to live theater earlier in this century (not to mention what they did to the audience for printed fiction), the VCR and cable TV are doing to the movie houses and to some extent to the film industry. That's just a fact of technological life. Of more interest to me is a different analogy: If movies and television have affected the art of prose fiction in the 20th century in something like the way that still photography affected the art of painting in the latter 19th, then we can reasonably expect that the development of interactive television and high-tech "virtualism" in the century to come will have a comparable effect on movies and videos as we know them today. We are told by another of my fellow American scribblers, Robert Coover, that electronic fiction and computer hypertext generally will have a comparable revolutionary impact on what remains of printed-book culture, with its obsolescent notions of author, reader, text, publisher, copyright, and the like.[10] I confess that I won't at all regret missing that particular technological revolution, which along with electronic virtuality offers to do to the audience for "p-fiction" what the rise of the novel since the 17th century did to the audience for poetry. It gives me some comfort to note, however, that while in my lifetime I've had to replace my 78 rpm records with 45s and then with 33.3 LPs, and then those with audiocassettes and then those with compact disks, each time discarding and expensively rebuilding the Barths' recorded-music library, the oldest volumes in our *book* library remain by and large as conveniently accessible as they were on their publication-day, perhaps centuries ago. If fewer and fewer people read printed fiction in the century to come, that won't be because the marvelously low-tech, high-protein medium of the book is outmoded, but because the pleasures of reading will have been displaced by glitzy and evanescent high-tech distractions for which civilization may on balance be the poorer. If thus it must go, then I shall with some small relief go first.

That curmudgeonly sentiment brings me to the last of these evolving but nevertheless routine questions, after which we'll move on to a couple of less routine ones and then have done.

Q: What effect does your university teaching have on your novels?

A: My reply to this gee-whizzer used to be, "It delays their completion." In this case, however, although the question remains the same, the respondent's altered circumstances require a different answer. As afore-established, I was indeed for four decades a full-time teacher as well as a full-time writer, and for the first two of those four decades I was a full-time parent as well—when you're young, you can full-time it on several fronts at once. Then my children grew up and (just as my late friend and I had foretold) my academic workload eased off, so that for several years I taught only one semester out of two, and for a few years after that only one graduate-level seminar every second semester. More lately, for the first time since kindergarten I've been out of the classroom altogether. To my total unsurprise, in these progressively time-richer circumstances my literary output has remained almost exactly what it was 40 years ago, when I was teaching four sections of freshman composition, six days a week, and helping to raise three small children, and moonlighting in a dance band on weekends for extra cash. Back then I *stole* time to write, and my larceny was sufficiently grand that I was able to go straight later on. Now that I have all the writing-time I want—in a day, in a week, in a year, if never in a lifetime—I find that although I enjoy generating sentences and stories as much as ever, I don't spend any more time at it than I did when I wished that I had a lot more time to spend. One's musely metabolism, evidently, is what it is almost regardless of circumstances, and so I infer that what used to delay the completion of my novels was not university teaching after all; it was (and it remains) living that part of life that doesn't consist of writing fiction—the part of life without which, in my case anyhow, there wouldn't be any fiction to write, even though that fiction seldom has to do directly with its author's biographical experience.

Does that, too, go without saying, I wonder? In any case, there it is: said.

SO MUCH FOR those profoundly routine questions, which I seem to find routinely profound. Of the non-routine sort I shall instance just one, and then ask myself one myself, and then we're done. Now and then, in the post-reading or post-lectorial Q&A, someone will come up with something at least as perceptive, and on occasion as unsettling, as anything that my most attentive critics have laid on me. It was an anonymous member of some audience a quarter-century ago who in the Q&A observed that my books thus far (of which there were back then only six) tended to come in pairs, the second member of each pair a sort of complement or corrective to the first. Inasmuch as the questioner understood me to be one half of a pair of opposite-sex twins, she wondered how programmatic on my part might be this metaphor of more-or-less-paired books, and what I took to be its significance.

Well, I was floored; I had never until that moment noticed what now seemed evident, even conspicuous—the more so since the theme of twinship itself comes up in a couple of those books. Moreover, although I've never regarded my twin sister and me as complements other than anatomically, and certainly not as reciprocal correctives,[11] I was so intrigued, even charmed by the unintended metaphor that I resolved perversely to defy it. And so I did in Book #7 (a monster novel called *LETTERS*), to which the slender novel that followed it had only the most tenuous connection; and Book #9, a collection of essays, was surely no twin to either of those—so there. But then Book #10, I noticed after writing it, can fairly be regarded as dizygotic not to Book #9 but to Book #8, and Books #11 and #12 to each other, and Book #13 (a second essay-collection) to the aforementioned Book #9, and Book #14 (a story-series) as trizygotic to Book #5 on the one hand and to Book #15 (another story-series, currently in progress) on the other, and so it would appear that only that gargantuan *Mittelpunkt*, Book #7, remains (so far) untwinned—although, come to think of it, it contains within its intrications sequels to all six of its predecessors. . . .

Make of all this, too, what you will; I myself have come to shrug my shoulders—first the left, and then, complementarily, the right. . . .

LET US RETURN to the country of Things That Go Without Saying. One Q that I've never had a chance to A in these public circumstances is the perhaps most basic and apparently elementary of all—which is why I used frequently to put it to my coachees (especially the most advanced apprentice writers among them) and why I put it still to myself, most often in the well-filling interval between books: What is fiction? What's a *story*?

Okay, so that's two questions, really, and for the long replies thereto I refer anyone who's interested to an essay of mine called "It Goes Without Saying," in the collection *Further Fridays*[12]—one of those dizygotic twin volumes afore-referred-to. The *short* answer to the question "What's a story?" was provided me by some member of yet another audience past, who after the show pressed upon me a treatise on something called Systems Philosophy and urged me to read it on the flight home. As I had no idea what Systems Philosophy might be, I did indeed leaf through that gift-book up there in the stratosphere, and although I landed not much wiser as to its subject, it did provide me with some wonderful jargon, out of which I constructed the following rigorous definition of the term *story*: A story (it goes without saying) consists of *the incremental perturbation of an unstable homeostatic system and its catastrophic restoration to a complexified equilibrium.*

I confess to being in love with that definition[13]—which in fact quite accurately describes classic Aristotelian dramaturgy. The "unstable homeostatic system" is what I've called elsewhere the Ground Situation of any story: a dramaturgically voltaged state of affairs preexisting the story's present action, like the ongoing feud between the Capulets and the Montagues. Its "incremental perturbation" is the "rising action" or complications of the conflict following upon the introduction of a Dramatic Vehicle into the Ground Situation (Romeo Montague and Juliet Capulet fall into star-crossed love, a turn of events that precipitates Bandello's tale and Shakespeare's play out of the Ground Situation; the couple's incrementally more desperate attempts to consummate that love comprise the story's action). The "catastrophic restoration" is the climax or Aristotelian *peripateia*, catastrophic in its relative swiftness and magnitude even in the quietest of stories. And the "complexified equilibrium" thereby restored is the classic denouement, dramaturgically consequential vis-à-vis the original Ground Situation or else no story has been told or sung or written down or played out (the lovers' death, e.g., puts the interfamily squabble at least temporarily on Hold).

All that sort of thing really does go without saying for most storytellers, who work at least as much by the hunch and feel of experienced talent as by articulated theory, and who are likely to find it easier to make up a story than to explain the difference between stories and non-stories or not-quite stories. If such high-tech theorizing makes no more sense to you than, say, much of life does, then I offer you another pet maxim from my inventory, to wit: *Of of what one can't make sense, one may make art.* May I repeat those eleven quasi-stammering monosyllables? *Of of what one can't make sense, one may make art.*

O self-demonstrating bliss.

BUT WHY *does* one make art? Specifically, what accounts for the odd circumstance that people in every time and place appear to enjoy, whether as individuals or as cultures, making up non-factual yarns, for example, and telling or writing or acting them out and hearing or reading or spectating them? Why is it that we *Homo sapiens* pleasure in the incremental perturbation of imaginary unstable homeostatic systems and their catastrophic restoration to complexified equilibria? In the vicarious turning of screws on cooked-up predicaments until those quantitative increments effect a comparatively sudden and significant qualitative change?

Damned if I know. In the Friday-piece mentioned above ("It Goes Without Saying"), I itemized some two dozen of fiction's feasible functions, from reality-testing and -mapping to reality-avoidance, from aphrodisia through anaphrodisia to mere linguistical futzing around. Behind all of those catalogued functions, I believe (as well as any of the many that I no doubt missed), lies a neuroscientific argument that strikes me as both plausible and pleasing, and with which I'll close my spiel. The self-styled "neurophilosopher" Daniel C. Dennett, of Tufts University, maintains that human consciousness itself has an essentially narrative aspect, grounded in the biological evolution of the brain. I won't attempt here to summarize Dennett's thesis, but I am immediately persuaded of its validity—at least as an explanatory fiction. To me it seems a short and plausible step, though a consequential and doubtless an intricate one, from the "if" propositions characteristic of computer and neural programming—*If x, then y*, et cetera, which in animal behavior might be called the Four F-propositions: whether Stimulus or Situation X prompts one to Flee, Fight, Feed, or, you know, Mate—it's a short and plausible step, I was saying, from these to the *what if*s and *as if*s of fictional narrative. I second the motion that the "neural Darwinism" by which consciousness may evolve—evolve not only to recognize and act upon stimuli but to reflect upon, disport with, and be moved to aesthetic pleasure by certain of them—has an inherently narrative aspect. Professor Dennett goes even further, conceiving of consciousness as essentially a "multi-draft scenario-spinner," or "Joycean machine"; of the self itself as an *as if*, a "posited Center of Narrative Gravity"— in short, as an intricate, on-spinning fiction. "We *are* the stories we tell ourselves and others about who we are," he concludes (in his treatise *Consciousness Explained*[14]): stories that we edit continually, and that continually edit us.

Amen to that, say I. Whether or not one goes the whole way with Dennett's neurophilosophy (and some very prominent neuroscientists do not), he has I think established at very least that when we make up stories or take pleasure in made-up stories, we are literally doing what comes naturally.

Now, THEN, I ask you: Did the pondering of questions like these ever make anybody a better writer? Wouldn't any fictionist be just as well off following the example of Norman Mailer, say, who in his 1984 Hopwood Lecture declared his tendency "to mumble about technical matters like an old mechanic"? "'Let's put the thingamajig before the whoosits here,'" said Mailer, "is how I usually state the deepest literary problems to myself." Same here, more often than not, when I am in actual intimate congress with the muse. It's in the recovery-time between such sessions that I incline to put such questions more formally to myself and to entertain them from others. And I happen to believe that when we do *that*, too, we're doing what comes naturally—perhaps more naturally to some people than to others.

But I suppose that that goes without saying.

Any further questions?

Incremental Perturbation

Some further "Further Questions." This little essay—written for and first published in an anthology on fiction-writing compiled by one of my former graduate students[1]—should be skipped by any who've heard enough already about the mechanics of storytelling.

*W*hat's a story?

Storytellers (it goes without saying) tell stories. Fiction-writers write them; playwrights and screenwriters script them; opera singers sing them; balletists dance them; mimes mime them. But what's a story?

Damned if I know, for sure. "A whole action, of a certain magnitude," says Aristotle in effect in his *Poetics*. "A meaningful series of events in a time sequence," say Cleanth Brooks and Robert Penn Warren in their New-Critical textbook *Understanding Fiction*.

Yes, well. But . . .

Most working writers of fiction—myself included when the muse and I are at it—operate less by articulated narrative theory than by the hunch and feel of experience: our experience of successfully (sometimes unsuccessfully) composing, revising, and editing our own stories and, prerequisite to that, our experience of the tens of thousands of stories that all of us audit, read, spectate, and more or less assimilate in the course of our lives. But it's another matter when, as teachers of novice fiction-writers and coaches of more advanced apprentices in the art, we find ourselves in the position of trying to explain to them and to ourselves why the manuscript before us, whatever its other merits, lacks something that we've come to associate with *stories*, and is in our judgment the less satisfying for that lack. "Gets off on the wrong foot," somebody in the room may opine. "Something askew in the middle there. . . ." "The *ending* bothers me. . . ."

Okay: But exactly what *about* the beginning, the middle, the ending, fails to satisfy? What keeps the thing from achieving proper storyhood? Freud remarks that he didn't start out with such peculiar notions as the Oedipus Complex; that he was driven to their articulation by what he was hearing from the psychoanalytical couch. That's how I feel with respect to dramaturgical theory.

What's dramaturgy?

In my shop, "dramaturgy" means the management of plot and action; the architecture of Story, as distinct from such other fictive goodies as Language, Character, Setting, and Theme. Be it understood at the outset that *mere* architectural completeness, mere storyhood, doth not an excellent fiction make. Every competent hack hacks out complete stories; structural sufficiency is hackhood's first requirement. On the other hand, about a third of Franz Kafka's splendid fictions, for example, and a somewhat smaller fraction of Donald Barthelme's, happen to be "mere" extended metaphors rather than stories—metaphors elaborated to a certain point and then, like lyric poems, closed—and they are no less artistically admirable for that.[2] Such exceptions notwithstanding, the fact is that most of the fiction we admire is admirable dramaturgically as well as in its other aspects.

If we admire a piece of prose fiction despite its non-storyhood, we are, precisely, admiring it *despite* its non-storyhood. Even the late John Gardner—by all accounts a splendid writing teacher despite his cranky notions of "moral fiction"—used to advise, "When in doubt, go for dramaturgy." Amen to that.

Back to Aristotle: The distinction between Plot and Action can be useful to what we might call clinical dramaturgical analysis, since a story's problems may lie in the one but not the other. As a classroom exercise, one can summarize the story of Sophocles's *Oedipus the King*, for example, entirely in terms of its plot with little or no reference to its action: "A happily married and much-respected head of state comes to learn that his eminent position is owing to his having unwittingly broken two major-league taboos, and in a day his fortunes are reversed." Clearly, any number of imaginable sequences of action might body forth that summarized plot. One then proceeds to examine for efficiency and effect the particular sequence chosen by Sophocles to do the job. Indeed, one may summarize the drama contrariwise, entirely in terms of its action with little or no reference to its plot: "A delegation of Theban elders complains to King Oedipus that a plague has fallen upon the place. The King sends his brother-in-law to the Delphic oracle to find out what's going on. That emissary returns with news of the gods' displeasure. The chorus of elders sings and dances apprehensively," et cetera.

Aristotle's stipulations that the action be 1) "whole" and 2) "of a certain magnitude" can be at least marginally useful, too: A "whole" action includes everything necessary to constitute a meaningful story and excludes anything irrelevant thereto—got that? "Of a certain magnitude" means that the action of fiction ought not to be inconsequential, however much it might appear to the characters to be so.

But if we ask "What's the meaning of *meaningful*?" or "What do you mean by *consequential*?", it turns out that *meaningful* means "*dramaturgically* meaningful" and *consequential* means "*dramaturgically* consequential," and around we go (likewise with Brooks and Warren's "meaningful series of events," even without their redundant "in a time sequence"). One is tempted to chuck the whole question and go back to good old Hunch and Feel—but these preliminary distinctions and definitions are worth bearing in mind as we try to spiral out of their circularity, mindful that what we're interested in here is not "mere" theory, but practical dramaturgy: Applied Aristotle.

The curve of dramatic action.

Not all fictive action is dramatic, either in the colloquial sense of "exciting" or in the practical sense of advancing the story's plot. And drama, to be sure, involves those other elements aforementioned— character and theme and language as well as action—although it's worth remembering that the Greek word *drama* literally means "deed," an action performed by a character, and that Aristotle declares in effect that it's easier to imagine a drama without characters[3] than one without action, the without-which-nothing of story. Dramatic action is conventionally described as "rising" to some sort of climactic "peak" or turning-point and then "falling" to some sort of resolution, or denouement. In short, as a sort of triangle—not really of the isosceles variety sometimes called "Fichte's triangle" after the late-18th-century German philosopher, but more like a stylized profile of Gibraltar viewed (in left-to-right cultures, anyhow) from the west: A ramp, let's say, which the story's "rising action" rather gradually ascends to a peak and then precipitately descends (punch lines are normally shorter than their jokes). Add to this ramp a bit of an approach and a bit of an exit—— and you've graphed the

Ingredients of Story as conventionally formulated: *Exposition* (the information requisite to understanding the action, or, as I prefer to put it, the "ground situation": a dramatically voltaged state of affairs pre-existing the story's present time), *Conflict* (or, in my shop, the introduction of the "dramatic vehicle": a present-time turn of events that precipitates a story out of the ground situation), *Complication* (of which more presently), *Climax*, *Denouement*, and *Wrap-Up* (the little coda, closing fillip, or dolly-back shot often appended to the denouement like a jazz drummer's "roll-off" at the end of a number, and usually suggestive of what the story's completed action *portends* for the principal characters).

Seems arbitrary, doesn't it, this curveless classic curve: an un-comfy-looking Bed of Procrustes upon which the action of fiction must be stretched or chopped to fit, or else. Or else what? Why not a story whose action graphs like this—— or this—— or that tracks more or less like Lawrence Sterne's diagrammed flourishes of Uncle Toby's walking-stick in *Tristram Shandy*—— or that simply flat-lines start to finish (_____)? In fact, that question touches a genuine mystery, in my opinion—and of course one can readily point to stories like the aforementioned *Tristram Shandy* that *appear* to proceed aimlessly, randomly, anyhow un-Aristotelianly; that digress repeatedly while in fact never losing sight of where they're going: up the old ramp to their climax and denouement. For practical purposes, however, the matter's no more mysterious than why one doesn't normally begin a joke with its punch line, a concert program or fireworks display with its *pièce de résistance*, a meal with its *chef d'oeuvre*, a session of lovemaking with its orgasm: Experience teaches that they simply aren't as effective that way, and "the rules of art," as David Hume remarked, are grounded "not in reason, but in experience."

Edward Albee has declared his preference for stories that have a beginning, a middle, and an end, "preferably in that order." Quite so—once one allows for another classical tradition, this one best articulated not by Aristotle but by Horace in his *Ars Poetica*: the tradition of beginning *in medias res*, in the middle of things rather than at their chronological Square One. To tell the story of the fall of Troy, says Horace, we need not begin *ab ovo*: "from the egg" laid by Leda after her ravishment by Zeus-in-the-form-of-a-swan, and from which hatched among others fair Helen, whose face launched a thousand ships, et cetera, et cetera. We might begin not even with the opening hostilities of the Trojan War itself, but rather—like Homer—in the ninth year of that disastrous ten-year enterprise, and then interstitch our Exposition retrospectively as we proceed.

In other words, the dramaturgical Beginning need not be and in fact seldom is the chronological beginning, and a story's order of narration (or a play's order of dramatization) need not be the strict chronological order of the events narrated. Dramatic effect, not linear chronology, is the regnant principle in the selection and arrangement of a story's action.

Isomorphs.

Apprentice story-makers may need reminding, however, that the world contains many things whose structure or progress resembles ("is isomorphic to" has a nice pedagogical ring) that of traditional dramaturgy. I have mentioned jokes, concert programs, pyrotechnical displays, multicourse meals, and lovemaking when things go well; one could add coffee-brewing (an old percolator of mine used to begin my every workday with a rising action that built to a virtual percolatory orgasm and then subsided to a quiet afterglow), waves breaking on a beach—you name it, but don't confuse those same-shapes with stories. In truth such isomorphy can be seductive; many an apprentice-piece hopefully substitutes the sonority of closure, for example, for real denouement; the thing *sounds* finished, but something tells us—a kind of critical bookkeeping developed maybe no more than half-consciously from our lifetime experience of stories—that its dramaturgical bills haven't been paid. Similarly, mere busyness in a story's Middle does not necessarily advance the plot; an analogy may be drawn here to the distinction in classical physics between Effort and Work. Dramatic action, as afore-established, need not be "dramatic," although a little excitement never hurt a story; it does need to turn the screws on the Ground Situation, complicate the conflict, move us up the ramp. Otherwise it's effort, not work; *isomorphic* to storyhood, perhaps, but not the real thing.

So how do we tell . . . ?

By never again reading your own stories or anybody else's—or watching any stage or screen or television-play—*innocently,* but always with a third eye monitoring how the author does it: what dramaturgical cards are being played and subsequently picked up (or forgotten); what waypoints (and how many, and in what sequence) the author has chosen to the dramaturgical destination, and why; what pistols, to use Chekhov's famous example, are being hung on the wall in Act One in order to be fired in Act Three. By learning to appreciate the often masterful dramaturgic efficiency of an otherwise merely amusing TV sitcom, for example, while on the other hand appreciating the extravagance-almost-for-its-own-sake of Rabelais' *Gargantua and Pantagruel.* Maybe even by reciting like a mantra this definition of Plot, which I once upon a time concocted out of the jargon of Systems Analysis: *the incremental perturbation of an unstable homeostatic system and its catastrophic restoration to a complexified equilibrium.*

Come again?

With pleasure. The "unstable homeostatic system" is that aforementioned Ground Situation: an overtly or latently voltaged state of
affairs pre-existing the story's present time; one that *tends* to regulate
itself toward equilibrium but is essentially less than stable (otherwise
there could be no story). The city of Thebes appears to be doing quite
satisfactorily under its new king, who fortuitously routed the Sphinx
and married the widowed queen (somewhat his elder) after the old
king was mysteriously slain at a place where three roads meet . . .
et cetera. No ground situation, no story, however arresting the action to come, for it is its effect upon the ground situation that gives
the story's action meaning. On the other hand, if the system merely
continues on its unstable homeostatic way, there'll be no story either.
Another child born to Oedipus and Jocasta? What else is new?

"And then one day," as the narrative formula puts it, the
Dramatic Vehicle rolls into town: A murrain descends upon Thebes
and environs and is determined to be owing to the gods' displeasure at
the unsolved murder of old King Laius. Because most stories originate
in some arresting experience or event—"Wait'll you hear what happened to *me* last night!"—it's a common failing of apprentice fiction
to be more interesting in its action and characters than in its point;
to launch an arresting or at least entertaining (potential) dramatic vehicle without a clearly established and thought-through ground situation, as ripe as Sophocles's Thebes for Incremental Perturbation—

Which is to say, for the successive complications of the conflict. That crazy old prophet Tiresias reluctantly claims that Oedipus
himself was old King Laius's murderer, and then. . . . The conflict-
complications comprising a story's Middle may in some cases be
more serial than incremental: One can imagine rearranging the order

of certain of Don Quixote's sorties against Reality or of Huck's and Jim's raft-stops down Old Man River without spoiling the effect. Even in those cases, however, the overall series is cumulative, the net effect incremental; the unstable homeostatic system is quantitatively perturbed and re-perturbed, until. . . .

In the most efficiently plotted stories, these perturbations follow not only *upon* one another but *from* one another, each paving the way for the next. In what we might call a camel's-back story, on the other hand, the complicative straws are simply added, one by one, as the story's Middle performs its double and contradictory functions of simultaneously fetching us to the climax and strategically delaying our approach thereto. In both cases, however—as Karl Marx says of history and as one observes everywhere in nature—enough quantitative change can effect a comparatively swift qualitative change: The last straw breaks the camel's back; one degree colder and the water freezes; at some trifling new provocation the colonies rebel. You say the ditched baby had *a swollen foot*, like, uh, mine? And that the uppity old dude I wasted back at that place where three roads meet was actually . . . ?

How many perturbatory increments does a story need? Just enough: Too few leads to unconvincing climax, faked orgasm; too many is beating a dead horse, or broken camel. And how many are just enough? Just enough—although one notes in passing the popularity of threes, fives, and sevens in myths and folk-stories.

The climax or turn, when it comes, happens relatively quickly: It's "catastrophic" in the mathematicians' Catastrophe Theory sense, whether or not (as Aristotle prescribes) it involves the fall of the mighty from the height of fortune to the depths of misery. Even in the most delicate of "epiphanic" stories, the little epiphany that epiphs, the little insight vouchsafed to the protagonist (or perhaps only to the reader), does so in a comparative flash—and for all its apparent slightness, is of magnitudinous consequence.

Which consequence we measure by the net difference it effects in the ground situation. Like some pregnancy tests, the measurement is only one-way valid: If nothing of consequence about the ground situation has been altered, no story has been told; the action has been all Effort and no Work. If the ground situation has unquestionably been changed (all the once-living characters are now dead, let's say), then a story *may* have been told. The follow-up test is whether that change—be it "dramatic," even melodramatic, or so almost imperceptible that the principals themselves don't yet realize its gravity—is dramaturgically/thematically meaningful, in terms of what has been established to be *at stake*. The "equilibrium" of a story's denouement is not that of its opening: Order may reign again in Thebes, for a while anyhow, under Kreon's administration; but Jocasta has hanged herself, and Oedipus has stabbed out his eyes and left town. It is an equilibrium complexified: qualitatively changed even where things may appear to all hands (except the reader/spectator) to be Back to Normal.

Otherwise, what we have attended may have its incidental merits, but for better or worse (usually worse) it's not a story.

"The Parallels!": Italo Calvino and Jorge Luis Borges

This record of encounters with two of my literary navigation stars was delivered to a conference on Calvino at the University of California at Davis in April 1997 and subsequently published in the inaugural issue of the journal *Context* in 1999. I include it here among these essays "On Reading, Writing, and the State of the Art," but it could as fittingly appear in the later "Tributes and Memoria" section of this volume.

MY PERSONAL REMINISCENCES of the writer we here celebrate can be covered in short order, for I didn't come to know the man nearly so well on that level as I wish I had. Italo Calvino's fiction I discovered in 1968, the year *Cosmicomics* appeared in this country in William Weaver's translation.[1] I was teaching then at the State University of New York at Buffalo and had fallen much under the spell of Jorge Luis Borges, whom I had discovered just a couple of years earlier. In that condition of enchantment I had published in '68 a sort of proto-postmodernist manifesto called "The Literature of Exhaustion"[2] and also my maiden collection of short stories, entitled *Lost in the Funhouse* and subtitled *Fiction for Print, Tape, Live Voice* (that particular deployment of the term "fiction" is a salute to Borges's *ficciones*). In short, the ground had been prepared for my delight in Calvino's *Cosmicomics* and then in his *T-Zero* stories, which appeared in Mr. Weaver's English the following year. Here, I thought, was a sort of Borges without tears, or better, a Borges *con molto brio*: lighter-spirited than the great Argentine, often downright funny (as Sr. Borges almost never is), yet comparably virtuosic in form and language, comparably rich in intelligence and imagination.

I was sufficiently impressed—and the university was sufficiently well funded in those Lyndon Johnson/Nelson Rockefeller years—to write soon after to Signor Calvino at his Paris address, inviting him to visit Buffalo as Señor Borges had recently done, also at my eager invitation. Indeed, I urged Calvino to be my professorial replacement for a semester or even a whole academic year. At that time I was the lucky sitter in a brand-new and peculiarly endowed professorial chair whose generous income I was not permitted to draw as additional salary, but *was* allowed to use to hire a visiting writer to replace me from time to time. The first of these eminent succedanea had been Donald Barthelme; I much wanted the second to be Italo Calvino. In due time I received a cordial reply—in Italian, which I gathered (and a bilingual colleague confirmed) to say that while Calvino was gratified by the invitation, he was not yet confident enough of his English to preside over a "creative writing" course at our university. Such enterprises were and are, of course, quite foreign to our European brethren. My enthusiasm for Calvino's fiction, however, was sufficiently shared by others at that lively place in that lively time (imagine having Don Barthelme and Michel Foucault as simultaneously visiting professors, as we did in Buffalo in 1972) to inspire the drama department to mount a charming stage adaptation of *Cosmicomics* in honor of the author; and having made each other's epistolary acquaintance, Calvino and I exchanged books and occasional letters thereafter. He sent me *Invisible Cities* and the *Tarots*, both of which I found wonderfully good; I sent him *Lost in the Funhouse* and *Chimera*.

A few years later, in 1976, I was able to re-extend my come-visit invitation, this time from Johns Hopkins, whereto I had moved and wherefrom we contrived to extract some special funding for distinguished visitors in connection with the university's centennial festivities. And this time, to our interdepartmental delight, Calvino accepted. Indeed, he accepted in English, declaring that he now felt confident enough in our language to give the thing a brief try. And at the close of his letter of acceptance I was charmed by . . . *Friendly yours*.

In the event, he was with us in Baltimore for about two weeks in March of that year: a dapper, courteous, reserved but entirely cordial fellow whose alert, rather intense mien reminded me of a sharp-eyed bird's. To my apprentice fiction-writers he read his essay on fiction as an *ars combinatoria* within a closed field. To the university's Italian community he lectured in Italian on Manzoni's *I Promessi Sposi* (but he politely declined an invitation from the Italian consulate in Baltimore to attend a reception there in his honor, on the grounds that he was visiting as a writer, not as a *paisano*). To the university community at large he gave a public reading from *Cosmicomics*, *T-Zero*, and *Invisible Cities*, which my wife and I remember with particular warmth despite the strain of his fallible and often hesitant English. I had let Calvino know, earlier, that his fiction had been among my courtship materials in the wooing of my bride—especially the lovely closing story from *Cosmicomics*, called "The Spiral"—and in acknowledgment of his unwitting role as our *Galeoto*, he included that story in his program, dedicating it to us. Finally, to our literature students and faculty he gave a delightful talk in English on his adventures with the Tarot cards, illustrating his remarks with the deck itself. A student of mine from those days remembers his accidentally dropping the whole pack in mid-demonstration; I myself cannot imagine Italo Calvino ever dropping a card or missing a trick—and sure enough, when I recently reviewed the videotapes of that occasion, I was gratified to see vindicated both my memory and Calvino's manual dexterity.

Of that too-brief Baltimore sojourn I recall little else. We pointed out to Calvino our city's funky Bromo-Seltzer Building, which Baltimoreans declare to resemble a Sienese tower. Calvino politely opined that it did not look remarkably Sienese to him, even without the giant blue trademark bottle that used to crown its clock (with the letters B-R-O-M-O-S-E-L-T-Z-E-R instead of numerals). We showed him a particularly bleak nighttime stretch of featureless East Baltimore rowhouses, their cornices lined with hundreds of chattering starlings; to me the scene looked very like de Chirico, but Calvino, delighted with it, said, "It's all Edward Hopper!" Both impressions, I think, are defensible. Off he presently went to join his wife up in New York City, which he loved, then down with her to Mexico City, which he didn't love (although he much admired the smaller towns and the Mexican countryside, and was an avid collector of pre-Columbian artifacts), and then back to his home turf, the Paris/Torino axis along which he regularly commuted in those days. We continued to exchange books and occasional letters (such a lover of "lightness" and "quickness" cannot have admired my enormous novel called *LETTERS*, which I sent him in 1979, although I'm confident he would have approved its formal design). My wife and I looked forward to a reunion with him and Mrs. Calvino during his

Norton lectureship at Harvard in 1985/86: a reunion and a lecture-ship that, alas, never came to pass.

Two final reminiscences, and then on with the story. Just a week or so after the news reached us of Italo's death on September 19, 1985, Umberto Eco happened to be our guest at Johns Hopkins, and of course we spoke of our mutual lost friend (a much closer friend of Eco's, to be sure; Calvino had been Eco's "chaperon," as Eco himself put it, for the Strega Prize). He had it on good authority, Eco told me, that despite the damage of the massive stroke that had felled Calvino a fortnight earlier, the man managed to utter, as perhaps his final words, "*I paralleli! I paralleli!*" ("The parallels! The parallels!"). Kindly perpend that wonderful exit-line, to which I shall shortly return.

A year or so later, Esther ("Chichita") Calvino telephoned to ask whom I might recommend to write a foreword to the Harvard University Press's forthcoming publication of her husband's never-delivered Norton lectures, *Six Memos for the Next Millennium.* Promptly and warmly I recommended myself for that melancholy last rite, but she explained that the Press was insisting on the introduc-er's being someone from the Harvard community. On that I drew a blank, and in the event she wrote the touching and altogether admi-rable foreword herself—the first of several that she has since written for posthumous editions of her husband's work.

In those five lovely *Memo* lectures—"Lightness," "Quickness," "Exactitude," "Visibility," and "Multiplicity"[3]—Calvino voices sev-eral times his admiration for Jorge Luis Borges, an admiration that he and I had shared in our Baltimore conversations. The story-series *Lost in the Funhouse*, I had told Calvino, was my attempt to assimi-late my encounter with Borges's narrative imagination; the *T-Zero* collection, Calvino had replied, was his endeavor to do likewise. If parallel lines can be bent non-Euclideanly back upon themselves, I shall circle now back to this lecture's starting-place and draw a few *paralleli*—also some anti-*paralleli*—between the fiction of those two superb writers, who were born a quarter-century apart (both, as it happens, in Latin America) but who died, alas for literature, within nine months of each other (both as it happens, in Europe).

FIRST, SOME NOT particularly literary *paralleli.* The two gentlemen shared that dignified, polite, even somewhat courtly but altogether approachable and good-humored sociability that I mentioned earlier; nothing in the least rowdy, "bohemian," or as some might say, re-demptively vulgar about either of them, at least in my limited experi-ence of their company. Compared for example to Vladimir Nabokov, Gore Vidal, or John Gardner (to name three very dissimilar anti-types), both Borges and Calvino were nonbelligerent with respect to their fellow writers. I note with some envy that Calvino's fiction in particular—rather like García Márquez's, but perhaps a touch less than Borges's—is mutually admired by writers who might agree on very little else. Vidal, Gardner, Mary McCarthy, John Updike (whom I have the honor of having introduced to Calvino's fiction)—all are or were warm *Calvinistas* along with us alleged Postmodernists, even though Mr. Vidal, in my opinion, gets things wrong even when sing-ing the writer's praises, which characteristically he cannot do with-out disparaging other of his contemporaries. Borges and Calvino shared moreover not only their Latin American nativity—Calvino was born in Cuba, where his father was doing agronomical work in 1923—but also a specifically Argentine connection: Borges was born in Buenos Aires and lived most of his life in that city; Esther Judith

Singer Calvino was likewise born in Buenos Aires, but spent most of her adult life in Europe—an Italian citizen living and working in Paris as a translator until the Calvinos resettled in Rome. Borges, it occurs to me to mention, declared himself pleased to have a Jewish component in his ancestry (not a very direct one, it turns out, though a consequential: One of his English grandmother's sisters married an Italian-Jewish engineer who immigrated to Argentina with his bride and with Borges's grandmother-to-be), and he said that only once did he break his own rule against political writing: He wrote two pro-Israel poems at the time of the Six-Day War. A fair number of his stories deal with explicitly Jewish themes and characters—"The Aleph," "Deutsches Requiem," "Emma Zunz," and "The Secret Miracle," among others—and in conversation he once gently corrected my mispronunciation of the word *Kabbalah*. To the best of my recollection, Calvino's Jewish connection nowhere surfaces in his fiction; perhaps his wife wasn't particularly interested in that aspect of her ethnicity, or perhaps Italo wasn't. His double Latino connection, on the other hand, notably does surface from time to time—for example in the wonderful story "The Jaguar Sun"—but its contexts are typically more Central American than Argentinean, distinctly removed from Borges's pampas and *milongas* and Buenos Airean suburbs. In Calvino's early story specifically entitled "The Argentine Ant," the setting and the characters are thoroughly Italian; only the eponymous ants are said to "come from South America."

It is Italy, of course, that plays the role in Calvino's fiction that Argentina plays in Borges's, and we note at once another parallel: While both writers draw strongly and eloquently upon their respective national cultures, the literary orientation of both is decidedly more international than regional, in their aesthetics as well as their subject matter. Borges was a lifelong Anglophile with a passion for *Beowulf* and a particular fondness for the England of Robert Louis Stevenson, G. K. Chesterton, and H. G. Wells, but his literary acquaintance was encyclopedic. Calvino valued highly his extended residence in Paris and his association with Raymond Queneau's OULIPO group (*L'Ouvoir de la litterature potentielle*, to which I'll circle back presently); while he wrote knowledgeably about Italian literature from various periods, his most strongly felt affinities (after the comic books and Hollywood movies of his youth) were with Italian folktales, the *novellini*, and such ingeniously structured tale-cycles as Boccaccio's *Decameron*. Both writers, I'm happy to point out, shared my fondness for Scheherazade and company. In Calvino's case, rather more than in Borges's though not more than in mine, this fondness extended to tale-cycles and narrative framing devices in general; in our final literary exchange, in 1984, I sent Calvino a half-serious essay of mine on Scheherazade's menstrual cycle as a key to *The 1001 Nights*,[4] and he sent me his 1982 essay in *La Repubblica* on Nezami's medieval Persian tale-cycle *The Seven Princesses*.

This "internationalism" caused Borges to be criticized at home for being not Argentinean enough in his literary preoccupations: a criticism which Borges quietly devastates in his essay "The Argentine Writer and Tradition." I doubt that Calvino was ever criticized for being insufficiently Italian, but I recall being told by an Italian colleague that his earlier, realistic works were knocked by the local Catholic critics for being too sympathetic to the Communists, and that his later, fabulistic fictions were knocked by the Communist critics for their abandonment of socialist realism. Although Calvino came to describe himself as a "political agnostic," he maintained a lively interest in the Italian political scene and wrote scathingly of the assassination of Aldo Moro. Borges was by temperament apolitical, although he despised Perón and got himself into hot water with many of his Latino literary comrades by welcoming the junta that displaced Perón and by accepting a Chilean literary award from the bloody hands of General Pinochet himself. He even permitted himself on that latter occasion some unfortunate disparagements of democratic government: as embarrassing though not incomprehensible a lapse, in its way, as García Márquez's buddyhood with Fidel Castro, which inspired the Romanian-American writer André Codrescu to remark that one can be simultaneously a great artist and a political idiot.

In sum, sort of, both Borges and Calvino were men of formidable literary sophistication who wore their learning lightly in conversation as well as in their art; unabashed "intellectuals" who were never pedantic or snobbish in their intellectuality (as their great peer Nabokov decidedly sometimes was). Before we leave these relatively personal for more strictly literary *paralleli*, I suppose it might be noted that both men's youthful lives were marked by a discreet, respectful ambivalence toward their fathers. Borges writes touchingly about his (and his military forebears) in the mini-memoir "An Autobiographical Essay"; Calvino likewise in *his* mini-memoir "The Road to San Giovanni." Both to some extent felt themselves to be letting the old man down in their pursuit of (in Borges's case) purely bookish interests and values or (in Calvino's) nonscientific ones; and both maintained a distanced fascination with what they had "rejected": swords, knives, and military history for Borges, the physical and natural sciences (but not agronomy) for Calvino. By way of anti-*paralleli*, before we move on: In part but surely not entirely because of his increasing blindness, Borges remained very much his mother's son during her long life and his long bachelorhood, which ended (the bachelorhood) only at age

68, when his then quite old mother felt unable to accompany him to Cambridge for the Norton lectureship. That late marriage lasted scarcely longer than Harvard's academic year; when *Madre* Borges succumbed in her mid-90s, Jorge Luis was admirably managed by his all-purpose assistant Maria Kodama, whom he married shortly before his death in Geneva at age 86. What Calvino's connection with his mother was, I have no idea (she scarcely figures in the "San Giovanni" memoir, although its author acknowledges that with "silent authority" she "looks out from between the lines"). On the evidence, however, he was altogether a more physically and psychologically independent fellow: a youthful veteran of the antifascist partisan resistance in World War II, a loving husband and father who wrote with amused affection of his domestic life—in the pretty essay "La Poubelle Agréé,"[5] for example, as well as in his letters. Perhaps that is why, to some of us at least, Calvino's fiction surpasses that of Borges in warmth and emotional range, if not in virtuosity and profundity.

BUT ENOUGH INDEED of this: The muses care not a whit about our personal profiles, and not much more than a whit about our politics; their sole concern is that we achieve the high country of Mounts Helicon and Parnassus, whether despite or because of where we're coming from, and this these two elevated spirits consistently did. The *paralleli* of their achievement are mostly obvious, the relevant anti-*paralleli* no doubt likewise. To begin with, both writers, for all their great sophistication of mind, wrote in a clear, straightforward, unmannered, non-baroque, but rigorously scrupulous style. ". . . crystalline, sober, and airy . . . without the least congestion," is how Calvino himself (in the second of his *Six Memos*) describes Borges's style, and of course those adjectives describe his own as well, as do the titles of all six of his Norton lectures: "Lightness" (*Leggerezza*) and deftness of touch; "Quickness" (*Rapidità*) in the senses both of economy of means and of velocity in narrative profluence; "Exactitude" (*Esatezza*) both of formal design and of verbal expression; "Visibility" (*Visibilità*) in the senses both of striking detail and of vivid imagery, even (perhaps especially) in the mode of fantasy; "Multiplicity" (*Molteplicità*) in the senses both of an *ars combinatoria* and of addressing the infinite interconnectedness of things, whether in expansive, incompletable works such as Gadda's *Via Merulana* and Robert Musil's *Man Without Qualities* or in vertiginous short stories like Borges's "Garden of Forking Paths"—all cited in Calvino's lecture on multiplicity; and "Consistency" in the sense that in their style, their formal concerns, and their other preoccupations we readily recognize the Borgesian and the Calvinoesque. So appealing a case does Calvino make for these particular half-dozen literary values, it's important to remember that they aren't the only ones; indeed, that their contraries have also something to be said for them. Calvino acknowledges as much in the "Quickness" lecture: ". . . each value or virtue I chose as the subject for my lectures," he writes, "does not exclude its opposite. Implicit in my tribute to lightness was my respect for weight, and so this apology for quickness does not presume to deny the pleasures of lingering," et cetera. We literary lingerers—some might say malingerers—breathe a protracted sigh of relief.

Reviewing these six "memos" has fetched us already beyond the realm of style to other parallels between the fictions of Borges and Calvino. Although he commenced his authorial career in the mode of the realistic novel and never abandoned the longer narrative forms, Calvino, like Borges, much preferred the laconic short take. Even his later extended works, like *Cosmicomics*, *Invisible Cities*, *The Castle of Crossed Destinies*, and *If on a Winter's Night a Traveler*, are (to use Calvino's own adjectives) modular and combinatory, built up from smaller, quicker units. Borges, more from aesthetic principle than from the circumstance of his later blindness, never wrote a novella, much less a novel.[6] And in his later life, like the doomed but temporarily reprieved Jaromir Hladik in "The Secret Miracle," he was obliged to compose and revise from memory. No wonder his style is so lapidary, so . . . memorable.

On with the parallels: Although one finds flavors and even some specific detail of Buenos Aires and environs in the corpus of Borges's fiction and of Italy in that of Calvino, and although each is a major figure in his respective national literature as well as in modern lit generally, both writers were prevailingly disinclined to the social/ psychological realism that for better or worse persists as the dominant mode in North American fiction. Myth and fable and science in Calvino's case, literary/philosophical history and "the contamination of reality by dream" in Borges's, take the place of social/psychological analysis and historical/geographical detail. Both writers inclined toward the ironic elevation of popular narrative genres: the folktale and comic strip for Calvino, supernaturalist and detective-fiction for Borges. Calvino even defined Postmodernism, in his "Visibility" lecture, as "the tendency to make ironic use of the stock images of the mass media, or to inject the taste for the marvelous inherited from literary tradition into narrative mechanisms that accentuate their alienation"— a tendency as characteristic of Borges's production as of his own. Neither writer, for better or worse, was a creator of memorable characters or a delineator of grand passions, although in a public conversation in Grand Rapids, Michigan, in 1975, in answer to the question "What do you regard as the writer's chief responsibility?" Borges unhesitatingly responded, "The creation of character." A poignant response from a great writer who never really created any characters; even his unforgettable Funes the Memorious, as I have remarked elsewhere, is not so much a character as a pathological characteristic. And Calvino's charming Qwfwq and Marco Polo and Marcovaldo and Mr. Palomar are archetypal narrative functionaries, nowise to be compared with the great pungent *characters* of narrative/dramatic literature. A first-rate restaurant may not offer every culinary good thing; for the pleasures of acute character-drawing as of bravura passions, one simply must look elsewhere than in the masterful writings of Jorge Luis Borges and Italo Calvino.

Attendant upon those "Postmodernist tendencies" aforecited by Calvino—the ironic recycling of stock images and traditional narrative mechanisms—is the valorization of *form*, even more in Calvino than in Borges. At his consummate best, Borges so artfully deploys what I've called the principle of metaphoric means that (excuse the self-quotation) "not just the conceit, the key images, the mise-en-scène, the narrative choreography and point of view and all that, but even the phenomenon of the text itself, the fact of the artifact, becomes a sign of its sense." His marvelous story "Tlön, Uqbar, Orbis Tertius" is a prime example of this high-tech tale-telling, and there are others. Borges manages this gee-whizzery, moreover, with admirable understatement, wearing his formal virtuosity up his sleeve rather than on it. Calvino, on the contrary, while never a show-off, took unabashed delight in his "romantic formalism" (again, my term, with my apology): a delight not so much in his personal ingenuity as in the exhilarating possibilities of the *ars combinatoria*, as witness especially the structural wizardry of *The Castle of Crossed Destinies* and *If on a Winter's Night a Traveler*. His extended association with

Raymond Queneau's OULIPO group was no doubt among both the causes and the effects of this formal sportiveness.

For reasons that will deliver me to the conclusion of this little homage, I regard Calvino as by far the finest writer in that lively Parisian group, which included the French/Polish Georges Perec and the American Harry Mathews, along with Queneau himself and a number of "recreational mathematicians" disporting with algorithmic narratives, or narrative algorithms. Calvino's skill at and delight in combinatory possibilities, a sort of structural *molteplicità*, led him into enthusiasms that I cannot always share—e.g., for the aforementioned Georges Perec, whose "hyper-novel" *La vie mode d'emploi* (*Life, a User's Manual*) Calvino calls "the last real event in the history of the novel thus far" (surely he means "latest," not "last") and which I myself find not only vertiginously ingenious but almost *merely* vertiginously ingenious. I read about a quarter of it, got the intricate idea (with Calvino's help), nodded my official approval, and could not force myself through the remaining three-quarters, confident as I was that the author would not miss a trick. Likewise, I have to confess, with Perec's algorithmic earlier novel *La Disparition* (translated as *A Void*), which so ingeniously manages not to use even once the most-used alphabetical letter in both French and English that at least some of the book's reviewers failed to notice that stupendous stunt. I shake my head in awe, but agree finally with the Englishman who said, vis-à-vis some other such feat, "It's a bit like farting *Annie Laurie* through a keyhole: damned clever, but why bother?"

That question happens to be answerable, but I prefer to move on to Calvino's superiority, in my view, to such near-mere stunts; to his transcension of his own "oulipesque" enthusiasms; and to the close of this talk. At his Johns Hopkins reading in 1976, Calvino briefly described the conceit of his *Invisible Cities* novel and then said, "Now I want to read just one little . . ." He hesitated for a moment to find the word he wanted. ". . . one little *aria* from that novel." Said I to myself, "Exactly, Italo, and *bravissimo!*" The saving difference between Calvino and the other wizards of OULIPO was that (bless his Italian heart and excuse the stereotyping) he knew when to stop formalizing and start singing—or better, how to make the formal rigors themselves sing. What Calvino said of Perec very much applied to his own shop: that the constraints of those crazy algorithms and other combinatorial rules, so far from stifling his imagination, positively stimulated it. For that reason, he once told me, he enjoyed accepting difficult commissions, such as writing the *Crossed Destinies* novel to accompany the Ricci edition of *I Tarocchi* or, more radically yet, composing a story *without words*, to be the dramatic armature of a proposed ballet (Calvino made up a wordless story about the invention of dancing).

To COME NOW to the last of these *paralleli*: Both Jorge Luis Borges and Italo Calvino managed marvelously to combine in their fiction the values that I call Algebra and Fire (I'm borrowing those terms here, as I have done elsewhere, from Borges's *First Encyclopedia of Tlön*, a realm complete, he reports, "with its emperors and its seas, with its minerals and its birds and its fish, with its algebra and its fire"). Let "algebra" stand for formal ingenuity, and "fire" for what touches our emotions (it's tempting to borrow instead Calvino's alternative values of "crystal" and "flame," from his lecture on exactitude, but he happens not to mean by those terms what I'm referring to here). Formal virtuosity itself can of course be breathtaking, but much algebra and little or no fire makes for mere gee-whizzery, like Queneau's *Exercises in Style* and *A Hundred Thousand Billion*

Sonnets. Much fire and little or no algebra, on the other hand, makes for heartfelt muddles—no examples needed. What most of us want from literature most of the time is *passionate virtuosity*, and both Borges and Calvino deliver it. Although I find both writers indispensable and would never presume to rank them as literary artists, by my lights Calvino perhaps comes closer to being the very model of a modern major Postmodernist (not that *that* very much matters), or whatever the capacious bag is that can contain such otherwise dissimilar spirits as Donald Barthelme, Samuel Beckett, J. L. Borges, Italo Calvino, Angela Carter, Robert Coover, Gabriel García Márquez, Elsa Morante, Vladimir Nabokov, Grace Paley, Thomas Pynchon, *et al.* . . . . What I mean is not only the fusion of algebra and fire, the great (and in Calvino's case high-spirited) virtuosity, the massive acquaintance with and respectfully ironic recycling of what Umberto Eco calls "the already said," and the combination of storytelling charm with zero naiveté, but also the keeping of one authorial foot in narrative antiquity while the other rests firmly in the high-tech (in Calvino's case, the Parisian "structuralist") narrative present. Add to this what I have cited as our chap's perhaps larger humanity and in-the-worldness, and you have my reasons.

All except one, which will serve as the last of my anti-*paralleli*: It seems to me that Borges's narrative geometry, so to speak, is essentially Euclidean. He goes in for rhomboids, quincunxes, and chess logic; even his ubiquitous infinities are of a linear, "Euclidean" sort. In Calvino's spirals and vertiginous recombinations I see a mischievous element of the non-Euclidean; he shared my admiration, for example, of Boccaccio's invention of the character Dioneo in the *Decameron*: the narrative Dionysian wild card who exempts himself from the company's rules and thus adds a lively element of (constrained) unpredictability to the narrative program. I didn't have the opportunity to speak with Calvino about quantum mechanics and chaos theory, but my strong sense is that he would have regarded them as metaphorically rich and appealing.

DID THESE TWO splendid writers ever meet?[7] Calvino's esteem for Borges is a matter of record; I regret having neglected to ask Borges, in our half-dozen brief conversations, his opinion of Calvino. My own esteem for both you will by now have divined. In Euclidean geometry, *paralleli* never meet, but it is among the first principles of non-Euclidean geometry that they *do* meet—not in Limbo, where Dante, led by Virgil, meets the shades of Homer and company, but in infinity.

A pretty principle, no? One worthy of an Italo Calvino, to make it sing.

Italo Calvino and Jorge Luis Borges. From *Album Calvino*, ed. Luca Baranelli and Ernesto Ferrero (Milan: Arnoldo Mondadori Editore, 1995).

My Faulkner

First delivered at a conference on William Faulkner at the University of Mississippi in 1999, this brief appreciation of that novelist's importance to this one was subsequently included (along with more scholarly presentations by other participants in the conference) in the volume *Faulkner and Postmodernism*, published later that year.[1] Reviewing my amateur remarks in the context of theirs, I'm reminded of what Flannery O'Connor is reported to have said about her work's being compared to Faulkner's: "Best get off the track when the Dixie Special's coming down the line."

I T'S UNDERSTOOD, I trust, that I'm with you today not in my capacity as a Faulkner specialist, for I have no such capacity, but merely and purely as a writer of fiction, who will presently read a short passage from a not markedly Faulknerian work in progress.[2] But the great American writer celebrated by this annual conference happens to have been among my first-magnitude navigation stars during my literary apprenticeship, and I'd like to speak a bit to that subject before I change voices.

In 1947, virtually innocent of literature, I matriculated as a freshman at the Johns Hopkins University. I can scarcely remember now what I had been taught before that in the English courses of

our semi-rural, semi-redneck 11-year county public school system
on Maryland's lower Eastern Shore; I certainly don't recall having
been much touched by any of it, or inspired by any of my pleasant,
well-meaning teachers. I borrowed books busily from the available
libraries[3]—Tom Swift, Edgar Rice Burroughs—and indiscriminately
from my father's small-town soda-fountain/lunchroom, whose stock
in trade included magazines, piano sheet music, and the newfangled
paperbound pocket books: Ellery Queen, Agatha Christie, Raymond
Chandler, and my favorite of all, the Avon Fantasy Reader series
(Abe Merritt, John Collier, and H. P. Lovecraft, *inter alia*). I remember being baffled but intrigued by an item called *Manhattan Transfer*,
by one John Dos Passos, and by another called *Sanctuary*, by somebody named William Faulkner, when they turned up randomly in
my borrowings. Those were, I came to understand later, my accidental first exposures to modern lit; I sensed their difference from
my regular diet, and even found and read some other items by that
Faulkner fellow in the pile: *The Wild Palms*, *Soldier's Pay*, and *Pylon*.
On the whole, however, I was more intrigued by another anthology
series just then appearing on Dad's shelves, called *The Ribald Reader*:
pretty spicy stuff by my then standards, and illustrated with titillative
line-drawings. What I only dimly registered at the time was that those
naughty anthologies were of considerable literary quality and admirable eclecticism: Their ribaldry was culled from the *Decameron*,
Pentameron, and *Heptameron*, from *The 1001 Nights* and the *Gesta
Romanorum* and the *Panchatantra*, among other exotic sources—all
news to me, and not to be found in either the Dorchester County
Public or the Cambridge (Maryland) school libraries (where *The
Arabian Nights* was a much-abridged and expurgated edition illustrated by N. C. Wyeth).

My declared major as a very green Hopkins freshman was Journalism: One was obliged to choose *something*, and I had done a humor column for our school newspaper in my senior year. Never mind how I stumbled from journalism into fiction-writing; what's relevant here, in retrospect, is that the literature most provocative to my adolescent curiosity, apart from the mystery novels and Tom Swifties, was not the canonical classics, but Modernism on the one hand (as represented in its American grain by the Dos Passos and those early, mostly minor Faulkners) and on the other hand the venerable tale-cycle tradition, as represented ribaldly in those Avon Readers. At Hopkins I had professors both excellent and inspiring and was at last baptized, though not totally immersed, in the canonical mainstream—but two circumstances, fortunate for me, reinforced those earlier, fugitive, extracurricular samplings.

The first, as I've written elsewhere,[4] was my very good luck in having to help pay my way by filing books in the university library. "My" stacks happened to be the voluminous ones of the Classics Department and of William Foxwell Albright's Oriental Seminary, as it was then called; the books on my cart therefore included not only Homer and Virgil and other such standard curricular items, but also Petronius and Apuleius and the unabridged Scheherazade and the *Panchatantra* and *The Ocean of the Streams of Story* and the *Vetalapanchavimsata* as well as, by some alcove-gerrymandering, Boccaccio and Rabelais and Marguerite of Angouleme and Giovanni Basile and Poggio Bracciolini and Pietro Aretino—hot stuff, which I sampled eagerly as I filed, and often borrowed from the book-cart to take home and read right through: what I think of as my *à la carte* education.

The second lucky circumstance is that in Hopkins's literature departments at that time, one did not generally study still-living or even recently dead authors; but our brand-new and somewhat frowned-upon Department of Writing, Speech, and Drama (later renamed the Writing Seminars) broke ranks and energetically held forth on Proust, Joyce, Kafka, Mann, Eliot, Pound, Hemingway, and Faulkner—this last via my very first fiction-writing coach, a Marine-combat-veteran teaching assistant from the deep South at work on the university's first-ever doctoral dissertation on the sage of Oxford, Miss.

Let's cut to the chase: For the next three years I imitated everybody, badly, in search of my writerly self, while downloading my innumerable predecessors as only an insatiable green apprentice can. Owing to some tension between our writing operation and the English Department, my curricular reading in literature was freighted with the Greek and Roman classics, with Dante and Cervantes and Flaubert, and with the big Modernists aforementioned, while my library cart supplied me with extracurricular exotica. What I never got, for better or worse, was the standard fare of English majors: good basic training in Chaucer and Shakespeare and the big 18th- and 19th-century English novelists, though there had been some naughty Canterbury Tales in those *Ribald Readers*, and I reveled in Fielding and Dickens on my own. So many voices; so many eloquent and wildly various voices—none more mesmerizing to me (thanks to that ex-Marine T.A. writing coach, the late Robert Durene Jacobs of Georgia State University) than Faulkner's. I read all of him, I believe—all of him as of that mid-century date—and I saw that the Faulkners I'd stumbled upon in high-school days were mostly warm-ups for such *chef d'oeuvres* as *The Sound and the Fury*, *As I Lay Dying*, *Light in August*, and *Absalom, Absalom*. It was Faulkner at his most involuted and incantatory who most enchanted me, and while I had (and have) never thought of myself as a capital-S Southerner—nor a

Northerner either, having grown up virtually astride Mason's and Dixon's Line—I felt a strong affinity between Faulkner's Mississippi and the Chesapeake marsh-country that I was born and raised in. My apprentice fiction grew increasingly Faulknerish, and when I stayed on at Johns Hopkins as a graduate student, my M.A. thesis and maiden attempt at a novel was a heavily Faulknerian marsh-opera about sinisterly inbred Chesapeake crabbers and muskrat trappers. The young William Styron, visiting our seminar fresh from winning his National Book Award for *Lie Down in Darkness*, listened patiently to one particularly purple chapter, a mishmash of middle Faulkner and late Joyce, and charitably praised it; but the finished opus didn't fly—for one thing, because Faulkner intimately *knew* his Snopeses and Compsons and Sartorises, as I did not know my made-up denizens of the Maryland marsh. A copy of the manuscript made the rounds of Manhattan in vain until my agent gave up on it; I later destroyed it as an embarrassment. The original languished in the dissertation-stacks of the Hopkins library for a couple of decades until, to my indignant half-relief, some unprincipled rascal stole it. Thanks anyhow, Bill Faulkner and Bill Styron.

AND WHERE WERE Scheherazade and company all this time? Singing in my other ear and inspiring my second and final major apprentice effort: A Faulknerian/Boccaccian hybrid this time, called *The Dorchester Tales*: 100 tales of my Eastern Shore Yoknapatawpha at all periods of its human history. This, too, failed, at round about Tale 50, and this manuscript too, lest it come back to haunt me, I later destroyed except for a few nuggets that worked their way, reorchestrated, into *The Sot-Weed Factor*. But I like to think that it was a step in the right direction: an attempt to combine the two principal strains of my literary DNA. In hindsight, as I've declared elsewhere,[5] it's clear to me that what I needed to do was find some way to book Faulkner, Joyce, and Scheherazade on the same tidewater showboat, with myself at both the helm and the steam calliope. Another way to put it is that I needed to discover, or to be discovered by, what later came to be called Postmodernism. With the help of yet another fortuitous and highly unlikely input—the turn-of-the-century Brazilian novelist Joaquim Machado de Assis, whose works I stumbled upon in the mid-1950s, this came to pass.

In the decades since, I am obliged to report, although the figure of Ms. Scheherazade has remained so central to my imagination that merely to hear one of the themes from Rimsky-Korsakov's suite is enough to deliquesce me yet, Mr. Faulkner's currency in my shop has had its ups and downs. My wife used to teach *Light in August* to her high-school seniors; while rereading it periodically for that purpose, she would recite memorable passages to me, and a time came when the rhetoric that had once so appealed to me now seemed . . . overpumped. I would tease her (and Faulkner, and myself) by wondering, for example, whether it was the Immemorial Wagon-Wheels going down the Outraged Path or the Outraged Wheels on the Immemorial Path, and what final difference there was between those sonorous propositions.

¿Cien Años de Qué?

The following was delivered (in English) in 1998 at Spain's León University as part of the conference described below and published two years later in Volume I of that conference's proceedings.[1]

W HAT A REMARKABLE occasion for a pan-American literary conference at a Spanish university: the centennial of the Spanish-American War and of Spain's consequent loss of her last American colonies; the end of her enormous empire, which, as the British historian Hugh Thomas recently declared, "in its duration and cultural influence . . . overshadows the empires of Britain, France, Holland, Belgium, and even Russia."

At first one might wonder, Why commemorate such an historical setback with a literary conference? But then one remembers that when a newspaper reporter once asked William Faulkner what, in his opinion, accounted for the impressive literary flowering of the North American Southland after our Civil War, Faulkner replied: "We lost." And does not Homer somewhere remark ironically that "Wars are fought so that poets will have something to sing about"? Perhaps we can revise that *obiter dictum* to read "Wars are *lost* so that" et cetera. Clearly, the aphorism applies with particular poignancy to Spain after 1898. I shall return to it after expressing my gratitude to this university, to the Fulbright Commission, and to the organizers of this conference for providing my wife and me with an occasion to revisit España: a country for which we share a longstanding affection; a country that we have visited a number of times over the decades, and that has been of some importance to me as a writer of fiction.

Indeed, for reasons that I shall presently make clear, one of my tentative titles for this talk was "One Hundred Years of Gratitude" (*Cien Años de Gratitud*: The rhyme with *solitude* works in English, though not in Spanish). Reflecting upon the literary activity in North and South America since 1898 and upon literary relations between the two continents as well, I also considered "One Hundred Years of Plenitude." But then, shaking my head at some unfortunate aspects of our *political* relations through that period, I thought perhaps "One Hundred Years of Turpitude" might be more appropriate. (Do we have the word *turpitud* en español? No? We certainly have it in English.) And then, considering what my more knowledgeable friends tell me of the vigor and diversity of contemporary *Spanish* literature, I considered "The (Re)Generation of '98;[2] or, Forget the *Maine*!" To this subject, too—I mean the infamous event that triggered the Spanish-American War—I shall return.

What a formidable *cien años* ours has been! As a novelist, I make occasional use of what are called in English "time lines": those reference books and computer software programs that attempt to show, like an orchestral concert score, what was happening more or less simultaneously in various fields in various parts of the world at particular periods of history. To look back upon the closing years of the 19th century and at the year 1898 in particular with the help of these time lines is to be impressed by their *busyness*, by their sheer activity in just about every area of human endeavor, and by what their remarkable accomplishments can now be seen to have portended for the century that followed. Perhaps the same could be said of virtually any decade in recent centuries if one examines it through the lens of hindsight; but just consider: The years 1890 through 1899 gave us the Nobel prizes and the modern Olympic games, Social Darwinism, the Dreyfus Affair, Gobineau's "scientific" racism, and the Klondike Gold Rush. They saw the triumph of Europe's colonization of Africa (except for Ethiopia and Liberia) and the suppression of our North American Indians at the battle of Wounded Knee, along with our westward expansion into the new states of Idaho, Wyoming, and Utah. They gave us the Sino-Japanese War and the Cuban Revolution and Queen Victoria's Diamond Jubilee; they gave us the first cinema and the first comic strip; they gave us the discovery of radioactivity and the invention of wireless telegraphy, the diesel engine, the automobile, electromagnetic sound recording, rocket propulsion, synthetic fibers, electric subways, the clothing zipper, the safety razor, and the "safety bicycle." They gave us Frazer's *Golden Bough* and Freud's *Studien über Hysterie* and Havelock Ellis's *Psychopathia Sexualis*; Karl Marx's *Das Kapital* (Volume 3) and Bergson's *Matiere et Memoire* and Herzl's *Der Judenstraat* and John Dewey's *School and Society*. It was the decade of Post-Impressionism and Art Nouveau; of Debussy and Puccini and Richard Strauss and Sibelius and Mahler and Massenet; of Chekhov and Darío and young Yeats and old Tolstoy, of Ibsen and Shaw and Conrad and Henry James and Machado de Assis.

As for our "baseline" year: The timelines tell us that 1898 saw the opening of the Paris Metro, the construction of Count Zeppelin's first dirigible, the discovery of radium and xenon and neon and the dysentery bacillus, and the first successful photography with artificial

light. In China, the Boxer Rebellion against Western influences began. Bismarck and Gladstone died that year; so did Lewis Carroll
and Stefan Mallarmé. On the other hand, Bertolt Brecht and Ernest
Hemingway were born (as was my mother), and, if my obstetrical
arithmetic is correct, both Jorge Luis Borges and Vladimir Nabokov
were conceived in 1898. Zola's "*J'Accuse*" was published that year,
as were Henry James's *The Turn of the Screw* and Knut Hamsun's
Victory and H. G. Wells's *War of the Worlds* and Oscar Wilde's
Ballad of Reading Gaol and Bernard Shaw's *Caesar and Cleopatra*
and J. K. Huysman's *La Cathédrale*.

All very impressive and rich in promise. But then we reflect upon
the staggering century that followed—two world wars and abundant
smaller but also dreadful ones; poison gas, automatic weapons, aerial
bombing, nuclear and biological weapons; totalitarianism and massacre on an unprecedented scale, despite which our species overruns
and despoils the planet and its atmosphere, et cetera ad nauseam—
and I am reminded of a cartoon in our *New Yorker* magazine a few
years ago: Our astronauts have landed on a beautiful, verdant new
planet, a virtual paradise; indeed, as they step out of their space vehicle they see in the near distance a fruit tree, under which stand a
man and a woman, naked; there is a serpent in the tree; the woman
holds an apple in her hand, from which she seems about to take a
bite—and one of the astronauts runs toward her, shouting "Wait!"
Looking back at the timelines for the pre-dawn of this century, I feel
like that astronaut: "*¡Cuidado! ¡Un momento, por dios!*"

Too late: *Consummatum est*, or almost so—for who knows what
may yet happen to us in the small remaining interval between today
and the next century, not to mention what *that* century may have in
store for us?

Cien años de plenitud; cien años de turpitud (I'll use the word, even though it doesn't exist in Spanish and doesn't rhyme with *soledad*). As for *gratitud* . . . well: In the face of our century's human catastrophes—the hundreds of millions of victims of militant nationalism and colonialism, of ideology in general and totalitarianism in particular—one feels that there is something unseemly, perhaps even obscene, about reviewing its *positive* accomplishments in science, technology, and the arts, including the Hundred Years of Literary Plenitude that inspired this conference: the century of *modernismo* and of Modernism; of Postmodernism and Magic Realism and *El Boom*.[3] As if, for example, the scientific and cultural enrichment of the United States (and the world) by refugees from European Fascism and Russian Communism—by Albert Einstein and Thomas Mann and Pablo Casals and Vladimir Nabokov and dozens of others in every field, including my own Johns Hopkins professors Leo Spitzer and Pedro Salinas—as if their achievements somehow mitigate the evils that they fled! Or, to come closer to home, as if, in some humanistic double-entry bookkeeping, Pablo Picasso's *Guernica* can somehow be balanced against the Guernica of Francisco Franco. Something obscene, I say, about that. And yet. . . .

AND YET, SINCE Guernica was destroyed in any case, we are surely no *worse* off for having Picasso's rendition of that atrocity to contemplate in Madrid. If, in Ezra Pound's bitter formulation, all that the ravages of history have left to us of classical Greece and Rome are "a gross of broken statues and a fewscore battered books," then we are not only no *worse* off for having those souvenirs; we would be considerably worse off if we *didn't* have them, much as we may lament what was lost of these cultures in the Christian Dark Ages, for example.

Consider the case of my compatriot Raymond Federman, an avant-garde North American writer and my former colleague at the State University of New York in Buffalo: Born in Paris to a family of modest French-Jewish tailors, Federman was destined to be apprenticed to his father's trade; but when the Nazis invaded France, he and his family were rounded up along with most other French Jews and shipped off to the death camps. Young Raymond and some other boys in his boxcar managed to escape almost accidentally before the train crossed the border; he made his way somehow to the south of France, where he worked as a farm laborer while his family and the rest of European Jewry were being exterminated in the Holocaust. Ultimately and fortunately he got himself to the USA, where he was able to finish high school, attend Columbia University, complete a doctorate in French literature at the University of California, and become a respected American university professor and writer instead of a small-time Parisian neighborhood tailor. "So what am I supposed to do?" Raymond once asked me: "Thank Hitler?"

Well, no, of course not. If we could magically undo the Holocaust by giving up the collected works of Raymond Federman, I am quite sure that even the author would consent.[4] William Faulkner, whom I've quoted already, once made the casually cruel remark that one poem by John Keats is worth "any number of old ladies." One would like to have asked him, *Any* number? Six million, for example? Or perhaps just a mere handful, but including your own mother and grandmother? Fortunately for us, history doesn't offer such options—at least not to most of us—and so we are free to be grateful for Raymond Federman and Anne Frank and Primo Levi without having to be grateful to Adolf Hitler. We can thank Vladimir Nabokov for his beautiful novels in English without thanking Lenin and Stalin for dispossessing him of pre-Revolutionary Russia. *Muchas gracias*, Pablo Picasso *y* Pablo Casals; no *gracias* necessary to the Generalissimo. And (to circle back toward my subject) *I* can thank Poet-Professor Pedro Salinas for leading us ignorant undergraduate gringos through *Don Quijote* and *Lazarillo de Tormes* and Lope de Vega and Calderón de la Barca and Unamuno and Ortega y Gasset without thanking the *Loyalistas* for driving Salinas into American exile.

INDEED, ON THE assumption that I have by now made my position clear enough not to be mistaken for Voltaire's Dr. Pangloss, I am tempted to return to 1898, as follows: Even the United States Navy, I understand, has come virtually to admit that the explosion that sank our battleship *U.S.S. Maine* in Havana Harbor at 9:40 PM on 15 February 1898 and killed 268 of its crew was almost certainly caused not by a Spanish anti-ship mine, but by an accidental fire in the vessel's coal bunkers, next to its reserve gunpowder magazines. Our own distinguished Admiral Hyman Rickover, commander of the U.S. nuclear submarine fleet, came to that conclusion in his official reinvestigation of the matter in 1976; Rickover's report (which our government in general and our Navy in particular received with loud silence) confirmed what Spanish investigators had been saying all along. But ah, my friends: If the powerful U.S. newspaper publisher William Randolph Hearst, along with President McKinley's hyper-*macho* Assistant Secretary of the Navy, Theodore Roosevelt, had not seized that opportunity to whip up American war hysteria with their cry "Remember the *Maine!*" there would have been no Spanish-American War to deprive Spain of its last colonies in the Western Hemisphere, and hence no *Generación de Noventa y Ocho*, and hence perhaps a different set of historical circumstances in Spain from those that led to the Guerra Civil and Franco's dictatorship, and hence no exile for the likes of Pedro Salinas (first in Puerto Rico, then in the USA), and hence no quietly inspiring exemplar for this particular 18-year-old Yankee fumbling his way toward a literary vocation: the first living, breathing *writer* of any sort, not to mention the first bona fide internationally distinguished poet, whom I had ever been in the gentle, dignified, good-humored presence of. . . .

Voltaire's Candide asks his friend Martin, "For what purpose was the world formed?" "To infuriate us," Martin replies. Also, I would add, to dismay and humble us with its staggering *contingencies*, both general and specific: Had it not been for the anti-Semitic pogroms in Russia and Eastern Europe and the relative poverty of village life in Germany toward the end of the 19th century, my wife's grandparents would not have immigrated to America from Minsk and Latvia and my own grandparents from Sachsen-Altenburg, and Shelly and I would not exist, much less have met each other. If not for a certain snowstorm in Boston at the end of the 1960s, we would not have re-met in romantic and happily consequential circumstances. A different sort of spontaneous combustion aboard the *U.S.S. Maine* in 1898 may be imagined to have led to my reading *Don Quijote, en español*, with Pedro Salinas in Baltimore 50 years ago and, thanks in part to that fortuitous experience, to my subsequent evolution into a novelist sufficiently attracted to things Iberian and Iberian-American to be powerfully affected by Joaquim Machado de Assis at the beginning of my career and by Jorge Luis Borges at its midpoint, and to visit Spain and Portugal (if not Brazil and Argentina) at every opportunity. Therefore, while I duly regret the death of those 268 U.S. Navy personnel aboard the *Maine* and the later casualties on both sides in Theodore Roosevelt's "splendid little war," not to mention the horrors of the Guerra Civil, it bemuses me to think of my *obras todavía no completas* as part of the fallout from—shall we say—*el boom* of 15 February 1898.

SPEAKING OF *El Boom*—that literary phenomenon so impressive that it prompted my comrade William H. Gass to declare not long ago that we *Yanquis* "no longer own the Novel; we just rent it from South America"—I must confess that although I would not go quite *that* far in my admiration for all those wonderful writers, it is the case that whereas Iberia (especially Spain) has been of perhaps more interest and importance to me than its contemporary literature has been, Latin-American literature from Machado de Assis to García Márquez has been, perhaps regrettably, of more interest and importance to me than have been the countries of its origin—or at least of its authors' origins, inasmuch as a considerable percentage of *El Boom* was detonated in either voluntary or involuntary expatriation. Reading Cervantes with Salinas made me yearn to come to Spain as soon as possible, and as soon as possible thereafter (on my first sabbatical leave from teaching) I came, even though in 1963 *el patriarca* was still in his long *otoño*, and the scars of the Guerra Civil, both physical and human, were still quite in evidence. Reading Machado de Assis and Borges and García Márquez, on the other hand—and Allende, Cortázar, Donoso, Fuentes, Piñon, Puig, Vargas Llosa, et cetera almost ad infinitum—seems *not* to have inspired me with any comparable craving to visit the locales of their excellent fiction, any more than reading Franz Kafka makes me yearn for the Czech Republic or reading William Gass impels me toward the American midwest.

No offense intended, comrades—and, after all, if I had in fact traveled to Chile, Argentina, Peru, Colombia, or Cuba in search of you, as I came to Spain in search of Cervantes, I would have found many of you not at home, whereas here in Spain I encounter Don Miguel or his characters again and again. I have sat at what is supposed to have been his writing-desk in Valladolid, and I have drunk deep from the little water fountain in his courtyard there. And I have, in fact, had the privilege of meeting and conversing with Jorge Luis Borges, José Donoso, Manuel Puig, Mario Vargas Llosa, and Nelida Piñon, for example—not on their home grounds, however, but on mine, as guests of my university or as fellow conferees at other U.S. universities.

AND HERE I shall digress for a moment from my expression of *gratitud* for all this literary *plenitud* in order to praise our *Yanqui* university system as an indispensable facilitator of cultural interaction. It was in our universities, after all, that the likes of Einstein and Spitzer and Salinas and Nabokov found supportive sanctuary, and that the likes of Borges and Donoso and Fuentes and Vargas Llosa found their most appreciative North American audiences (my daughter, for example, though not officially enrolled at Harvard University, was able to sit in for a whole semester on Carlos Fuentes's lecture-course there called "Time and the Novel"—a course that I would gladly have attended myself). Moreover, whatever one might think of the peculiar Yankee phenomenon in the second half of this century of university programs in "creative writing" and the related phenomenon of novelists and poets as university professors—a phenomenon about which I myself have mixed feelings, although I have been one of its grateful beneficiaries—it cannot be doubted that two generations of apprentice writers in the United States have thereby been enabled and encouraged not only to read and study such writers as *los Boomeros*, but in many cases to hear and meet and speak and even work with them. My own apprentices at Johns Hopkins, for instance, were thus exposed and introduced to all of those writers whom I mentioned a moment ago—and one interesting consequence of this contact is that they sometimes asked our distinguished visitors questions that I myself would have considered undiplomatic, although I listened with interest to the replies. Thus for example during Jorge Luis Borges's last visit to Johns Hopkins in 1984, we were all disappointed that the old fellow had been passed over once again for the Nobel Prize, but of course none of us mentioned that subject to him—until one of our students asked him publicly how he felt about being passed over once again for the Nobel Prize. While we blushed with embarrassment, Borges himself merely smiled as if happy to have been asked that question, and then replied, "Well, you know, I have been on their short list for so many years now that I suspect that they think that they've already *given* me the prize." *¡Olé, Jorge!* And why did Manuel Puig choose the epistolary form for his novel *Heartbreak Tango*? Because (so he mischievously declared to my students when one of them asked him that question) he had been working for so long as an airline ticket-clerk in New York City that he had lost confidence in his Spanish; in the epistolary mode, he reasoned, any mistakes in his spelling, grammar, or punctuation would be attributed to the fictional authors of the letters. *¡Bravo, Manuel!*

Et cetera. And of course, like any young artists in any medium, these university apprentice writers must undoubtedly have sometimes found from their exposure to such eminent visitors and their works the sort of navigational assistance that I myself found in the works of Machado de Assis and Borges. Just recently, for example, I picked up a new novel by one of our distinguished alumnae from the Johns

Hopkins Writing Seminars—a novel called *The Antelope Wife*, by
Louise Erdrich[5]—and I read its marvelous opening passage, called "A
Father's Milk," in which a U.S. cavalry troop in the 1880s slaughters
a village of Ojibwa Indians (Ms. Erdrich herself is of half Ojibwa
and half German ancestry). One of the soldiers, for reasons that he
himself does not understand, deserts his company in mid-massacre,
rescues an Indian baby girl, and flees with her into the wilderness.
Unable to feed her or to silence her crying, in desperation he puts
the infant to his own breast, which she suckles with fierce content-
ment but without nourishment—until, *mirabile dictu*, "half asleep
one early morning [with] her beside him, he felt a slight warmth, then
a rush in one side of his chest, a pleasurable burning. He thought it
was an odd dream and fell asleep again only to wake to a huge burp
from the baby, whose lips curled back . . . in bliss, who . . . looked,
impossibly, well fed. . . . He put his hand to his chest and then tasted
a thin blue drop of his own watery, appalling, God-given milk." The
renegade soldier believes that his breast-milk has come from God;
my strong suspicion is that although North American Indian cultures
have their own sorts of Magic Realism, this particular miraculous
lactation came from Ms. Erdrich via Gabriel García Márquez, whose
fiction she would certainly have been exposed to, and was perhaps
nourished by, during her apprenticeship at Johns Hopkins.

I wonder whether that benign and nourishing *leche de padre*
flows in both directions. Have any young Latin-American writers
been inspired by the likes of Flannery O'Connor, Donald Barthelme,
Robert Coover, Thomas Pynchon, Grace Paley, John Hawkes, Philip
Roth, or Toni Morrison? I don't know. I do know that it pleased me
a few years ago to hear Sr. García Márquez acknowledge Hemingway
and Faulkner to have been "[his] masters," and even more to hear

him remark (in an interview in the *Harvard Advocate*[6]) that Faulkner "is really, you know, a Caribbean writer"—an observation that certainly gave me a fresh perspective on the sage of Oxford, Mississippi. Here is a conspicuous instance of a great writer "creating his own precursors," as Borges said with respect to Franz Kafka: One reads Faulkner somewhat differently after reading *Cien Años de Soledad*. Even a few such seminal exchanges (excuse the expression: "seminal exchanges" comes more naturally to me than "father's milk") may suffice for cultural cross-fertilization. If there are traces of Faulkner in the literary DNA of Gabriel García Márquez, then no literary paternity suits should be filed by chauvinistic critics who see Magic Realism in Toni Morrison and Louise Erdrich.

We are speaking here, after all, of admiration and inspiration, not of international trade balances. 20th-century Modernist and Postmodernist fiction owe much to Ireland, for example, for giving us James Joyce and Samuel Beckett; but Joyce's and Beckett's own navigation stars were from all over the literary firmament, and so it's futile and pointless to try to calculate cultural trade deficits and surpluses—all the more so when we bear in mind my dictum that a writer's navigation stars are not to be confused with his or her destination. 45 years ago, the brilliant novels of Joaquim Machado de Assis helped me to find my own first voice as a novelist. But much of what I borrowed from Machado to write *The Floating Opera*, Machado had borrowed in turn from Laurence Sterne's *Tristram Shandy*, which I had not yet discovered for myself at that time, and which anyhow might not have had the impact on me that it did when reorchestrated by Machado's Romantic pessimism. A dozen years later, Jorge Luis Borges's *Ficciones* inspired me to imagine the possibilities of a Literature of Exhausted Possibility and what came later to be called Postmodernist fiction; but Borges's own navigation stars were chiefly English, from Beowulf through G. K. Chesterton and Robert Louis Stevenson. Apollo be praised for such happy cross-cultural miscegenation!

Perhaps this mixed metaphor—international trade balances, celestial navigation, and DNA analysis—is itself a metaphor for my point: I have steered my own writerly course by the various lights of Faulkner, Joyce, Machado, and Borges, not to mention Cervantes, Boccaccio, Rabelais, and Scheherazade; my muse's DNA, like that of most writers, is a *mestizo* smorgasbord of these and many other literary-ethnic inputs, and while I freely acknowledge my debt to them and to the assorted literary traditions that produced them, it is not the sort of debit that requires repayment. My books, whatever their worth, are my only intercultural bookkeeping. If, on some literary-critical balance sheet, those books show a net cultural deficit to Ireland, Brazil, Argentina, Spain, Italy, France, and medieval Araby, that debit is a debt merely of gratitude. And of gratitude I have a plenitude: if not yet quite *cien años de*, at least *cinquenta años de gratitud*.

Thank you; *muchas gracias*; et cetera.

A Window at the Pratt

Winners of the Enoch Pratt Society's Lifetime Achievement in Letters Award, established in 1997, are expected to say a few words upon their accepting that distinction at Baltimore's fine old Enoch Pratt Free Library and then, the following evening, to say a few more before giving a reading from their work. My receipt of that honor in 1999 prompted the following remarks on literary awards and then, the next day, the mini-essay after this one, on public readings—both published here for the first time.

J OHANN WOLFGANG VON Goethe once remarked to the Duke of Weimar—no doubt on the occasion of accepting some ducal honor—that refusing a distinction (as Boris Pasternak and Jean-Paul Sartre, for different reasons, declined their Nobel prizes in 1958 and 1964) can be as immodest as chasing after it. Philip Roth, upon accepting a New York Book Critics Circle Award, observed that since he, like many another writer, often feels that such prizes go to the wrong guy, this must be his night to be the wrong guy. John Updike's character Henry Bech, upon accepting the Nobel Prize that his author surely deserves but has yet to be graced with,[1] declares that *that* prize "has become so big, such a celebrity among prizes, that no one is worthy to win it, and the embarrassed winner can shelter his unworthiness behind the unworthiness of everyone else." That reminds me of how the undergraduates at Washington College over in Chestertown, where my wife and I live, feel about the college's prestigious Sophie Kerr Lit Prize, a $35,000 plum awarded annually for quite a few years now to one of their number, none of whom thus far (so they tell me) has subsequently evolved into a professionally publishing writer: So convinced are the student competitors that the Kerr Prize is cursed ("Sophie's Curse," they call it) that upon my being appointed a Senior Fellow of the college a few years back, I made it my first official act to pronounce that curse lifted. We'll see what happens.[2] And a writer friend of mine—as we were either applauding Gabriel García Márquez's receipt of the Nobel in 1982 or else shaking our writerly heads at someone else's receipt of it in some other year, I forget which—observed sagely that there are on the one hand those who do honor to the prize, and on the other hand those to whom the prize does honor.

Well: In the short history of the Pratt Society's Lifetime Achievement award, my two forewinners (Saul Bellow and Joyce Carol Oates) have done enough honor to the prize to permit me simply to be honored by it—as I hope you'll disagree. In any case, my thanks to the adjudicating committee, whoever you are, the difficulties of whose task I can appreciate, having paid my dues on a similar committee of the American Academy of Arts and Letters. Indeed, after doing three years' hard time on that awards committee, while at the same time tisking at the Swedish Academy for passing over such contemporary giants as Vladimir Nabokov, Jorge Luis Borges, and Italo Calvino in favor of one or another lesser entity, I was led to what I think of as the Tragic View of Recognition: namely, that a worthwhile literary prize is one that will at least occasionally be bestowed upon an author *despite* the fact that she or he happens to deserve it. By that stringent definition, the Pratt Prize has a high credit rating indeed, to which I hope tonight's occasion will not do lasting damage.

That said, I must confess to feeling a slight chill in the presence of any "Lifetime Achievement" award. Since I persist in still going to my writing-table every weekday morning to see what my muse has on her mind, I can't help wishing that the thing would say "Lifetime Achievement *Thus Far*." In any case, as I used to tell my apprentice fiction-writers up at Johns Hopkins, lit prizes are a bit like PhDs: They don't invariably equate with excellence (in some cases they may barely equate with proficiency), and some of the very best practitioners don't have them. But if you're going to be shrug-shouldered about either literary prizes or doctoral degrees, it's better to be so after winning them, so that your shrug-shoulderedness can't be mistaken for sour-grapes envy.

ALLOW ME NOW a very brief reminiscence, and then we're done. As an undergraduate apprentice myself at Johns Hopkins in the late 1940s, my comrades and I would often take the bus downtown from the university's Homewood campus to the Pratt, where in addition to using this library's splendid resources we would admire and envy the authors whose works were honored back then with displays in the building's street-side windows. Libraries, after all, as William H. Gass somewhere remarks, "acquire what we cannot afford, retain what we prize and would adore, restore the worn, ignore fashion, and repulse prejudice." Your typical would-be writer, says W. H. Auden, "serves his apprenticeship in a library [*I* certainly did—but that's another story]." "Though the Master is deaf and dumb,"

Auden continues, "and gives neither instruction nor criticism, the apprentice can choose any Master he likes, living or dead; the Master is available at any hour of the day or night; lessons are all for free; and his passionate admiration of his Master will ensure that he work hard to please him." Especially to those of my fellow apprentices who (unlike me) had grown up in Baltimore and had made excursions to the Pratt all through their childhood, there seemed to be no more incontrovertible affirmation and validation of one's writerly calling than to earn, one day, "a window at the Pratt." I'm honored to regard tonight's award as *my* Pratt-window; although I hope that I may have a few stories left to tell, I accept with pleasure this recognition of The Stories Thus Far.

On Readings

YESTERDAY EVENING, IN the course of accepting the Enoch
Pratt Award,[1] I delivered myself of a few remarks about the
pros and cons of literary prizes in general. *This* evening, before reading to you a short section from the nearly-finished "millennium"
novel that I've been at work upon since 1995,[2] I want to make a few
remarks about Public Readings in general.

What prompts me this evening is an observation by my distinguished fellow fictioneer Kurt Vonnegut, Jr., as quoted some
few weeks ago in the "Today" section of the Baltimore *Sun*: Mr.
Vonnegut allowed as how he gives "talks" here and there from time
to time (indeed, he has done so as our guest in the Johns Hopkins
Writing Seminars, for example), but "I've never done a reading," he
declared, and then added: "It's the lowest art form imaginable."

Well, now. This sentiment echoes that of some other notable
writers I've heard on the subject: I think, e.g., of Mr. Mark Helprin,
who voiced a similar opinion to his audience up at Hopkins (in fact,
Mr. Helprin devoted his whole allotted public hour with us to ex-
plaining why he wasn't going to give a reading). I think of Gore
Vidal's remark somewhere that public readings by authors, especially
on the campus circuit, are "just a form of show biz." And Baltimore's
own Anne Tyler, who once did a well-received reading for us from
her then-new novel *Morgan's Passing*, decided subsequently that

fiction-readings are a bad idea, and although she visited our Writing Seminars again thereafter, she confined herself to chatting with a roomful of apprentice writers.

In certain cases, I suspect, a writer's disinclination to public readings may stem from simple platform-shyness or the circumstance of that writer's not happening to be an effective public reader of his or her work. (Neither of those factors, let me say at once, applies to Ms. Tyler, whose presentation was confident and capable, a pleasure to attend.) But some more general objections to public readings are worth considering apart from those circumstances, and I'd like to review them before I myself descend to this "lowest form of art."

It is a matter that I feel reasonably qualified to address. For one thing, in my years of professoring at Penn State, State University of New York at Buffalo, and especially Johns Hopkins—where my job-description included inviting writers to visit the campus, confer with our students, and give public presentations—I have heard every sort of delivery: from the masterful to the inept, from the histrionic to the eye-glazingly monotonous, from the exhilarating to the embarrassing, or the intoxicating to the intoxicated, and including the over-long, the inaudible, and the all but unintelligible, whether owing to the speaker's accent, the room's acoustics, the nature of the material, or possibly some foreign substance in the lectern water-pitcher. Moreover, I confess to being guilty myself, over 40-plus years as a publishing writer, of 400-plus public readings from my output, whether of work already published, or of work "finished" but not yet published, or (as is the case with tonight's material) of work not-yet-even-quite-finished but close enough thereto to risk reading from it without tempting the muses to strike, or to go on strike. What's more, I have almost invariably found the experience agreeable, despite the occasional fouled-up airline connection and the occasionally disappointing, disappointed, or less than entirely comprehending audience—as in, say, Tokyo or Tangier.

Part of my pleasure in reading publicly from my fiction (or from other folks' fiction, as I've done in homages to Samuel Beckett, Italo Calvino, Jorge Luis Borges, and other of my heroes) has nothing to do with the pros and cons of readings as an art-form but rather with the biographical circumstance that I happen to be a once-upon-a-time jazz drummer and orchestrator who still enjoys the opportunity of trying selected riffs on a *live* audience instead of a merely living one, as is the normal case with writers and their readers. What's more, aside from affording me the occasional change of scene and a modest supplement to what for most of my academic history was a fairly modest teaching salary and what remains, in the nature of my literary case, a blushingly modest royalty income, these reading/lecture sorties have brought me quite unexpected other boons as well, of which I will mention only the most blessed and life-altering one: On a snowy night in February 30 years ago, after a hairy flight from my Buffalo campus to Boston to do an evening gig at Boston College—a reading that I started at least half an hour late, on an empty stomach, because of snow delays at the airports and on the streets of Boston—it was my extraordinary good fortune to re-meet and renew my acquaintance with a former student from Penn State days who had loyally shlepped across town through the snowstorm to hear her old teach's spiel, and who subsequently became and to this hour remains my bride, my keenest-eyed reader, and my editor of first resort.

BUT THAT'S ANOTHER story, which—like the circumstance of one's happening to be a good, bad, or middling public reader—has nothing to do with the pros and cons of "readings" themselves as a form of art and entertainment. Let me quickly review those pros and cons, offer my own opinions themupon, then read my reading, and then, I hope, respond to your questions or comments on this or any other reasonably pertinent subject.

First, the Cons: The printed word can reasonably be argued to be meant for the silent eye, not for the ear: a private, "privileged" transaction between author and individual readers, not a communal experience like theater, or like the oral tale-telling tradition out of which written and eventually printed fiction evolved. The reader of print proceeds at his/her own pace—lingering, considering; perhaps rereading a particularly striking or puzzling passage before going on; perhaps skimming a bit to cut to the chase, so to speak, or to cut *out* the chase if one so chooses; perhaps peeking ahead to check the distance to the next space-break or chapter-division (what might be called "chasing to the cut"); perhaps leafing back to remind oneself where a particular character or image last appeared, and reading neither more nor fewer minutesworth of pages than one has the time and motivation to ingest at a given sitting. In short, the medium of print is *interruptible*, *referable*, and *pace-adjustable* by the individual reader, as theater and film are not (setting aside the function-buttons on videocassette players), and as the oral tale-telling tradition was not (unless you were the king ordering Homer to do a high-speed encore of his Catalogue of Ships, I suppose, or a grandkid begging Grandma to do the wolf-in-the-bed scene one more time). Interruptibility, Referability, and Pace-Adjustability: three terrific virtues of the print medium, and of course they're lost in public readings.

Lost too is the absence of the possibly distracting physical presence of the Author, along with our imagination of the narrative "voice" and the voices of the several characters. We often speak of a writer's having a distinctive *voice*—languid, eloquent, restrained, jazzed-up, tender, forceful, whatever—but the voice we're speaking of is a figurative, not a literal one. And the narrative voice that so moved and/or entertained us on the silent page may turn out in authorial person to be bothersomely lisping, or hesitant, or strident, or perhaps female baritone or male soprano when it's doing dialogue. In the same way, we may have an agreeable image of the author of our pleasure and then find ourselves disappointed if not altogether turned off by his/her actual speaking presence. And finally, of course, we *can* go read the thing for ourselves, if not immediately then whenever it hits the stands, in the medium for which it was presumably designed; so why bother hauling out to watch and hear its perpetrator perp a portion of it in person?

The answer, of course, is that there is no reason at all, if that's the way one feels. And it goes without saying (but let's get it said anyhow) that some reasons for going to hear a writer read have little or nothing to do with the art of literature, however defensible they may be otherwise: innocent curiosity about the live performing presence of a literary celebrity, or of a non-celebrity whom we happen to admire or be merely curious about; curiosity about an author's work in progress, if we've enjoyed earlier fruits from the same tree; the opportunity, perhaps, to ask or anyhow attend a question or two or three (as I much hope you'll do in Part Three of our time together); to turn the monologue of printed fiction into a dialogue.

ET CETERA. BUT none of these considerations has to do with public readings as an art form. They may justify, even partially vindicate, my presence here onstage this evening and yours in the audience, or my presence in the audience some other evening to hear some other writer onstage. But is it art, or art of other than the lowest order?

IN THE CASE of a great many fine poets, it unquestionably *is* art, of a very high order. The utterance of lyric poetry is no doubt more intimately bound to speech than is the recitation of prose; one remembers somebody-or-other's definition of poetry as "memorable speech," and any of us fortunate enough to have heard the likes of Dylan Thomas or Robert Frost or Anne Sexton speak their poems has experienced an unforgettable dimension of that verbal art beyond its silent presence on the printed page. But what about poor old fiction? Here are three things that I believe:

1. That the art of reading it publicly is different from the art of writing it. The well-written story and the well-spoken story are two different entities, although a given text may happen to be suitable for both.

2. Or it may not be, since a gifted reader may breathe life into an indifferent text, and an ineffective reader can make humdrummery out of a passage that might quite move us on the silent page. And there are passages of world-class fiction that one would be ill-advised to choose for "performance": the exhaustive and exhausting catalogues in Francois Rabelais' great *Gargantua and Pantagruel*, for example, or those deliberately grueling, unparagraphed, relentless stretches in some of the late Thomas Bernhard's first-rate novels.

3. That an excellent reading need not at all be histrionic or "dramatic" in the popular sense of that adjective. The art of theater is not the same as the art of public reading, and indeed some of the most memorable author-readings of my experience—the late Donald Barthelme's, for instance—were delivered in a downright

anti-histrionic, even deadpan style perfectly appropriate to the material and wonderfully effective. I have heard John Updike read memorably despite his occasional, fleeting, and actually quite endearing stammer, which only served to remind us that his extraordinary eloquence is after all human. I have heard Joseph Heller read the scene of Snowden's dying in *Catch-22* in the author's unreconstructed Coney Island accent, which at once became for me the voice of that novel, the way Grace Paley's New York Jewish intonations, once heard live, spring pleasurably thereafter from her pages to my ear. And my (alas!) also-late friend John Hawkes:[3] Who of us who've relished his sonorous cadences in the flesh, so to speak, does not hear them with a smile and a wistful headshake whenever our eyes fall upon any of his pages?

Oscar Wilde once mischievously declared that anyone who can read the death of Little Nell (from Dickens's *Old Curiosity Shop*) without laughing must have a heart of stone. I understand what he means, but all the same I wish I could have heard the great Charles read that passage, and I'll bet I'd have been moved if not to tears (as were the Victorian audiences of that most famous of author/readers) then at least to the exhilaration that comes from virtuoso instances of the oldest of narrative arts: the art of Homer and Scheherazade, of Uncle Remus and Garrison Keillor; the art not only of *story*telling but of story-*telling.*

The End Of The Word
As We've Known It?

A follow-up to "The State of the Art," delivered here and there on the lecture/reading circuit back at the turn of the millennium.

N OW THAT WE seem to have made the transition more or less safely into the new century and millennium, it may require some effort of memory to recall that back in the late Nineteen Hundreds—especially in the year we called "1999"—the word "TEOTWAWKI" was a popular acronym for the most apocalyptic of "Y2K" scenarios: TEOTWAWKI, The End Of The World As We Know It. Difficult as it may be to believe from this historical distance (a full twelvemonth later), chronicles of the period tell us that in certain precincts of Planet Earth it was seriously believed that either widespread critical computer failures or the Second Coming of Christ, perhaps both, would precipitate the collapse of our technology-dependent society, followed very possibly by literal or anyhow figurative Armageddon. The End Time! *Eschaton!* The end of the world as we'd known it! Convinced TEOTWAWKIs went so far in some instances as to build well-stocked refuges out in the boondocks and to arm themselves against the expected desperate hordes of a no longer civilized civilization. A few, of the Christian-apocalyptic persuasion, put everything behind them and followed their leaders or went on their own to Jerusalem or some comparably appropriate venue to await the Rapture and its *sequelae*. Even among the skeptical and conservative, we're told, many withdrew a wad of extra cash and laid in some daysworth of nonperishable food and jugged water, as their government's Y2K advisors recommended. For such as those (my wife and me among them) these precautions amounted to a scaled-down secular version of Pascal's famous Wager concerning the existence of God: The world as we knew it wasn't *likely* to end, we figured, but at least the weekend might be messed up; no harm in hedging our bets a bit. And so we did.

TEOTWAWKI: In my tidewater-Chesapeake ears, the word sounds like a large, rather ungainly waterfowl taking flight. Great Blue Herons, for example, make a sound like that when they take off or flap in for a landing: TEO*TWAW*-KI! Characteristically too, on lift-off they emit, along with the squawk but from their other end, a copious white jet of birdlime. And there was certainly no shortage of *that* back in '99, associated with what in our house was known as TEOTCAMATTGCACM: The End Of The Century And Millennium According To The Gregorian Calendar As Commonly Misconstrued.

ENOUGH, HOWEVER, OF all that. My advertised topic here is not TEOT*World*AWKI, but TEOT*Word*AWKI (with a question-mark after it): the here-and-there-speculated end of the Word— specifically the printed and bookbound fictive word—as we've known it. But I can't resist wondering for another paragraph or two how red-faced (or whatever) those folks must have been, must indeed still be, who really believed back in '99 that the show was

over, the end truly at hand. The rest of us could more or less sheep-
ishly redeposit our excess cash, draw down our hoard of trail mix
and bottled water, and go on with our lives, feeling that we had
after all merely been being prudent. But what of those (so my novelist's imagination wonders) who truly burned their bridges; who
put behind them, perhaps irretrievably, *everything* once dear in
order to follow—perhaps even to lead—a gaggle of like-minded
TEOTWAWKIs to wherever in preparation for The End, and then
saw Y2K-night embarrassingly come and go with no other fireworks than the jim-dandy ones televised from Sydney and London,
Times Square and the D.C. Mall?

One can hazard a few educated guesses about those folks.
Apocalypticism was not invented in 1999; indeed, what the novelist Salman Rushdie once called "endism"—the conviction that the
world's clock has just about run—has such a long and busy history
that back in 1956 a team of sociologists published a fascinating study
of what happens among dead-serious TEOTWAWKIs out in their
desert or up on their mountaintop the morning after, so to speak,
and the morning after that, as the world mortifyingly persists much
as before.[1] What they found—as one might have guessed—is that
while some disillusioned and disaffected disciples give their prophet
the finger and make their way back home to pick up what pieces
they can, the more common reaction is rationalization, followed by
even more radical commitment or coercion—for these folks are, after
all, *way* out on a limb, their entire self-respect at stake, their "belief
structure" in crisis. So okay, they're likely to say, or to be told by
their leader: The *timetable* may require a bit of tweaking, but the essential prophecy remains valid. Curtains-time is coming soon, don't
you doubt it; what may appear to our merely mortal eyes and minds

to be delays and postponements are simply errors in our human reckoning, perhaps even tests to weed out the weak of faith. We did not pray hard enough; we did not burn *every* bridge behind us, purge ourselves of *every* reservation. Here's our chance to show the world (and our Leader, and our fellow followers) what *real* commitment is! Et cetera.

The pressures in that line must be tremendous. Back in November of 1978, when 914 disciples of the guru Jim Jones more or less voluntarily drank poisoned purple Kool-Aid in their Jonestown Guyana commune, the novelist James Michener happened to be our guest at Johns Hopkins, and was asked by someone in his audience what he thought of that prodigious autodestruction. Michener's reply—a quite sage reply, in my opinion—was that the first 50-or-so "victims" didn't surprise him; it was at that enormous remainder that he shook his head in sad amazement. But after all, their world *had* ended: not only the world of their previous lives and the life-connections put behind them, but also the isolated world of voluntary submission and exploitation that they had seen fit to commit themselves to under their charismatic leader's spell, which seemed about to be dispelled by congressional investigators of the Rev. Mr. Jones's reported abuses of his position.

Well: Worlds are always ending, are they not? Not only such catastrophically beleaguered worlds as that of the Zealots besieged by Roman legions at Masada in 73 c.e., for example, or that of European Jews before Hitler's Final Solution; not only such more gradually beleaguered worlds as that of the Algonquin Indian tribes upon the arrival of English Colonists in Virginia and Maryland, but likewise the temporarily victorious worlds that displaced these unfortunates: the worlds of Imperial Rome and the Third Reich and the prosperous

18th-century colonial tidewater tobacco plantations that supplanted the indigenous Native Americans. The small-town Maryland neighborhood in which I was born and raised during the Great Depression and World War II is a world long since gone, although most of its streets and trees and houses spookily remain in place. From the microworlds of the Harlem Renaissance and F. Scott Fitzgerald's Jazz Age to the macroworlds of Victorian England and the Soviet Union, or for that matter the worlds of Earth's Pleistocene era and its fast-fleeting successor, our very own Holocene; from MGM musical extravaganzas of the 1940s to our local solar system, whatever lives in time dies in time, and can be considered ipso facto to be always in the process of ending. So?

SO LET'S CONSIDER whether—or, rather, *how*—the same applies to the world in which we meet here today: the world that fetches people like me to college campuses to speak to people like you, and that fetches you from your other pleasures and concerns to come hear what I have to say. I mean, of course, the world in which *literature*, for example, is written, published, and at least occasionally read and discussed: literature in general, but more particularly prose fiction, and most particularly what we're accustomed to calling *novels*. *Printed* novels, as it used to go without saying: the dramatic interactions of imaginary characters narrated at some length by their author in language printed in ink on paper pages numbered sequentially and bound into books, to be read by presumably though not necessarily individual readers who (also presumably though not necessarily) begin on page one and proceed thence to page two, page three, et cetera, in typically though not necessarily silent transaction with the printed text. Will that do as a working definition of the form? It is a category of art and entertainment, please permit me to remind you, that more or less developed in the 17th century, although there are notable earlier instances even before the development of print technology; that then flowered in the 18th and 19th centuries, fertilized by the Industrial Revolution and the ascendancy of a middle class with the time, means, and ability to read; and that then in the 20th century was believed in many quarters to have become more or less moribund, an endangered species, its niche in the culture's aesthetic ecology usurped by successive new technologies of narrative/dramatic entertainment such as movies, network radio, television, videocassette recorders, and, at that century's close, by the interactive pleasures of the Internet, including online magazines, "e-books," and even hypertextual multimedia electronic fiction, of which more presently. Toward mid-century especially—at the apex of what was called High Modernism in the arts of what was called Western Civilization, before Postmodernism and personal computers had even hit the fan—it became so fashionable for literary theorizers to titillate themselves with the subject of The Death of the Novel that I used half-seriously to warn aspiring fiction-writers, in the universities where I coached them back then, that they were apprenticing themselves in an art perhaps destined soon to become as passé as vaudeville, as quaint as the Magic Lantern and the Stereopticon, as limited and "special" in its range of audience as is equestrian dressage, say, or narrative poetry since the ascendancy of the novel. While busily writing novels myself, I took it as my coachly duty in those days to familiarize my coachees with such mordantly witty Cassandras of our medium as the European critic E. M. Cioran, from whom I would quote cautionary tidbits like this one, from his essay "Beyond the Novel":

. . . the material of literature grows thinner every day, and that of the novel, more limited, vanishes before our very eyes. Is it really dead, or only dying? My incompetence keeps me from making up my mind. After asserting that it is finished, remorse assails me: what if the novel were still alive? In that case, I leave it to others, more expert, to establish the precise degree of its agony.

And then I would encourage them, and myself, with the critic Leslie Fiedler's heartening observation that the novel was, after all, *born* a-dying, like all of us (Fiedler had in mind the genre's European origins in parody and satire, such as Cervantes's transcendent satire of chivalric romances in *Don Quixote* and Henry Fielding's hilariously scathing *Shamela*, a parody of Samuel Richardson's pioneering epistolary novel *Pamela*); that it has gone on dying vigorously for several centuries since, and that we may hope to enjoy its continuing terminality for some time to come. I would suggest to my charges that like the doomed tubercular sopranos dear to 19th-century Italian opera, the Novel might be reserving its best arias for the end of Act Three, its ring-down-the-curtain swan song. And since neither I nor they had been on hand to compose Act One, mightn't it be something to score that curtain-closer?

Having thus encouraged and inspirited them, however, I felt obliged to remind my young Novelist Aspirants that the art of made-up stories appears to have managed quite nicely for a very long while before the invention of *writing*, even, not to mention before the inventions of paper, ink, movable-type printing, general literacy, and mass-produced book-bound extended prose fictions borrowable from public libraries or purchasable online as well as from mega-bookmarts along with croissants and cafe latté; and that that art would doubtless survive the supersession of any or all of those inventions. The Death of the Novel, in short—if that so-long-heralded, almost anticlimactic expiration should finally come to pass—would not likely be the end of story-making, story-transmission, and story-reception by one means or another. Even TEOTWordAWKI, the end of the word as we've known it, would not spell the doom of Storying, although it would certainly leave us old-fashioned print-novelists in an awkward position.

So: Is OUR soprano still robustly melodious in her terminality, like Violetta in *La Traviata* and Mimi in *La Bohème*, or has her song all but given way to last-gasping? One notes that the literal tuberculosis that was such a grim staple of 19th-century life, and therefore of 19th-century novels as well as operas, made an ominous curtain-call toward the end of the 20th, thanks to international air travel, but that it has (at least for the present) been largely contained by antibiotics.[2] Could it be that some cultural-historical-technological equivalent of the TB-pharmaceutical Isoniazid has appeared like a *deus ex machina* to save the Novel's life, or at least to postpone The End? And why should anybody care one way or the other, except the few people who happen to devote their lives to the writing of fiction, and the slightly larger number engaged in editing, publishing, and selling it, and the larger yet but by no means overwhelming number who still read it for pleasure? What did those literary-critical Cassandras mean anyway, back there in the 20th century, by "the death of the novel"? That the likes of John Grisham and Danielle Steel and their millions of readers are dinosaurs unaware that the asteroid of their extinction has already struck? Or merely that the Heroic Age of the

novel—the age of Jane Austen and Charles Dickens, of Tolstoy and
the Brontë sisters, Balzac and Victor Hugo and Mark Twain—had
given way to the brilliant decadence of Modernism, to Proust and
Joyce and Kafka, Virginia Woolf and Gertrude Stein and Thomas
Mann (whose 1924 novel *The Magic Mountain* happens also to be
the great culminating gasp of Tuberculosis as a literary and thence
operatic motif)?

I shall speak to those questions, perhaps even systematically, after a classical digression—by which I mean a digression into classical
lit, not a classical instance of wandering from the subject. In Spain a
few years ago, by the way, my wife and I stopped in the attractive old
hill-town of Úbeda, in the Andalusian foothills of the Sierra Morena,
where the 11th-century soldiers of King Alfonso VI were besieged by
the Moors until the legendary El Cid belatedly arrived with reinforce-
ments to lift the siege. "What took you so long?" the exasperated
king is said to have demanded of his tardy rescuer—to which El Cid
is said to have replied, "I have been wandering the hills of Úbeda."
Spanish friends of ours told us subsequently that that phrase is still
used to describe a lecturer, for example, who strays from his or her
announced subject: "*Se marcha por los cerros de Úbeda.*" Awhile
back I referred to those mid-century Death-of-the-Novel types as
"Cassandras," invoking the apocalyptic prophetess in Homer's *Iliad*
who foresees the destruction of Troy but can't get anybody to take
her seriously. Now that I've used the word *apocalyptic*—a much-
heard word indeed at the close of the past century and millennium—
it occurs to me to point out that while many of us were reminded in
print and on television, as Y2K approached, that *apocalypse* comes
from the Greek *apo*, meaning "reversal," and *kalupsein*, meaning "to
cover," hence an uncovering, an unveiling, or (as every reader of the

New Testament knows) a *revelation*, perhaps fewer of us remember that the sexy sea-nymph Calypso in Homer's *Odyssey*, who detains the hero for seven lusty years on his erratic homeward voyage from ruined Troy, takes her name from the same root. Calypso is "she who conceals," metaphorically speaking, Odysseus's proper objective from him—his return to faithful Penelope and their troubled estate—by her long-term seduction of that errant though resourceful fellow. Calypso is the alluring aspect of Melville's "great shroud of the sea," which rolls on and covers everything at the end of *Moby-Dick*; she can also be thought of as the Goddess of Digression—to whom I have now paid more than adequate homage, and from whose embrace I now return to my apocalyptic subject: TEOTWordAWKI.

Back to the burning questions, beginning with whether the novel is toast as a major mode of popular narrative entertainment in what we call the advanced industrialized world or merely passé as a major genre of literary art. I myself would say "Neither," although the answer obviously depends on what's meant by Major. Indisputably, most people in the world we're speaking of spend more time spectating stories via television and movies nowadays than reading them off the printed page or the pixelated computer monitor. And indisputably the popular audience for the noble genre of the *short story* has all but disappeared by comparison to the palmy days of periodicals like *The Saturday Evening Post*, when an Edna Ferber or an "O. Henry" could acquire an enormous readership on the basis of magazine publication alone—quite apart, in Ms. Ferber's case, from her success as a popular novelist. But the short story is a whole 'nother story. Back at Barnes & Noble and Amazon.com, however, the commerce in printed book-length fiction evidently remains brisk, although the institutions of trade fiction publishing, distribution, and sale are less kind than they were half a century ago to non-blockbuster, "mid-list" novelists of high literary quality. One still sees occasionally, though perhaps less often than once upon a time, novels of impressive literary merit and low advance promotion, written by previously unknown authors, make their way onto the bestseller lists by sheer word-of-mouth advertising: Charles Frazier's admirable *Cold Mountain* (1998) comes hearteningly to mind. And I believe that the aesthetics of literary Modernism, with its notorious tendency to divide novels, for example, into either High Art on the one hand or pop entertainment on the other, is far enough behind us now so that I, for one, am gratified at the sight of people still reading *any* kind of fiction for pleasure, in airports and airplanes and on beaches and for all I know in the privacy of their homes as well, between surfing the Web and surfing the cable channels. Competition from glitzy and convenient alternative media has no doubt reduced the novel's share of literate-audience attention (I mean "literate" here in both senses of that adjective); but the fiction alcoves of our public libraries remain fairly busy still, with wait-lists for popular titles; one hears that community book-clubs are on the rise; and even noncommercial fictors like me may learn to their surprise that there exist websites for our books out there in Cyberland. On a continuum of species-imperilment extending from starlings and rabbits on the safe end to pygmy owls and rhinoceri on the other, I'm inclined to position the capital-N Novel somewhere in the neighborhood of the bald eagle or maybe even the osprey, its numbers unquestionably reduced from its glory-days by habitat loss and other ecological pressures, but its status still considerable and its reasonably vigorous continuation in no apparent short-term danger. I'll return to this zoological analogy later.

Very well: But if that is the case, where, then, are the Charles Dickenses and the Mark Twains of our postmodern era; our novelists at once popular and excellent, acclaimed widely in their own time by critics and lay readers alike and likely to be so by generations to come? If the genre's Golden Age extended some 100-plus years, from Fielding to Flaubert, let's say, *Tom Jones* to *Madame Bovary*, and its more self-conscious Silver age through the big Modernists—certainly excellent, though scarcely popular—from Proust and Joyce to Nabokov and Beckett, aren't we by comparison Bronze-Agers at best, maybe even (biodegradable) plastic? My reply is that I don't know, really, although several considerations come to mind. Alternative media really have altered the audience for printed fiction, not only since Dickens and Twain, who didn't have movies to compete with, but since Hemingway and Faulkner as well, who weren't in the ring with television, really, not to mention with VCRs and the Internet. And we ought to remember, e.g., that while Twain was indeed a popular success, the novel of his that we most treasure nowadays had a rough critical lift-off indeed, and is still found offensive by distressingly many Americans. We should remember too that the likes of Cervantes and Dickens and Tolstoy and Twain are not common in any era—pre-modern, modern, or postmodern. And that in J. D. Salinger's *The Catcher in the Rye*, for instance, Joseph Heller's *Catch-22* and Gabriel García Márquez's *One Hundred Years of Solitude* (even in translation), we have after all at least three classics from the past half-century that meet our criteria: a not-inconsiderable number, to which other novel-aficionados will certainly rush to make additions or substitutions. So maybe things are just fine, anyhow quite okay, though less so than formerly?

I half-suspect that to be the case; but an abiding sense of malaise 'round about our subject resists dispelling. What will the effect on print-lit be of *hypertext*, for example, whose evangels have called it "the third great advance in the technology of writing, after the alphabet and the printing press," but whose nature precludes the fixative of print? And how about *e-fiction*, those ingenious interactive hypertextual computer-novels that effectively redefine the job-descriptions of Author and Reader? This is the medium that prompted Robert Coover's landmark 1993 essay "The End of Books?" in the *New York Times Book Review*, which prompted in turn a little essay of mine called "The State of the Art"—to which I refer any who thirst for my extended take on the subject of e-fiction. For now let's merely ask, "Aren't e-novels the *coup de grace* for the old-fashioned p-variety? Don't Hypertext & Co. render all print-lit more or less obsolete—The End Of The Word As We've Known It?"

After much and deep consideration, I reply: Nah. It's a fascinating medium indeed, is hypertext; and electronic fiction is an intriguing genre for sure. Just a few years ago, when one couldn't take for granted that everybody in the room understood what *hypertext* is, I used to illustrate it by asking my auditors to imagine on their computer-screens the innocent old test-proposition *The quick brown fox jumps over the lazy dog*, its key elements "loaded" in such a way that

> *"clicking" on any of them opens a window menu of associations available for exploring, from the relative nimbleness of temperate-zone quadrupeds, through the history of fox hunting and its representation in painting, music, and literature, to soundtracks of hounds in full cry (with or without expert commentary) and disquisitions on animal rights—and every one of those associated "lexias" similarly loaded, another ring of keys with which one may open yet further*

doors, and on and on and on—no two routes through the
maze ever likely to be the same, and every venturer thereinto
not only a Theseus but a Daedalus, remodeling the labyrinth
at will en route through it.

End of quote from that aforementioned "State of the Art" essay. A recent communication from my aforementioned fellow print-novelist Robert Coover informs me that one of the "writers," if that's the correct term, in his Electronic Fiction seminar at Brown University has in fact taken that Quick Brown Fox of mine and run with it: An electronic multimedia *QBF* is now several years into its elaborate gestation, Coover reports, and not finished yet. Stay tuned.

But aside from a general curiosity about all Edges of the Envelope of the art I practice, my own interest in the medium of e-fiction is mainly metaphorical. Hypertext, like the World Wide Web itself, reminds us of the real interconnectedness of things, and the many-layeredness of our experience of life: It reminds us that to "click," figuratively speaking, on anything we pause to consider—the water-glass on this lectern, the pattern of that fellow's necktie, the earrings that his companion chose to wear this evening—is to open stories within stories, "hot-linked" to further stories, et cetera literally ad infinitum: what I've called elsewhere the Hypertextuality of Everyday Life. I like that sense of narrative depth, that vertiginous dimension of nonlinearity; so too, I believe, would my muse like it, the all-but-inexhaustible Ms. Scheherazade. And so, in the same way that those earlier digressions of mine on Calypso and the hills of Úbeda could be said to have been an awkward linear approximation of hypertext, I have sportingly included in a forthcoming novel [*Coming Soon!!!*] some *faux*-electronic menus and option-buttons, for example, the

way my Modernist forebears incorporated *faux*-newspaper headlines
and such into their novels.[3]

HOWEVER (AS I'VE remarked elsewhere), while much of our life-
experience is inarguably of a non-linear character—all our senses
operating at once—it happens that on the other hand much of our
experience is decidedly linear: *this* apparently leading to *this,* evidently followed by *that.* It is an aspect of our living ineluctably in linear time, which is the basis of all narrative no matter how we might
diddle its linearity for effect. 2000 years ago the Roman poet Horace[4]
was already recommending, in his Epistle on the Art of Poetry, that
storytellers would do well to hit the ground running by starting their
stories *in medias res*, "in the middle of things" rather than way back
at Square One. But even when we heed that sage advice, as more
often than not most storytellers do, we still necessarily proceed sequentially from unit to unit of action, event to event in time, as language proceeds linearly word by word and our lives proceed linearly
from birth to death. For rendering or at least suggesting *simultaneity*, film is unquestionably a better medium than either printed or
pixelated language: Onscreen, several people can talk at the same
time, as they often do in life but can't on the page; what's more, they
can do so as we see their car moving through city streets, with attendant urban sights and sounds and a musical score to enhance the
effect. But even the camera can "narrate" only one scene at a time
(split-screen or multiple-screen effects can *show* simultaneously oc-
curring though spatially separated segments of action, but our minds
can't simultaneously follow them unless they're radically simplified
and abbreviated). In film-narrative as well as print-narrative, it's usually "Meanwhile, back at the ranch . . ."—and in print we have to

read, one word at a time, *While Myrtle fiddled with the fancy new microwave and tried once more to tell Fred about that afternoon's scary phone call, her loser of a husband unfridged and deflowered yet another St. Pauli Girl beer, wondering dully which lie he would tell his wife this time. . . .*

I could deliver a whole separate talk on what's being done in that rudimentary narrative sentence that can't be done as readily if at all with a camera: the interpretations ("fiddled," "fancy," "loser," "scary"), the expository information ("*new* microwave," "tried *once more*," "her *husband*," "*yet another* beer," "tell his wife *this* time"), the voltaged metaphor (his "deflowering" a "St. Pauli Girl"), the transcription of interiority ("wondering dully which lie," et cetera)— but never mind. My point is the unexceptionable one that various narrative/dramatic media have their various virtues and limitations. Just as you can do things on-page that you can't on-screen and vice-versa (and I haven't even mentioned such great paginary virtues as proceeding at one's own pace, lingering over choice or difficult bits, thumbing back or even forward, making marginalia if the book is your own, marking passages for later reference or for sharing with a pal), so too the printed fictive page, for all its sensory limitations and its inability to let you wander the interactive hills of Úbeda, has virtues that hypertexted, interactive, even multimedial e-fiction lacks. Among them, for the present at least, is relative portability, convenience, and user-comfort. But even when, as is rapidly coming to pass, new technologies permit us to recline in our recliners with hypertexted pages almost as comfortable in the hand as a well-printed book and no harder on the eyes, the latter will still have things going for it that the former, by its very nature, will not. Allow me, please, a final self-quotation:[5]

Interactivity can be fun; improvisation and collaboration
can be fun; freedom is jolly. But there are dominations that
one may freely enjoy without being at all masochistic, and
among those, for many of us, is the willing, provisional, and
temporary surrender of our noisy little egos to great artistry:
a surrender which, so far from diminishing, quite enlarges
us. . . . Reading a splendid writer, or even just a very en-
tertaining writer, is not a particularly passive business. An
accomplished artist is giving us his or her best shots, in what
she or he regards as their most effective sequence—of words,
of actions, of foreshadowings and plot-twists and insights
and carefully prepared dramatic moments. It's up to us to
respond to those best shots with our minds and hearts and
spirits and our accumulated experience of life and of art—
and that's interaction aplenty, for some of us, without our
presuming to grab the steering wheel and diddle the driver's
itinerary. The kind of reading I've just described requires not
only [what the critic Sven Birkerts has called] "meditative
space" but, as Birkerts observes, a sense that the text before
us is not a provisional version, up for grabs, the way texts in
the cyberspace of a computer memory always are, but rather
the author's very best: what he or she is ready to be judged
by for keeps.

Those virtues, I believe, are sufficient to keep hypertext, e-fiction, and other electronic wonders from being The End Of The Word As We've Known It, even before we play our ace: print's marvelous low-technicity. Back in the late evening of the past century, the *New York Times Magazine*'s final wrap-up-the-millennium issue (in December

1999) featured a panel of experts discussing the best medium for storing information in a "Times capsule," to be opened a thousand years hence. After considering a very wide array of high-tech possibilities, they decided that nothing in the nature of Zip disks and CD-ROMs would do, because the hardware required to run the software for accessing the "content" evolves so very rapidly, and the disks themselves have nothing like so long-term a shelf life. For the very long haul, they agreed, nothing beats plain old high-quality ink on plain old high-quality paper.

That sounds encouraging to us POB's—"print-oriented bastards," as followers of the late Marshall MacLuhan used to call us even back in the pre-computerized 1960s. But before we break out the champagne and raise a toast to the Health of the Novel-in-Print, we need to remind ourselves that the persistence of our medium for long-term infostorage and other special applications does not in itself mean the persistence of a substantial audience for a particular art-form. Granted that what Joyce Carol Oates has called "pop apocalypses" usually turn out to be false alarms: Thomas Edison's confidence, for example, that the invention of motion pictures would soon make textbooks obsolete in our schools; the publisher Henry Holt's concern that the development of the bicycle might spell the end of reading books for pleasure. Granted too that one must guard against conflating one's personal advanced age with the Decline of the West or the senescence of print-lit. All the same, it doesn't seem at all unimaginable to me that reading novels may continue to become an ever more specialized pleasure for an ever-smaller "niche" audience, like (alas) the audience for short stories and for poetry: literary support-groups, really, akin to those for the clinically addicted and the terminally ill.

Should we care?

Yes and no. There are certainly graver concerns on the thoughtful citizen's agenda than the Death of the Novel: the death of the planet, for starters. Art-forms rise and decline in popularity with artists as well as with audiences, without thereby going extinct: New symphonies and operas are still composed, though not in 19th-century abundance, and the classical repertoire has a faithful following. Should something analogous become the case with novels for print—if books themselves should become, as one commentator recently put it, "the vermiform appendix of the communications system"[6]—civilization won't be the *better* for it, but it won't be the end of the word, much less the end of the world. There's more great stuff to read out there already than most of us can get to in a lifetime; and as for new novels, written by our contemporaries and speaking to the here and now, well: Unlike the rhinoceros and the pygmy owl or even the osprey and the eagle, the novel has from its beginnings been as elastic a critter as the octopus and as adaptable as the crow, the coyote, and the raccoon, able not only to survive but even to flourish in radically transformed environments. It cheers me that the population of Virginia white-tail deer where I come from is estimated to be larger nowadays than it was in the time of Powhatan and Pocahontas, when The Novel As We Know It was just being invented on the other side of the Atlantic. Those deer have become a downright nuisance: "rats with hooves," the environmentalist Tom Horton has called them. The emergence of e-fiction and of electronic publishing are instances of that kind of adaptability on the novel's part, and while I have no compelling interest in those phenomena myself, I take their appearance as a healthy development and do not doubt that there will be others, on and off the printed page.

The king is dead? Long live the king!

And the novel? *Encore! Encore!*

"I've Lost My Place!"

The popular Key West Literary Seminars, held each January at the southern tip of the USA, offer workshops for aspiring writers and guest appearances by more established ones. In 2001, the Seminar's theme (which changes annually) was "The Spirit of Place." That year's writer-speakers included, among others, Merrill Joan Gerber, Peter Matthiesson, Annie Proulx, Susan Richards Shreve, Lee Smith, and myself; we participated in a spirited symposium on "The Loss of Place in Fiction: The Homogenization of American Life," and then each of us delivered a talk on some particular aspect of the general subject. What follows are, in order, my symposium-statement and my presentation on the place of "place" in fiction.

I T MAY BE worth noting that the title of this symposium comprises two separate or at least separable topics: the first general, the second more specific, and both interesting. I'll make a few remarks first about the general subject of a writer's being cut off for whatever reason from a geographical/cultural place that had been important to his/her creative imagination, and then about the specific loss of place-identity to what we're calling "the homogenization of American life." Both, I'm going to argue, are non-problems—at least in themselves.

As for Topic 1: "I've lost my place!" is a lament almost as common among writers as among readers who neglect to use bookmarks. Among the former, the consequences of place-loss by voluntary or involuntary *exile*, for example, have historically been downright splendid for literature, however painful for particular writers as people. From Ovid through Dante to Joyce and Nabokov, and including the expatriate "Lost Generation" of Hemingway, Scott Fitzgerald, et al., the Literature of Exile is so rich a tradition that it might arguably be well for Place-Lit if *all* writers were obliged to spend a figurative Junior Year Abroad in the course of their apprenticeship, the way Professor Larry Chisholm at Yale used to require his doctoral candidates in American Studies to spend a year or two in Biafra or Zimbabwe, say, for the purpose of acquiring an anthropological detachment from their subject-matter. In my own case, it was when I left my native Chesapeake tidewaterland after graduate school to go teach in central Pennsylvania that the place I'd put behind me became the locale, if not quite the subject, of my first several novels. But of course writers are so different from one another that no generalizations about the benefits of exile will do. Getting out of Ireland worked as well for Frank McCourt (of *Angela's Ashes* fame) as it did for James Joyce; but whether that "Trieste/Zurich/Paris" at the end of Joyce's very Irish *Ulysses* would have been good for Eudora Welty or Flannery O'Connor, for example, is another story.

And as to our real subject—the literary consequences of a place's loss of its distinctive character to the "homogenization of American life"—I call it a non-problem for at least four reasons, while always acknowledging that *anything* might turn out to be a problem for some particular writer:

—First (a point I'll expand upon in my later remarks on "The Place of Place in Fiction"), although many good writers revel and even more or less specialize in the realistic rendition of some particular locale, such rendition is *not* prerequisite to first-rate fiction. Ernest Hemingway declared that "every writer owes it to the place of his birth either to immortalize it or to destroy it"; I would add that he/she may opt simply to ignore it, and to set her/his fiction in other real places, or in imagined or imaginary places, or nowhere in particular. I'm not *recommending* this, mind; only remarking it.

—Second, the loss of a place's once-distinctive character, whether to cultural homogenization or simply to the passage of time, is what leads to the Literature of Nostalgia: a genre as rich as, and often overlapping, the Literature of Expatriation. Thus Faulkner, for example, whose Mississippi remained central to his imagination even after he himself shifted to exotic Virginia in his latter years, enjoyed contrasting the Old Yoknapatawpha with the New, where automobiles now zip down the streets "with a sound like tearing silk." All grist for his mill.

—Third, the Homogenization of American Life and consequent attrition of place-identity can itself be a viable literary subject—as can anything, I daresay, in the hands of an appropriately inspired writer.

—And fourth, "homogenization" is always a matter of degree, and can cast what distinctiveness remains into higher relief than formerly. The film-director Jean Renoir observed that "the marvelous thing about [Hollywood] Westerns is that they are all the same movie. That gives a director unlimited freedom."[1] "Unlimited" is doubtless an exaggeration, but it's a truism about any genre-art that its practitioners and fans become connoisseurs of small differences within the generic parameters. Against a background of the perceived homogenization of American life, the same might apply to non-generic art as well—as witness the title of Larry McMurtry's recent essay-collection, *Walter Benjamin at the Tasti-Freeze*. A once-"wild" West that now has the usual constellation of strip developments and franchise businesses is admittedly less different from other places than it used to be; I submit, however, that a Tasti-Freeze in Archer, Texas, with a Larry McMurtry in it reading the late French literary critic and theoretician Walter Benjamin, remains a distinctive place indeed and (Q.E.D. by the book afore-cited) may be a fit subject for fiction, nonfiction, drama, or verse.

MIND YOU, I'M not arguing in *favor* of homogenization. But even biological clones are identical only genetically—and our DNA, as we all know, is by no means our whole story.

The Place of "Place" in Fiction[1]

JOHN O'HARA ONCE remarked that when he was between plots, all he had to do was take his imagination for a stroll down the streets of his native Pottstown, PA, remembering the families who lived in each house along the way, and soon enough he'd have the makings of his next story. One can scarcely imagine Flannery O'Connor's muse in Ontario instead of Georgia, or William Faulkner's singing sweetly of Down-East Maine. Fiction, whether narrative or dramatic, requires characters, action, theme, and setting, and for a great many writers of it—especially from the 18th century onward, with the ascendancy of the novel and the tradition of literary realism—*setting* becomes not only inseparable from those other components, but a virtual player itself, in numerous instances even a kind of authorial trademark: Thomas Hardy's Wessex, Anne Tyler's Baltimore.

This is so clearly the case that it's worth remembering that the richly "textured" rendition of geographical locale is *not* prerequisite to great literary art. It was enough for Homer to invoke Odysseus's Wine-Dark Sea and Rock-Bound Ithaca without going much beyond those formulaic epithets; we may get some pungent flavors of 14th-century Florence from Dante's *Divine Comedy* or of 16th-century France from Rabelais' *Gargantua and Pantagruel*, but it's not from any Henry Jamesian "composition of place." And in modern times, writers like Franz Kafka, Samuel Beckett, Jorge Luis Borges, Italo Calvino, and Donald Barthelme achieved first-rate literary art that in many instances is all but placeless. Indeed, one does well to bear in mind Borges's memorable objection[2] that to be an "Argentine writer" one need not lay on the tangos and gauchos and pampas and such, any more than the author of the Koran felt obliged to load that sacred text with camels (Borges cites Edward Gibbon's observation that there is no mention of camels in the holy book of Islam, and then speculates that had its author been an Arab nationalist, there would be caravans of camels on every page).

One might go even further and perpend some writerly cautions about the risks of *too much* dependence upon Place, especially upon any one particular place. Larry McMurtry, at an earlier stage of his career than the present, good-humoredly complained that critics had so often called him a "good minor regional novelist" that he'd had (or was going to have, I forget which) a T-shirt made for himself with that damningly qualified praise: a T-shirt that he has most certainly outgrown, if it ever fit him in the first place. And Joyce Carol Oates, speaking in my seminar room at Johns Hopkins to a group of apprentices from all over the map, warned that it can be perhaps all too easy to become the Sweet Singer of Saskatchewan, say, with an audience that may not extend beyond that doubtless songworthy place. The difference between a "good minor regional writer" and a Faulkner or a Joyce (Joyce Oates or Wordsworth or a Frost, for this distinction applies to poets as well as to fictionists) would seem to be the evocation of Place as an end in itself versus its evocation as locus and focus of the writer's other and larger concerns. It no doubt has to do also with the strength, width, and depth of the writer's powers other than "the composition of place."

It's worth noting too that writers very good indeed at the evocation of Place may not be associated with one particular locale: Of the
likes of Hemingway, Steinbeck, Nabokov, Penelope Fitzgerald, Annie
Proulx, and Robert Stone, one is tempted to say that they choose,
from book to book, the locale that suits the project's theme and action. More likely, I'd bet, the connection is coaxial, the place suggesting the theme as much as vice-versa—as is the case dramatically, so
to speak, with Shakespeare's "Italy of the heart" and Denmark of the
soul in such plays as *Romeo and Juliet* and *Hamlet*: masterworks of
whose settings the author had no firsthand experience at all.

THAT SAID, IT remains the case that Place assumes uppercasehood,
for better or worse, more with writers like Eudora Welty, García
Márquez, Flannery O'Connor, and Robert Frost, whose virtually entire *oeuvre* is inspired by or at least grows out of one general locale,
than it does with writers who shift locations from project to project, or with writers like Jane Austen or Honoré de Balzac or Henry
James or Marcel Proust, whose evocation of place is more social
than geographical. Take Africa away from Hemingway or Italy from
Henry James and you've still got a lot of Hemingway and James; take
Mississippi away from Faulkner and you've got a Displaced Person.

A good many writers, of course, are somewhere between these
polar examples: Their muse may return more or less frequently to
some home base (Twain's Mississippi River, John Updike's small-
town Pennsylvania), but also enjoy notable excursions from it
(Twain's *Connecticut Yankee* and *Innocents Abroad*, Updike's Bech-
books, his Brazil and medieval Denmark). It's in this category that
I locate myself: Tidewater Maryland, especially the Eastern Shore
thereof, has been my muse's boggy home turf for five decades, from

my first published fiction to my latest. But if it is a place *to* which she much enjoys returning, that is at least in part because it is a place *from* which she has enjoyed considerable excursions: My first three books are set there, although Place is all but irrelevant to the second of those (*The End of the Road*). The next three are set mainly in Allegorica or Mythsville; most but not all of the ones after that return to Tidewaterland.

Why? Not because it's the only place that I know rather well: I housekept for a dozen years in central Pennsylvania, half a dozen in upstate New York, and two dozen in urban Baltimore, with shorter residences in Andalusia, Boston, and Los Angeles; my wife and I have traveled fairly extensively (by my lights, anyhow, though less extensively than my Mrs. wishes), and in recent years we've wintered on the Gulf Coast of Florida. In any case, one needn't necessarily know a place widely or deeply in order to be literarily inspired by it; one need only apprehend some aspect of it sharply and then render that aspect into artful language. How profoundly did Vladimir Nabokov know the American west, into which he made only the occasional lepidopteral foray? And yet his impressions of it in *Lolita*, however limited, are memorable indeed. On the coin's other side, we note that massive knowledge of a place is no guarantee of its immortal rendition: Nobody did his homework more thoroughly than James Michener as his muse shuttled him from the South Pacific to Hawaii, Korea, Spain, Poland, the Chesapeake, Texas, and even Outer Space—but one may respectfully question the long-term staying power of those knowledgeable and enormously popular place-novels of his.

Myself, I take my inspiration where I find it, and that Where more often than not turns out to be the only geographical place to which I feel genuine, like-it-or-not Connection. That like-it-or-not, warts-and-all qualification can be important, as with pain-in-the-ass members of one's family: It can safeguard one's commitment from contamination by sentimentality. At its most extreme, one notes that it was Thomas Bernhard's visceral *disgust* with aspects of his native Austria that largely fueled his novelistic imagination. My attachment to the region of my birth, upbringing, and re-residency—after a considerable and useful absence from it—is not an uncritical bond, but it's a warm and strong one. To its choice as the setting for a novel or short story, however, I try to apply the same qualification-test that one ought to apply to one's choice of characters, action, and every other component of the work: What's its relevance to the fiction's *sense*, the project's theme? What's it *for*?

The answers to such questions may not always be clear or pure to the author/asker; even hyper-self-conscious Postmodernists work by hunch and feel and habits of craft that have become second nature to them. But the questions ought always to be asked.

Liberal Education: The Tragic View

Commencement address delivered in 2002 to the graduating seniors of St. John's College, Santa Fe (an institution noted for its Great Books curriculum), and subsequently published in the Albuquerque, NM, *Tribune*:

A COMMENCEMENT ADDRESS MUST always commence with a joke, even if the somber-sounding title of that address is "The Tragic View of Liberal Education." As I happen not to have any appropriate jokes of my own, I'm going to borrow one from Bill Cosby, who gave the commencement address at Goucher College in Baltimore this time last year. It is a joke that, as Cosby warned his audience, contains one naughty word—and then he added, "At least it *used* to be a naughty word."

It seems that a distinguished physicist and a distinguished philosopher happened to die at the same time, and approaching Heaven's gate they were informed by the Gatekeeper that because of temporary overcrowding, God was admitting only those deserving souls who could ask Him a question that even He couldn't answer; all others would have to wait in Limbo indefinitely. The physicist reflected for a moment and then posed the most intricate, difficult problem in quantum mechanical theory—which God solved on the spot. The philosopher then put the most elusive question in metaphysical/ontological/epistemological theory—to which God unhesitatingly gave an irrefutable answer. As the two great thinkers shook their heads in awe, an elderly couple humbly approached and whispered in the deity's ear; He scratched His head, then shook it and promptly ushered them into Heaven.

"Excuse us, Sir," the physicist and philosopher then respectfully inquired: "We can't help wondering what in the world those folks asked that even You couldn't answer." To which God sighed and replied, "They asked me, *When will our kids ever get their shit together?*"

END OF JOKE (which anyhow I suspect applies less to graduates of this institution than to those of many others) and beginning of the Tragic View of Liberal Education. For me to natter on here about the importance of "Great Books" curricula like St. John's would obviously be preaching to the choir—but I'll do at least a paragraphsworth of that anyhow, for reasons to be set forth presently. Having been born, raised, and schooled in the state of Maryland, and having subsequently lived and worked there for more of my life than not, I became acquainted early on with the program at your original campus in Annapolis. If I ended up matriculating at Johns Hopkins instead, that was because from high school I had gone up to Juilliard's summer program to test against reality my then ambition to be a professional jazz drummer and orchestrator; I aced my courses but failed my reality-test with flying colors, came home to think what to do next, and found I had won a state scholarship to Hopkins that I'd more or less forgotten I'd applied for. So with a shrug of the shoulders I went there, *faute de mieux*—a most happy *faute*, as I came to realize later. In my undergraduate and graduate-school years there half a century ago, the St. John's curriculum was spoken of and its pros and cons debated, or anyhow discussed now and then, in class and out; we compared and contrasted it with our own quite admirable two-year lecture courses in Literary Classics and Classics in the History of Thought—mandatory in those bygone days for all Hopkins Arts & Sciences undergrads.

What were those pros? What were the cons, as we saw them from the perspective of Baltimore back at mid-century?[1]

The pros, as I've said already, go without saying in this venue— or would so go except that 1) some of them are even more evident now than they were 50 years ago, and 2) saying over and over what goes without saying (at least vis-à-vis the craft of fiction-writing) was for decades my pedagogical specialty. So what's to be said (once more, with feeling) for a curriculum devoted to the study of a more-or-less-agreed-upon roster of "the best that has been thought and said," in Matthew Arnold's famous formulation—or at least as representatively much of that Best as the ever-evolving consensus of a good college faculty believes can be fruitfully addressed between undergraduate matriculation and the baccalaureate?

Well: What's to be said for it, needless to say, is that it not only edifies and instructs—any old good curriculum does that—but permits *discourse* within a shared frame of reference richer and more stable than this season's pop music, films, and TV shows, which a colleague of mine used to lament were the only points of cultural reference that he could assume to be shared by his undergraduate students: not Homer and Sophocles and the Bible, not Virgil and Dante and Shakespeare, but *The Sopranos* and *Friends* and Britney Spears and N'Sync, all of which in just a few years will seem as quaintly dated and otherwise limited as *Leave It to Beaver* and Boy George and Tiny Tim (I don't mean Charles Dickens's Tiny Tim). It is this urge for a richer shared frame of reference that has prompted those "One City, One Book" programs that you may have heard about, in Seattle, Chicago, Buffalo, Rochester, and elsewhere: the urging by city officials that every adolescent and adult in town read, say, Harper Lee's *To Kill a Mockingbird* or Ernest J. Gaines's *A Lesson Before Dying*, their reading to be accompanied by discussions and other events in the city's libraries, bookstores, and community centers as a low-cost way to nurture civic pride and community spirit while propagandizing benignly against racism (in the case of the two novels just cited) and offering teenagers a healthy alternative to television and video games. Who could possibly object?

No show of hands necessary: One may fidget at the choice of Harper Lee and Ernest Gaines (serious and competent writers both) instead of, say, Flannery O'Connor and Ralph Ellison, finer literary artists with no less moral passion in the matter of racism. And one fidgets at the idea of *any* single book—instead of, say, Dr. Eliot's Five-Foot Shelf of 418 Harvard Classics, or the 88 distinguished names (who can resist saying "88 *key* names"?) on the St. John's College Reading List last time I looked—as a shared frame of reference for dialogue on racism or anything else, including the topic of Shared Frames of Reference. But one has to start *somewhere*, no? It's just a question of where—and in raising that question we find ourselves confronting possible reservations about Great Books curricula, which doubtless also go without saying in this venue, especially on this happy occasion, so let's review a couple of them anyhow:

NEVER MIND, FOR starters, the half-serious objection of my undergraduate mentor at Johns Hopkins, the late aesthetician and historian of ideas George Boas, who liked to tell us that the problem with
the Annapolis curriculum was that it left out not only all the *bad*
books—which, like bad art, may be indispensable to defining and
appreciating the good—but also all the arguably great books that
happen to disagree with the ones in the canon. We can dispense with
these teasing objections because (in the first instance) mediocre-to-
bad books and art are sufficiently inescapable that we needn't include
them in our curriculum, although it's certainly useful to point them
out from time to time and to argue with them. As for the second instance, any respectable clutch of Great Books will contain sufficient
contradiction or at least disagreement on, e.g., the nature of Truth,
Goodness, and Beauty to escape the curricular sins of pasteurization
and homogenization. The real problem, it goes without saying (and
this is what Professor Boas was good-humoredly pointing out to us
sophomores), is that there are so *many* great or at least important
books that no four-year undergraduate survey—much less his own
two-year survey—can be more than a radically selective, though not
arbitrary, sampling. And this, mind you, was the 1940s and '50s, before multiculturalism and political correctness hit the fan. Dr. Eliot's
aforementioned shelf (which I myself read, or at least thumbed right
through in numerical sequence, while working as a night-shift timekeeper in Baltimore's Chevrolet assembly plant one undergraduate
summer) had come to look quaint indeed by the century's latter decades: all those Protestant sermons, instead of the *Mahabharata* and
Gargantua and Pantagruel! Alessandro Manzoni's novel *I Promessi
Sposi* instead of Murasaki Shikibu's *Tale of Genji* and James Joyce's

Ulysses! For all its merits, by the 1960s it was as obviously dated a cultural artifact as its most judiciously updated and multiculturally sophisticated present-day counterpart would doubtless be seen to be half a century from now.

The difficulty, of course—as you probably knew before you enrolled at St John's but were no doubt reminded of during your freshman orientation here and every semester thereafter—is succinctly put in the title of Isaac Babel's earliest known work of fiction: *You Must Know Everything*. What a title: *You Must Know Everything*! That imperative implies, among much else, that you must *read* everything; must indeed *have read* everything, which of course you cannot; which you could not even if history refrained from growing both longer (as recorded time accumulates) and wider (as cultures evolve and intercultural connections multiply), thus ever enlarging the mass of what Umberto Eco calls "the already said." You cannot read everything; could not even if you were a certain fellow Hopkins graduate student who seemed to me and his other seminar-mates to have read nearly everything already; whom we suspected of staying up all night reading the corpus's few remaining unread volumes (in their original languages) while we lesser beings slept; and who I later learned *was*, in fact, doing just that, more or less, he being not only a polymath but a tireless insomniac: a charming and generous fellow of such cripplingly vast erudition that to this day he is scarcely able to complete a sentence or publish an essay, because every word he utters sets off so many synaptic hot-links in his mind that he has difficulty getting from subject to verb to object, astray in the hypertextuality of his splendid erudition.

Yet even he, as he'd be the first to insist, is far indeed from having read all the books worth reading, much less from having *re*-read them (we recall Vladimir Nabokov's insistence that "all great reading is rereading"—a dismaying idea when one has finally reached the end of Dr. Eliot's shelf or of the ten folio volumes of Somadeva's *Katha Sarit Sagara*, or *The Ocean of the Streams of Story*). No: We cannot read all the books, not to mention spectating all the important stage-plays, films, and graphic and plastic arts; auditing all the music; acquiring a working knowledge of all the languages and arts and sciences (a fascinating section of our Hopkins commencement program is the pages and pages of doctoral-dissertation titles in the several sciences: titles of which, more often than not, I cannot understand a single word; can only shake my head in awe at the staggering *multifariousness* of human intellectual curiosity). . . . We "must know everything," but we cannot, and inasmuch as we cannot, our pursuit of Higher Education both during and after our college years involves us in an exemplary paradox: Since time, attention, energy, and opportunity are all finite, we must radically exclude and delimit if we are to learn anything at all well; yet in so doing we may very possibly leave out things that, had we discovered them or they us, might have been keys to the treasure that we were scarcely aware we were seeking; or if not the keys, at least elements of the combination.

The Tragic View of life, and/or of history, is that there are no ultimate victories, just different ways to lose, the only "victory" being to go down heroically, or anyhow as nobly as we can. The Tragic View of liberal education is that even at its best, as at St. John's, it is so necessarily, unavoidably limited that all it can attempt is to afford us some experience of, for example, informed close reading and critical thinking, and to make us aware that there remain continents of knowledge out there that one lifetime could scarcely scratch the surface of, even were we to devote it all to reading and studying—which we must not, since education comes so much from hands-on doing and experiencing as well as from reading and study. Our Hopkins mini-version of your Great Books curriculum was commendable; but how fortunate for me that to make ends meet I worked as a book-filer in the university library, where I lost myself back in the stacks sampling what I was supposed to be reshelving, and thus discovered such extracurricular storytellers as Petronius and Boccaccio and Scheherazade, important to my eventual vocation. But who knows what-all I *didn't* happen to discover, or do or meet, that might have made me into a very different, not impossibly a quite better, writer, not to mention a better human being?

BUT THAT WAY lies fruitless discontent, and I do not at all intend the Tragic View of Liberal Education as a despairing or even a pessimistic view, only an unblinkered one. I remember wishing, as a green undergraduate and apprentice writer, that I could at least know the *names* of everything, if not the things themselves: "all trades," as the poet Gerard Manley Hopkins puts it, "their gear, tackle, and trim": every rock, bug, plant, star, body-bone, lingo, culture. I remember feeling like a newcomer to a party that had been going on for millennia, and worrying that maybe all the best jokes and stories had been told already. 25 centuriesworth of poets getting off good metaphors for the ocean and the sunrise, for example, since Homer's "wine-dark sea" and "rosy-fingered dawn": Could I or anybody hope to come up with yet another? And how would I know that I had, unless I reconnoitered the entire existing inventory? Which of course I could not; only comfort myself with the speculation that my tens of thousands of predecessors, so far from exhausting the stock of good dawn- and sea-images, might for all we know have scarcely made a dent in it. No doubt the number of possible zingers is finite, but then so is the number of stars in the galaxy, not to mention in the universe: finite, but astronomically large.

Therefore take heart, adviseth the Tragic View: One's education is at best fragmentary, and will never be anything like complete; but at least it can know itself to be so, and can achieve *some* compass and coherence. It has to start somewhere, and inasmuch as we happen to dwell in *this* historical/cultural latitude and longitude rather than some other, it seems not unreasonable to begin (although we will not end) with some judiciously chosen reading-list therefrom—recognizing it to be neither more nor less than our point of departure (or 88 or 418 points of departure), not our journey's end.

Will there be objections to the list? Of course there'll be, and welcome to the Great Conversation! Are there arguable alternatives to the Tragic View of Liberal Education? No doubt there are—including the Tragic View of the Tragic View. But that's a sermon for some other occasion than this: For now, my warm congratulations indeed on your Education Thus Far. Welcome to the party! *Gaudeamus igitur!* On with your stories!

The Relevance of Irrelevance: Writing American

This article—commissioned by the State Department in 2002 for inclusion in a book of essays to be distributed in U.S. embassies and consulates throughout the world "to illustrate American values through having various authors consider what makes them an American writer," but subsequently rejected for its "explicit commentary on the events of September 11"—first appeared in Italian translation[1] in the anthology *Undici settembre* (Torino: Einaudi, 2003).

S PEAKING AT JOHNS Hopkins University back when his country was riven by *Apartheid*, the eminent South African novelist J. M. Coetzee remarked that under such sorry historical circumstances, for him to publish a novel that made no political statement would be tantamount to his making a very conspicuous—and egregious—political statement. From my seat in the audience I nodded sympathetic assent, although Coetzee's observation was by no means a pitch for sympathy. And, not for the first time, I silently thanked Apollo and all the Muses for affording me the luxury of political irrelevance.

More exactly, I felt grateful to chance and history for affording me the *option* of writing fiction that intends no political/ideological statement; for the good fortune of living in a place and time that can regard as equally honorable the literary credos of, on the one hand, my fellow American fictionist Grace Paley, for example—a heroic protester of U.S. involvement in Vietnam in the 1960s and '70s, among her other good causes, who once declared to my students that "Art isn't important: *People* are important. *Politics* is important"— and on the other hand that of the late Vladimir Nabokov, himself a political refugee, who nevertheless maintained that his sole literary aim was "aesthetic bliss." It should be noted that one can savor a Grace Paley short story on its literary merits alone (I myself do not find her excellent fiction especially "political"), and that Nabokov's virtuoso novels are by no means oblivious to the political upheavals that drove him from his native Russia. But both authors felt free—as Coetzee by his own acknowledgment did not, and as artists in any politically convulsed or oppressed place and time may well not—either to engage their art in the service of some political/moral cause or to regard that art itself as their cause: Art for Art's sake, or more specifically, in the case of fiction, art for the sake of language, form, action, character, plot, setting, narration, and theme; Story (mainly though not exclusively) for Story's sake. For the freedom to be, in my writing, politically engaged or politically irrelevant, I feel as fortunate as for the happy accident of my having been born in just the right narrow historical "window" (the year was 1930) to miss direct involvement in all the U.S.-involved wars of the Terrible Twentieth Century: not here yet for World War I, in which my father served and my uncle died; too young for World War II, in which my older brother served; exempted by student- and then marital/parental deferments from service in Korea, where many of my age-group served; too old to be conscripted for the war in Vietnam (for which my male children, luckily, missed having their draft-lottery numbers called). May that cycle of good fortune be repeated for my children's children! Would that it could extend to all the world's children!

Which is not at all to say that I regard every one of those terrible wars as unjustified, any more than (as a citizen of my country and the world) I feel "above" engagement with political/social issues. Not at all. Although I happen to incline to the Skeptical-Pacifist persuasion, had I been born a few years earlier I would no doubt have enlisted patriotically in the 1940s, along with my brother, to oppose Nazism and its Japanese counterpart. I will even grant that if such had been the case, I might very well feel the experience to have been centrally important or at least significant to me as a writer: Most artists' work is affected in some measure by major experiences of their youth. But I do not regret having missed that particular category of convulsion. Indeed, Ernest Hemingway is the only American writer I can think of who professed a condescending *pity* for those of his countrymen who happened not to experience the trauma of warfare: I recollect his declaring somewhere or other that World War I was "the defining event of their generation, and they simply missed it." Hemingway, however, was by notorious disposition a *macho* adventure-seeker. If his admirable fiction happened to depend upon that appetite, so be it; the no less admirable fiction of William Faulkner, James Joyce, Thomas Mann, Marcel Proust, Virginia Woolf, Franz Kafka, and F. Scott Fitzgerald—to name only a few of his illustrious peers—did not.

My argument is simply that for an artist to be politically concerned and even politically active as a citizen does not—anyhow *should* not, ideally—mandate politically concerned art. I quite understand J. M. Coetzee's position as aforestated, which in his case has produced writing as commendable on its literary as on its moral/

political merits. But I admire at least equally the art of the late great Argentine Jorge Luis Borges, for example, who, though embarrassed and harassed by the Perón regime (at whose hands he was "promoted" from his post in the Buenos Aires municipal library to the rank of chicken-and-rabbit inspector in the public markets), was not moved thereby to write political allegories and anti-*Perónista* fables, as he quite justifiably might have been.[2] Borges admits (in "An Autobiographical Essay") to having danced in the streets of Buenos Aires when Perón was ousted in September 1955, and also to writing a couple of pro-Israel poems at the time of the Arab-Israeli war of 1967; more typically, however, when his fiction addresses contemporary political/historical matters—as in his short story "The Secret Miracle," for example, about a Czech playwright executed by the Nazis for the crime of being Jewish—the story is at least as much about art and metaphysics as about the Holocaust.

MY OWN MUSE happens to be the one with the grin rather than the one with the grimace. One of our recent collaborations, a comic-apocalyptic "Y2K" novel called *Coming Soon!!!*, coincidentally appeared just a few weeks after the Islamic terrorist attacks on the World Trade Center and the Pentagon, and in subsequent book-tour interviews and public appearances I was more than once asked whether I thought irony, even comedy in general, was perhaps *inappropriate*, to put it mildly, in the wake of that atrocity and the subsequent national emergency. Less in my own defense than in defense of artistic liberty and therapeutic laughter, I found myself invoking two of my longtime literary stars, *The Thousand and One Nights* and Boccaccio's *Decameron*. In the former, the King's anger at his wife's adultery turns into murderous misogyny, ruinous to the state as well as lethal to many of its female citizens: After killing his unfaithful wife and her paramour, King Shahryar "marries" a young virgin every night and has her executed the next morning lest she prove unfaithful, and after three bloodthirsty yearsworth of such misguided revenge, families with maiden daughters are fleeing the country in droves. To save her homeland, her remaining "sisters," and the King himself from his madness, Scheherazade volunteers herself (she has a Plan), and the 1001 suspenseful nights of her literally marvelous storytelling ensue. The *Decameron* opens with a scarifying description of the Black Death of 1348: the cataclysmic bubonic plague that in only a few years killed a third of Europe's population, just as the influenza pandemic of 1918 would claim millions more victims than the Great War itself—including that aforementioned uncle of mine, who died of it in France while serving with the American Expeditionary Force. Boccaccio's ten young Florentine lords and ladies retreat from the lawless horror of the dying city to their country estates, where they amuse themselves by swapping a hundred stories: one tale per person per day for ten days (fourteen days, actually, but they take Fridays and Saturdays off), until they deem it safe to return to Florence.

The point of my invoking these classics was that in both distinguished cases, the stories—told in horrific, indeed apocalyptic circumstances—so far from directly addressing those circumstances, are all but programmatically irrelevant to them. Scheherazade may slip in a tale or two about people unjustly threatened with death who are mercifully spared (e.g., Nights 1 and 2), but more typically she goes in for whiz-bang Special Effects like magic lanterns and bottled genies, along with erotica and even scatology: one of Goethe's favorite Arabian Nights was #410: "How Abu Hasan Farted."[3] After

Boccaccio's detailed description of the plague in Florence, his privileged gentry never speak of it again until their idyll's conclusion:
Their tales have to do with libidinous husbands and wives (and nuns
and friars), narrow escapes, flirtations, witty retorts; not a word
about how their less privileged *compaesani* are dying miserably by
the thousands back in town. Indeed, Romantic Interest grows among
several of the taletellers, and when they return to Florence and part
company at the book's close, it is not to aid the victims (who anyhow
could not be helped, since neither cause nor cure for bubonic plague
was known at the time), but to avoid the appearance of having fallen
into Vice and to go their separate ways, having judged the epidemic
to have passed its peak. A proper Marxist would be appalled, I suppose; even we mere liberal Democrats may be given pause by such
blithely oblivious elitism, and Boccaccio himself repudiated the book
in his elder years—but on moral, not ideological grounds. His merry,
ribald tales, however, along with the schedules, rules, and agendas
that their tellers improvise for ordering their pleasures, have served
as a therapeutic diversion for the lucky company, even as an *ad hoc*
social order until the larger world recovers. Their very irrelevance to
that world's crisis, like the general irrelevance of Scheherazade's tales
to her being in bed with the Guinness World Record Serial Killer,
may be said to be their relevance. Centuries after the horror that inspired and frames them, we read them for pleasure still.

NOW: AS A matter of biographical fact, I happen to be no fan of
the present administration in Washington, or of U.S. unilateralism
in foreign affairs: No anti-ABM or anti-landmine treaties or Kyoto
protocols or International Court of Justice for us Yanks, thanks!
Drill the Arctic, cut the parkland timber, bomb Saddam and *Roe v.*

Wade, torture the war-prisoners, and step on the gas! And while I quite understand the post-9/11 fever of patriotic display (as opposed to unostentatious patriotism) among my countrymen, it makes me uncomfortable, as does my government's ever more lavish military expenditure at whatever sacrifice of other deserving priorities. In my personal political opinion, the charges against Osama bin Laden and his al-Qaeda terrorists include, along with their more serious crimes, their having rescued an insecure and, to a great many of us, lamentable American presidency by permitting it to wrap itself in the Stars and Stripes and imply that criticisms of its right-wing heavy-handedness are unpatriotic. One worries that if the terrorists should strike again, some version of our infamous House UnAmerican Activities Committee of the 1950s could rise from its well-deserved grave and resume its deplorable witch-hunting. Already, one imagines, complaints like these of mine do not go unnoticed by the nation's reinvigorated agencies of domestic surveillance. . . .[4]

In the uncertain meanwhile, however, we Americans remain among that minority of the world's population blessedly free, both as citizens and as artists, either to strive for political relevance or—in our art especially—to savor the honorable privilege of Irrelevance. Long may that treasured banner wave!

"All Trees Are Oak Trees . . .": Introductions to Literature[1]

WRITERS WHO HANG out in academia to help pay the rent are likely to find that their job description comes to include inviting other writers to visit their campus and then hosting them through their visit, introducing them to their lecture audience, and sitting in on the informal sessions with students that typically complete the visitor's tour of duty. Such visitations are, I believe, a generally worthwhile feature of any college writing program: beneficial to the visitor, obviously, who gets paid or otherwise rewarded and may possibly gain a few additional readers; potentially enlightening for the visitor's audience (even those whose curiosity may be more sociological, anthropological, or even clinical than literary); and at least marginally beneficial for the host as well, as I shall attempt to illustrate.

Most certainly, as an undergraduate and then a grad-student apprentice myself at Johns Hopkins in the latter 1940s and early '50s, I was impressed, entertained, instructed, inspired, and chastened by spectating such *eminences grises* as W. H. Auden, e. e. cummings, John Dos Passos, and a decidedly intoxicated Dylan Thomas, who threw up in the wastebasket of our seminar room just prior to his public reading and had to be walked by our department chairman a few turns around the quadrangle to clear his head. After which—in a chemistry lecture-theater, with lab faucets flanking the podium and the old 92-element periodic table on the wall behind—he delivered himself flawlessly of perhaps the most eloquent, exhilarating, *intoxicating* poetry reading I've ever heard. Indeed, I can summon the cherub-faced Welshman's majestic voice yet, bidding us Yankee undergraduates *Do not go gentle into that good night . . . / Rage, rage against the dying of the light. . . .*

Farther down the academic road—on the faculties of Penn State, the State University of New York at Buffalo, Boston University, and then back at Hopkins—it devolved upon *me* to be the frequent host and introducer of visiting literary luminaries: more often than not an agreeable and even instructive chore for the glimpse it afforded of how very different from one another's and from one's own are the lives of fellow scribblers whom one respects; likewise for the obligation, in composing their introductions, to articulate in distilled form what one finds distinctive about their writing; and, not least, for their incidental remarks and advice to aspiring writers in the campus workshops.

I like to warn such aspirants that down their own roads, some of *them* will be saddled with this not-unpleasant responsibility. I trust they'll learn from it, as I did, to be wary of all generalizations about how fiction and poetry ought to be written or its author's life lived, since what's good advice for one writer may be counterproductive if not downright disastrous for another (*there's* a generalization they can trust). I hope further, I tell them, that those fortunate enough to one day find themselves *being introduced* instead of doing the introduction will likewise heed that advice about Advice: What worked for Emily Dickinson would not likely have served Lord Byron; Proust,

Kafka, Henry James, and Hemingway would in all probability not have flourished in one another's *milieux*.

It has been my happy case to be both introducer and introducee— so often the former that I once considered, half-seriously if only briefly, perpetrating a book to be called *Introductions to Contemporary Literature*, comprising my "takes" on (to name an alphabetized few) Edward Albee, Paul Auster, the brothers Barthelme (Donald, Frederick, and Steven), Ann Beattie, Jorge Luis Borges, Richard Brautigan, Italo Calvino, Raymond Carver, Robert Coover, José Donoso, Umberto Eco, Stanley Elkin, Ralph Ellison, Louise Erdrich, William Gass, John Gardner, John Hawkes, Joseph Heller, Larry McMurtry, James Michener, Joyce Carol Oates, Grace Paley, Richard Powers, Mary Robison, Anne Sexton, I. B. Singer, Robert Stone, William Styron, Anne Tyler, John Updike, Mario Vargas Llosa, and Kurt Vonnegut. In the second capacity—doing reading gigs myself as well as sitting in on fiction-writing workshops all over the republic—I often find myself quoting one or another of those introducees on some particular aspect of writing, usually though not invariably because they made their point so memorably; sometimes because, while memorable, their aphorisms seem to me to need a bit of qualifying, or at least glossing; and other times because I respectfully but firmly disagree and wouldn't want their recommendations or pronouncements taken as gospel.

WORKING BACKWARDS THROUGH those three categories: I remember Kurt Vonnegut's smiling, shrug-shouldered, but not unserious admission that "like all writers," he writes his fiction "in the secret utopian hope of changing the world," and my wanting to differ, politely: "Not *all* of us, Kurt; some of us just want to get a story told." I quite allow, however, that if like Vonnegut I had been a prisoner of the Nazi *Wehrmacht* in World War II and by the merest fluke had survived the Allied bombing of Dresden during my captivity, I might well approach the fictive page with the same "secret hope" as his.

In a similar humor, Donald Barthelme acknowledged to the room his private ambition to write "a book that will change literature forever." No objection there, especially as Barthelme was neither generalizing nor prescribing, only confessing—but I'd want it pointed out that ambitions of that sort belong to the general aesthetic of Romanticism, which, while not to be sniffed at, is by no means the only viable aesthetic: Virgil, for example, probably didn't intend his *Aeneid* to change either literature or the world, only to demonstrate that he and Rome and the Latin language could hold their own with Homer, Hellas, and classical Greek—no small ambition itself.

And then there was Grace Paley's spirited credo[2]—when one of my coachees asked her, back in Vietnam War days, how she managed to get any writing done amid her tireless anti-war protesting and occasional consequent jail-time serving—that "Art isn't important. *People* are important; *politics* is important." To which one wanted to demur, "Well, yes, of course, Grace, but . . ." But one held one's tongue, out of respect for such principled, selfless courage as hers. As one did likewise when Raymond Carver summed up his literary aesthetic for our Hopkins fiction-writing students in two words: "No tricks." One knew what that excellent realist-minimalist meant: no O. Henryish trick endings or suchlike jokers in the dramaturgical deck; no stunts; nothing fancy/flashy. Much as I admire Carver's plainspoken down-to-earthiness, however, I admire at least equally François Rabelais' unbuttoned verbal and imaginative excesses, and that brilliant trickster Laurence Sterne's *Tristram Shandy*;

what counts, I told those students later, is the quality and relevance of a writer's "tricks," not their presence or absence as such. For that matter, to the extent that "no tricks" may be taken to mean "no artifice," mightn't it be objected that Carver's finely-honed narrative simplicity, like Hemingway's, is as much artifice as Faulkner at his most incantatory or Henry James at his most syntactically baroque? Apprentices especially (I wanted to protest but did not, just then) should be encouraged to acquaint themselves open-mindedly with the literary corpus's whole bag of tricks while working out for themselves their own next-stage aesthetic.

And how hold one's tongue when a bellicose John Gardner, fresh from his kneecapping treatise *On Moral Fiction*, repeated in my seminar his distinction between what he called Primary Fiction ("fiction about life") and Secondary Fiction ("fiction about fiction"), and made it clear that for him this was not mere taxonomy, but a value-judgment? "King Priam weeping over the bloody corpse of Hector!" Gardner thundered, pounding the seminar table: "*That's* literature, damn it! The rest is bullshit!" Really, John? I wondered: What about the same bard's famous extended description, in Book 18 of the same opus, of the elaborate scenes forged by Hephaestos on Achilles's shield—scenes that bear poignantly upon the epic in progress and are a literally classic specimen of art about art? Or the fine reorchestration of that riff in Book 1 of Virgil's *Aeneid*, where refugee Aeneas sees in the unfinished frescoes of Queen Dido's Carthage-under-construction not only scenes from the Trojan War and its similarly unfinished aftermath, but the figures of his fallen comrades and even his protagonistic self? Art about art, for sure; fiction about fiction, including the Homeric fiction with which Virgil's epic-under-construction is very self-consciously in the ring—but it's also so affectingly "about life" that Aeneas (his own epic labor likewise far from finished) weeps at the spectacle, and his author is moved to the famous line *Sunt lacrimae rerum*: "there are tears in things"—even in so-called Secondary Fiction. Insofar as all the world's a stage and even our selves themselves may be said to be essentially the stories we tell ourselves and others about who we are—our Center of Narrative Gravity, as the "neurophilosopher" Daniel C. Dennett puts it—great literature (I wanted to say to the now-late Gardner then and there, but, being his host, did not until a later occasion) can be regarded as being Seldom Simply but Always Also about itself. In that sense, at least, *all* fiction is secondary fiction, and all "fiction about fiction," even the most programmatically and/or tiresomely "metafictive," is also fiction about life.

Got that, John? (Not every neuroscientist, I should add, agrees with Professor Dennett that human consciousness has evolved to be essentially a scenario-making machine; but we storytellers are likely to nod Yes to that proposition—always allowing for the venerable device of the Unreliable Narrator.)

I conclude this first category of my fellow scribblers' wisdom-pearls with the grand declaration made by Richard Brautigan at the close of his "reading" at SUNY/ Buffalo toward the end of the high 1960s. The author of *Trout Fishing in America*, *The Revenge of the Lawn*, and *In Watermelon Sugar* was at the peak of his literary fame then, a hippie icon warmly received on a campus that prided itself, in those years of anti-war sit-ins and tear-gassing riot police, on being "the Berkeley of the East," and various doomsayers were declaring the print medium moribund in the "electronic global village." In that spirit, after my introduction, Brautigan said hello to the packed hall, pushed the Play button on an old reel-to-reel tape recorder beside the lectern, and disappeared into the auditorium's projection booth, from where—as we-all sat for a *very* long three-quarters of an hour listening to our guest's recorded reading—the invisible author projected slides of giant punctuation-marks: five or ten minutes each of a comma, a semicolon, a period, entirely without bearing on the taped recitation. Had it been anybody but Brautigan, that audience would never have sat still for it—but still we sat, until when the eye-glazing hour was done at last, the shaggy, beaming author reappeared from the projection booth, gestured grandly toward the tape machine, and declared, "There you have it, folks: the Twentieth Century!" Whereat one of my seriously avant-garde graduate students sitting nearby turned to me and muttered "Yup: about 1913."

ON TO MY second category: visiting writers' *obiter dicta* to which I readily nod assent and find myself often quoting, but not without some amplification or qualification. I like Dylan Thomas's (sober, but playful) assertion, for example, that "all trees are oak trees—except pine trees": It serves to remind early-apprentice writers especially that to say *Patsy paused under a tree* or *Just then Fred's car zipped by* is almost always less effective than specifying what sort of tree and automobile were involved—specificity being one component of sensory texture, and sensory texture being usually a literary plus (but not invariably, I remind them: Don't forget Beckett). Whence one goes on to suggest—they having in revision paused Patsy under a Norway maple and zipped Fred into a milk-white Camaro—that it were well if those specifications turned out to be not only specific, but *relevant*. Why a Norway maple instead of a weeping birch? Why a "milk-white Camaro" (Mary Robison) instead of a "gamboge Cadillac" (Frederick Barthelme) or a "high, rat-colored car" (Flannery O'Connor, the mother of automotive specificity in American literature)?

Into this same middle category go the contradictory recommendations of Joseph Heller and E. L. Doctorow regarding dramaturgical advance planning. Heller declared to our seminar that he always wrote his novels' closing chapters first: How would he know how to get there, he asked rhetorically, if he didn't know where he was going? Mind you, he went on, these first-draft last chapters were proposals, not binding contracts; by the time he re-reached them, small or large changes might well be in order. But he could no more begin a novel without knowing how he meant to end it than he could launch into a joke without knowing its punch line. Doctorow, on the contrary (not in my seminar, but in one of his at Sarah Lawrence College decades ago, whence one of his students later came to us and retold the tale when I retold Heller's) is alleged to have said that a novelist "needn't see beyond [his] headlights"—which I take to mean that knowing the direction of the next plot-turn is navigational data enough; that bridges farther down the road may be crossed when one arrives at them. All very well, perhaps, I warned my seminarians, for a veteran professional like Doctorow with doubtless well-established work habits and seasoned intuitions, but dangerous advice indeed for apprentice novelists, a fair number of whom I've seen write themselves into all but inextricable cul-de-sacs. Something between Doctorow's improvisatory insouciance and Heller's to-me-unimaginably-detailed advance planning is probably soundest for most of us yarn-spinners: The aforecriticized John Gardner—by all reports a first-rate coach despite his wrongheadedness, by my lights, in certain areas—wisely observes (in his treatise *On Becoming a Novelist*) that most novels culminate in some sort of all-hands-on-deck Big Scene, and that it were well for the author to have at least *some* advance notion of that scene's lineaments. Something may be said for putting off the crossing of bridges until one reaches them, but it helps to know ahead of time that there's a bridge or two to be crossed, and whether it looks to be a footbridge or the Golden Gate.

I'VE SAVED FOR last that first category of authorial *obiter dicta:* observations about writing made by visiting authors that I find myself quoting without need of comment. With a sigh I recall a reluctant, taciturn, and very weary-looking John Dos Passos in Hopkins's Gilman Hall back in the early 1950s (he lived nearby then, a widower saddened further by the indignation of many liberals at what they saw as his turncoat right-wingery during the McCarthy era) warning us starry-eyed aspirants that writing was "a bad job." More cheering was Norman Mailer's reply when I reported to him, two decades later, Dos Passos's gloomy remark: "Granted, the pay's not so hot—but you can't beat the hours." Mailer, by the way, when he visited us at Buffalo just after publishing *Why Are We in Vietnam?*, preferred not to be introduced at all: At his request, we sparred or shadow-boxed or something for a few seconds in the lobby of the auditorium—my first and only experience of that alarming exercise— and then he sprang to the podium and introduced himself.

I like to repeat too Larry McMurtry's declaration (back at Hopkins again) that the reason he got along well during his Hollywood script-writing period was that he didn't give a damn whether his screenplays were finally produced or not, as long as he got paid; the main purpose of screenplays anyhow, he declared, is to give the producer some idea of how many locations are involved, for budget-and-logistical purposes. Stanley Elkin, too, after a stint in LaLa-Land, waxed eloquent on the inferior status of *words* in film as opposed to prose fiction: We writer-types, he said, are in the habit of thinking that stories are told with lines like Proust's "For a long time I went to bed early," or Joyce's "Stately, plump Buck Mulligan. . . ." Movies, on the other hand, said Elkin, tell stories *this* way—and he launched into hilarious extended wordless sound-effects: car screeching to a halt, doors slamming, footsteps approaching, other obscure but portentous noises. . . . Not easy for a wordsmith to adjust to.

Then there's William H. Gass's memorable response to a student who asked him whether a writer's first concern ought to be the reader's pleasure or the author's. Neither, Gass replied: To put the reader's pleasure first is pandering; to put the author's pleasure first is self-indulgence. A writer's first concern, he declared, ought to be for the verbal artifact that's trying, with the writer's collaboration, to get itself said. The author as midwife: I like that.

Ditto the so-prolific John Updike's response to my student who asked him . . . I don't recall exactly what; perhaps whether he had ever abandoned a project-in-the-works, for Updike's reply was to the effect that now and then he would set aside a fiction-in-progress because he didn't recognize its author as (quoting Updike) "nimble old me." *Nimble*, yes: That's him, for sure, a self-assessment as modest as it is exact. Likewise James Michener's response to the student who asked him what he regarded as his major strength and his most serious weakness as a novelist. The former, Michener replied unhesitatingly, was *information*: Whether writing about Iberia, Texas, Poland, or Outer Space, he prided himself on doing his homework. And his major weakness? "Human psychology," confessed our visitor with a smile and a shrug: "Don't know the first thing about it."

And that sort of authorial self-recognition informs—most touch-ingly, by my lights—the final item in this little anthology of *en pas-sants*. In the only conversation I ever had with Robert Frost, who visited us at Penn State on a wintry spring day some 40 years ago, the old poet invited us to ask him anything we cared to: He was too deaf to hear our questions anyhow, he said, but he would answer *some-thing*. I don't recall what my question was, but I remember clearly Frost's reply: that every spring for as long as *he* could remember, he would notice that the oak trees up his way still had a few forlorn brown leaves hanging on from the previous autumn. The sight of those weatherbeaten remnants, he declared, never failed to suggest to him the tatters of a blown-out sail on a ship limping into harbor after storms, and his professional intuition never failed to tell him that there was in that simile not merely a poem, but a *Robert Frost* poem—a Robert Frost poem that, alas, the poet of that name had yet to figure out. Nor did he ever, to my knowledge, although there is passing mention of oak leaves in several of his verses.

As might be expected, one supposes—given that *all* trees are oak trees (except pine trees).

The Inkstained Thumb

From *Rules of Thumb* (subtitled *73 Authors Reveal Their Fiction-Writing Fixations*), compiled by Michael Martone and Susan Neville.[1]

T HUMB-RULE #1 FOR aspiring writers, it goes without saying, is Be Wary of Writers' Rules of Thumb. Anton Chekhov liked the smell of rotting apples in his writing desk. Edna Ferber advised nothing more interesting on that desk's far side than a blank wall. Ernest Hemingway and Scheherazade, for different reasons, inclined to close their day's (or night's) output in mid-story, even in mid-sentence. I myself advise no more than that you merely perpend such advisements and predilections, including mine to follow, en route to discovering by hunch, feel, trial, and error what best floats your particular boat. Too many rules of thumb can make a chap all thumbs.

That said, I report that for this writer at least, *regularity* is as helpful with the Muse as with the bowels: a comparison to be taken just so far and no farther. Go to your worktable at the same time daily, establish your Personal Prep Routine, and you're likely to find that just as making breakfast (to change analogies) may sharpen your appetite, so some established little ritual of muse-invocation may get your creative juices flowing. I myself—after the breakfast afore-alluded-to with wife and newspaper, followed by that *toilette* likewise alluded to and a ten-minute routine of stretching exercises picked up half a century ago from an RCAF training manual—refill my thermal coffee mug and disappear into my Scriptorium no later than half past eight every weekday morning. It has separate workspaces for Creation, Production, and Business; ignoring the third of those (appointments calendar, file drawers, check registers and accounting ledgers, telephone, clock, and calculator, all relegated to Later), I pause at the second just long enough to boot up and then promptly anesthetize my more-or-less-trusty Macintosh, which will remain in Standby mode unless this morning's work is to be the revision and editing of an already first-drafted text—for me, the most enjoyable stage of writing, because it *feels* agreeably creative, but is so much easier than invention and composition. Turning then to the *sanctum sanctorum*, the worktable consecrated to Composition, I do the following routine preps, the musely equivalent of those earlier RCAF exercises:

1) Insert a set of Mack's earplugs from supply in worktable drawer: a habit carried over from that same half-century ago, when my now middle-aged children were high-energy tots and their father was an overworked, underpaid young college instructor obliged to snatch the odd hour of writing-time at a little desk in the bedroom. By the time the nest was empty and my work-area a more commodious and quiet Personal Space, the earplug habit was as fixed as Chekhov's requisite rotting apples. My muse sings only through ambient silence—her song not always clearly distinguishable, I confess, from the tinnitus familiar to many of us oldsters.

2) Ears plugged, slide selfward the worn, stained, and battered three-ring looseleaf binder procured during Freshman Orientation

Week at Johns Hopkins in 1947, in which has been first-drafted every page of my fiction since those green undergraduate days. It's as
weathered now as its owner, who however counts on its continuing
to hang together for at least as long as he does.

3) Open that "serviceable old thing" (as W. H. Auden fondly addressed his aging body) either to the Page in Progress or to the blank
Next Thing, and take from its nestling-place among the gently rusting
triple rings the somewhat less venerable but by me equally vener-
ated Parker pen bought 40-plus years ago in "Mr. Pumblechook's
Premises" in Rochester, England, in honor of the great Boz. Uncap
and fill that instrument with its daily draught of Permanent Jet Black
Quink, and then. . . .

Well, that depends. Like Hemingway & Co. aforementioned, I try
to end each morn's first-drafting while the going's good, with maybe
a brief penciled or ballpointed note of what's to follow (the Parker is
reserved strictly for Composition, not for notes, correspondence, and
suchlike mundanities). If today's session involves work in progress,
then reviewing and editing the print-out of yesterday's installment
usually suffices to reorient the imagination and pump the creative
adrenaline enough for me to resume first-draft penmanship—which a
couple of hours later I'll break off in mid-whatever, date in parenthe-
ses (with ballpoint pickup-note appended), and type into the waiting
word processor for ease of subsequent revision, already editing the
draft as I transcribe it. If, on the other hand, what awaited me back
there at 8:30 was the between-projects three-hole ruled blank page,
it's a whole 'nother story, so to speak: one in which I'm likely to have
recapped and renestled that refilled Parker, taken up Papermate and
clipboard instead, and scratched hopeful preliminary notes toward . . .
who knows what? Maybe a mini-essay on writerly Rules of Thumb?

Most prose-writers nowadays in every genre—perhaps most *poets*, even—dispense altogether with the venerable, to them perhaps
obsolete medium of longhand and compose directly on the PC. For
all I know, maybe even their preliminary note-making is done on
laptop or Palm Pilot. If so, so be it: As aforedeclared, whatever floats
the old boat. For Yours Truly, however, the equation of narrative
"flow" with the literal flow of ink onto paper, of the fountain pen
with the Fount of Inspiration, holds as firmly as my right hand holds
that maroon-and-brushed-silver Parker 51: a rule of (sometimes inkstained) thumb.

Future Imperfect

In the spring of 2008, for what it described as an upcoming Political Issue, the journal *Tin City* invited responses from a number of people to the following questions: 1) What is your greatest fear for the future? And 2) What is your greatest hope for the future? After due consideration, I replied (tongue at least partly in cheek) as follows:

1) My chiefest *fear* for the future is that, like past futures, it will become the present.

2) My main *hope* for the future is that when presently it becomes the present, and anon the past, the worst its relieved survivors in some future present will be able to say of it will be that although they had feared the worst, as now-past futures go it could have been worse.

I.

From *The Art of the Word*,[1] an anthology of essays by various scholars, critics, translators, novelists, poets, memoirists, essayists, editors, and others about some word that they find particularly fascinating, intriguing, poignant, irksome, whatever. . . .

S LIMMEST OF ENGLISH-LANGUAGE pronouns and yet most self-assertive, even self-important, the nominative-case first-person-singular *I* (identical in most type-fonts to the Roman numeral, as if to declare "I am Number One!") is always upper-case, unlike the more self-effacing Spanish *yo*, Italian *io*, French *je*, and German *ich*, for example, capitalized only when beginning a sentence, or even the English *me, my,* and *mine*—suggesting that in our tongue the self that is acted upon, or that merely possesses things, is less self-possessed than the self that takes action or possession.

The skinny thing's antecedent, its user's self, is at once obvious—*self-evident*, let's say—and teasingly elusive. "Myself": whose self is that? Who or what is the "self" that's conscious of self-consciousness, even of *being* conscious of self-consciousness, et cetera ad infinitum? The "I" who asks that not-unreasonable question—who tries to peer behind that so-slender vertical letter—finds him-/herself caught in the classic philosophical quandary of the Retreating Subject, the infinite regress of facing mirrors. *Gnothi seauton*, "Know thyself," advises the Delphic oracle: an incompletable project, sometimes vertiginous, in extreme cases even paralyzing, and commonly productive of unpleasant news. Professional storytellers like . . . *myself* . . . may incline to the "neurophilosopher" Daniel C. Dennett's definition of the Self as one's "center of narrative gravity"[2] (always allowing for the famous fictive device of the Unreliable Narrator). Not a bad idea, in "my" opinion, to sneak a peek from time to time in those funhouse mirrors. Having done so, however, better to turn away and ask, not "Who am I?", but "Who are *you*? Who are *we*, and *they*? What is *this*, and *that*, and *that*?"—and get on with the story.

"In the Beginning, Once Upon a Time, It Was a Dark and Stormy Night . . ."

Although it was first published before the three preceding essays, I'm placing this meditation on story-openers here so that its "dark and stormy night" will be followed by "The Morning After."

"HAPPY FAMILIES ARE all alike, but each unhappy family is unhappy in its own way." I don't particularly agree with that famous kick-off proposition of Tolstoy's *Anna Karenina*, but I'll carry it to my grave, along with a clutch of other jim-dandy story-openers.

A first sentence's job is to draw its reader into the sentences that follow it—while at the same time, in the case of fiction, maybe establishing the tale's tone and narrative viewpoint, introducing one or more of its characters, and supplying preliminary hints of setting, situation, and impending action. Some do their job so well that they remain in our memory long after we've forgotten most of the words that came after, even in a novel that may have changed our lives, or at least deeply engaged our minds and spirits in the way great literature can. *A Tale of Two Cities*, in this reader's opinion, is neither the best nor the worst of Dickens's novels, but it's the only one whose opening—"It was the best of times, it was the worst of times . . ."—has stayed with me. Likewise the so-casual "Call me Ishmael" that opens Melville's *Moby-Dick* (the first time I met the novelist Ishmael Reed, he smiled and said, "Call me Mister Reed"), and García Márquez's time-straddling fanfare to *One Hundred Years of Solitude*—"Many years later, when he faced the firing squad, Colonel Aureliano Buendía would remember that distant afternoon when his father took him to discover ice"—and a dozen more, from the bibliophilic beagle Snoopy's "It was a dark and stormy night" in Charles Schulz's *Peanuts* comic strip (a cliché opening by the 19th-century novelist Edward Bulwer-Lytton, which the poor mutt never gets beyond) to the slyly soporific first words of Marcel Proust's multivolume *Remembrance of Things Past*: "For a long time I used to go to bed early."

   "*Longtemps je me suis couché de bonne heure,*" that last one reads in the original, and the poet/translator Richard Howard thought it sufficiently important to preserve that opening's word-order, even at some slight cost to its sense, that he amended Scott-Moncrieff's earlier translation to read "*Time was* when I went to bed early," so that Volume One of Proust's epic about Time begins (as it will end) with that key word—and then, seven volumes later, outflanks its subject by having "Marcel," at the saga's close, set about to write the time-intensive tale that we've finally finished reading: a story about a storyteller's preparing himself to tell the story that we've just been exhaustively told.

   If that sounds too clever by half—too vertiginously "metafictive" or proto-Postmodern—it has some distinguished and comparably dizzying antecedents, none more offhandedly cunning than the opening of "Scheherazade's" *Kitab Alf Laylah Wah Laylah*, or *The Book of a Thousand Nights and a Night.* English translations from the anonymous compiler's 13th-century Persian vary considerably, but my two favorites—Sir Richard Burton's freewheeling and footnote-rich 1888 version, and Mardrus and Mathers's more rigorous one a half-century later—both begin by declaring (in effect, and *much* less directly), "Praise be to Allah, who has passed on to us the tales called *The Thousand Nights and a Night*, among which is . . . [the story of Scheherazade's telling her nightly postcoital tales to wean the cuckolded King from his serial-murderous revenge]." A double-take opener indeed: The book in our hands, whose introduction we've embarked upon, is not Scheherazade's book, but a book *about* Scheherazade's book, which will wind up multivolumes later (17 in Burton's edition, a modest four in M&M's) with the welcome news that King Shahryar relents, lifts his nearly three-year-old entertain-me-or-die ultimatum, marries Scheherazade (who has by that time delivered him three male heirs as well as a kilonightsworth of stories), and commands her to *tell them all over again* to the royal scribes—thus accounting not directly for the book we're finally at the close of, but for the book that that book is about: "And this is all that has come down to us concerning the origins of this book."[1]

Allah willing, Amen!

Which terminal imperative may remind us that this kind of ingenious once-upon-a-timery has been a storyteller's ploy from the beginning, so to speak. Whether or not the God of the Bible ever winked at the devoted audience of His own creation, His chronicler in the Book of Genesis sure did: What subtle, pre-proto-Postmodern *chutzpah*, to kick off the story of the world's beginning with the Hebrew word *Bereshith*, "In the beginning . . ."—anticipating Proust's merely Modernist "Time was" by nearly three millennia![2]

But then, the bards of the classical Greek oral tradition, arguably coeval with Genesis if not with the world's big-bang commencement, traditionally cleared their epic throats by saying, in effect, "Sing, O Muse, the tale that I'm here and now about to repeat: the one about [et cetera]." Which is *not* necessarily to say, "And while you're at it, begin at the beginning, okay?" Better to hit the ground running *in medias res*: advice worth perpending still in Tale-Telling 101.[3]

A dozen-plus centuries later, at about the same time that the great Persian Anonymous was setting down the story of the story of Scheherezade's stories, his or her fellow pre-Postmodernist Dante Alighieri, in exile from Florence, ratcheted up his countryman Horace's advice by beginning *his* divinely comic epic not only in the middle of its narrator's story instead of "In the beginning," but with the very words *Nel mezzo*. "In the middle of our life's road, I found myself lost in a Dark Wood": a quietly bravura overture to a work whose form throughout will figure its three-in-one, unity-of-the-Trinity content, from the traditional division of the Hereafter into Hell, Purgatory, and Heaven, through the allotment of (on average) 33 1/3 cantos to each of those departments, to the interlocking three-line stanzas' *terza rima* versification. Three cheers, *maestro!*

Tough acts to follow. But a mere six centuries later, James Joyce completes the movement from Genesis's "In the beginning" through Dante's "In the middle" by beginning his dream-epic *Finnegans Wake* not with "The end" but with "riverrun, past Eve and Adam's, from swerve of shore to bend of bay, brings us by a commodius vicus of re-circulation back to Howth Castle and Environs"—which odd, lower-case opener (so we learn 627 dream-dark pages later, unless we'd heard the news already) is the completion of that cyclical opus's un-finished closing sentence. In short, the author begins his story literally in the middle of its ending: a triple play at which Dante might have nodded approval, unless he'd nodded off. As a graduate student in the 1950s, I proposed in a Joyce seminar that the appropriate print-vehicle for *Finnegans Wake* would be not a conventionally bound book, but either a *very* long roller-towel or unnumbered pages fanning out from a central spindle, so that Beginning and Ending would literally conjoin.

Time was (excuse the expression) when some late-arriving epigones of the great Modernists did indeed chafe at what they felt to be the passé bonds of conventional print technology and experimented with alternatives, not necessarily to the print-medium itself, but to its customary modes of presentation: One thinks of Marc Saporta's 1962 novel-in-a-box *Composition 1*, its unnumbered and unbound pages packaged in any random "order" and thus *sans* any fixed opening sentence at all, or any other authorially-determined beginning, middle, or ending; likewise Daniel Spoerri's unpaginated *Anecdoted Typography of Chance*, from 1966. That rebellious, "countercultural" decade was particularly rich (if that's the right adjective) in this sort of post-Dadaist, pre-computer-era experimentation: Apprentice writing-workshoppers back then came up with such alternatives to conventional tale-telling as, e.g., a short story called "Serial," its several sentences typed on separate paper strips like extended fortune-cookie fortunes, shaken up in an appropriately refigured "cereal" box and dumped into a bowl, to be fished out and read in random order, any one of them potentially the story's opening sentence. After two or three such "serial" readings, one pieced together the tale's simple plot; its suspense then became not "What happened?" but "In what order will its component actions be recounted this time around?" And it worked, sort of, to hear a line like "Three months later they found what remained of Lizzie in the marsh" now as the story's open-ing, now as its ending, now as one mid-course complication—a bit like reassembling a familiar jigsaw puzzle or reconstructing a fos-sil skeleton from its scattered bones. One remembers too Spencer Holst's "Pleasures of the Imagination: 64 Beginnings," comprising just that: 64 more or less arresting openers like "The obese puppeteer washed the dishes in the dark," with no stories attached.

The advent of word processors, "hypertext," online interactive fiction, and even an Electronic Literature Organization may make such Marshall McLuhan-era innovations seem as quaint as tail-finned autos. But it may also remind us (if we need reminding) that the ma-ture and stable technology of the printed book, like the narrative/dramatical conventions of Beginning, Middle, and Ending—older than print, older even than writing—can be jiggered and redeployed to memorable effect as long as *homo sapiens* still savors the emi-nently human pleasure of hearing and recounting tales. As Donald Barthelme liked to say (and as I'm fond of repeating), the important question about a story isn't whether it's realistic or irrealistic, tra-ditionalist or "experimental," pre- or post-Modern: The important question is "Does it knock your socks off?"

To which one might add that a real socks-knocker of a story may have a deliberately low-keyed opening ("Call me Ishmael"), just as a first-rate movie may start with nothing more "dramatic" than a man shaving or a woman pouring the breakfast coffee. Contrariwise, a lapel-grabbing opening shot or sentence—car chase, pistol fired as if at viewer, string of Boldface all-caps obscenities!—may open an eminently forgettable yarn. The wannabe novelist Joseph Grand in Albert Camus' *The Plague* tinkers endlessly with his manuscript's first sentence (*"One fine morning in the month of May, an elegant young woman might have been seen riding a handsome sorrel mare along the flowery avenues of the Bois de Boulogne,*" among numerous other versions) in a vain effort to get it so exactly *right* that any editor must cry "Hats off!"—while Camus's *chef d'oeuvre* itself opens with the simple declaration that "The unusual events described in this chronicle occurred in 194_ at Oran."

    Do I have your attention, Reader? On with the story, then. . . .

The Morning After

In 2009, at the invitation of Penguin Books, I revisited my longtime narrative navigation star Scheherazade by writing the following introduction to their new Signet Classics edition of *The Arabian Nights, Volume II*, published in 2010.

D AVID BEAUMONT'S MASTERFUL Introduction to Volume I of the two-volume Signet Classics edition of *The Arabian Nights* opens in true Scheherazadean style: "The story of the book called *The Arabian Nights*, it has been said, is a story worthy of being in *The Arabian Nights*."

To that introduction-to-an-introduction, your present introducer of Volume II—no scholarly authority like Professors Beaumont and Jack Zipes (whose Afterwords to both volumes are likewise excellent), but a longtime yarn-spinning fan of Ms. Scheherazade—cannot resist adding that "the story of the book called *The Arabian Nights*" in fact *is* in *The Arabian Nights*, or anyhow just outside it. It's the frame that frames the frame, so to speak.

I mean this literally. The stories, stories-within-stories, and stories-within-stories-within-stories that comprise the *Kitab Alf Laylah Wa Laylah*, or, as it's variously called, "The Book of a Thousand Nights and a Night" or "The Arabian Nights Entertainment," are from all over the Indian/Persian/Arabic map. Over the centuries, like old-time merchant-traders traveling the Silk Road and adding to their stash of goods along the way, the book's innumerable compilers picked up yarns from here and there and stitched them into their narrative quilt. And they're famously framed by the best story of them all: the story of their teller, the courageous, canny, beautiful, and learned young daughter of the king's Grand Vizier—a monarch so murderously deranged by his wife's infidelities that after executing her he "marries" a virgin every night and has her killed in the morning before she too can cuckold him. For the story of that story, see Beaumont's preface to Volume I—and then read the opening story in that volume, "The Story of King Shahryar and His Brother," which explains why and under what circumstances Scheherazade will spin out, by my count, no fewer than 169 "primary" tales, at least 19 of which contain tales-within-the-tale: 87 "secondary tales" in all, at least four of which contain tertiary tales-within-the-tale-within-the-tale, for a total of some 267 complete stories, plus about ten thousand lines of verse in Sir Richard Burton's original unexpurgated ten-volume translation of the *Nights* (1885–1886), of which the present version is an artful two-volume abridgment. And that's before we even get to the seven volumes of Burton's later *Supplemental Nights*.

But this apparently outermost frame—the tale of King Shahryar of "the lands of India and China," his similarly-cuckolded and similarly-vengeful brother King Shah Zaman of Samarkand, and Scheherazade and her younger sister Dunyazade, which begins more than a thousand nights before Night 1 and winds up well after Night 1001—is itself framed, sort of, by an intriguing formulation (intriguing to some of us later storytellers, anyhow): In all versions, after the ritual invocation to Almighty Allah, the anonymous narrator-scribe declares in effect, not that "There once was a jealous king named Shahryar," et cetera, but that "There is a book called *The Book of a Thousand Nights and a Night*, in which one will find the story of King Shahryar and his brother Shah Zaman [and Scheherazade and Dunyazade], which goes like this. . . ." A thousand-plus nights later, after that so-productive young talester—talestress?—has delivered herself not only of those several hundred stories, but also of three male children ("one walking, one crawling, one suckling") sired by her entertain-me-or-die consort, and has delivered the king as well from his pathologically murderous, kingdom-wrecking jealousy, she successfully pleads for her life, officially weds the father of her children and inspirer of her stories in a regally elaborate joint ceremony with her now older and less innocent kid sister and Shahryar's up-till-then equally murderous kid brother, and the foursome are declared to have lived happily thenceforth—not "ever after," as in Western fables, but more realistically "until the Destroyer of Delights and Severer of Societies and Desolater of Dwelling-places came upon them": the standard wrap-up of Scheherazade's own stories. Whereupon the successor to Shahryar's throne (One of those three sons? We're not told) discovers in the late and no doubt unlamented king's treasury the tales that not only entertained him but saved his kingdom and their teller's life, and which grateful Shahryar had therefore obliged his scribes to record after the fact in thirty volumes for posterity (another story: imagine weary Scheherazade having to *recollect and re-tell* all those tales to the royal clerks!); and said successor is so delighted with them that he has *his* scribes re-copy the whole shebang and "spread them throughout the world."

Then comes the almost off-handed punch line: "As a consequence," concludes this story-of-the-story-of-the-stories, "the tales became famous, and the people called them *The Marvels and Wonders of the Thousand and One Nights*. This is all that we know about the origins of this book, and Allah is omniscient . . . FINIS. "

GET IT? THE book that we've just finished reading is not *The Thousand and One Nights*, exactly, but a book *about* a book called *The Thousand and One Nights*. FINIS indeed—and wow! But so lightly and engagingly does this outermost Scheherazade, so to speak, lead us into and out of the narrative labyrinth of tales within tales within tales, we're scarcely aware of all this structural complexity. Nor need we be, any more than venturers through an amusement-park funhouse need appreciate the intricate mechanics of its serial gee-whizzes: quite okay just to go along for the ride, at least the first time through. Closer examination has its rewards, however, and may well lead one not only through this expertly edited two-volume Signet Classics version, but on to the ten- or twelve- or thirty-volume feast of which it is a rich sampling. Ms. Scheherazade is, among other things, a storyteller's storyteller *par excellence*, whom writers as otherwise dissimilar as Johann Wolfgang von Goethe, Marcel Proust, Jorge Luis Borges, and Yours Truly have found irresistible. Goethe was impressed by the stories' mix of fantasy and realism, humor and terror, delicacy and ribaldry, even downright scatology: his journals note that the author of *The Sorrows of Young Werther* was particularly taken with Night 410, the Tale of How Abu Hasan Farted. And as David Beaumont notes in his introduction to Volume I, Marcel Proust—whose seven-volume *Remembrance of Things Past* is itself a fiction of Scheherazadean proportions, though not of *Arabian Nights* flavor—frequently refers to her epical narrative in his. Likewise the late great Argentinian Jorge Luis Borges (who, being blind, was himself necessarily a story*teller* rather than a story-writer, composing his splendid *ficciones* in his head and then, like Scheherazade after her narrative menopause, dictating them from memory for inscription), and many another storyteller from all over the globe.

That's no surprise to this one, who most certainly includes himself among the Vizier's daughter's long-time ardent admirers. As a child in the time before television, video games, and the Internet, I was charmed by a much-abridged and radically expurgated one-volume kiddie edition of the *Nights*, discreetly but handsomely illustrated by N. C. Wyeth. No gas-passing villagers in it, as in the tale that so amused Goethe (the unfortunate Abu Hasan, mortified by his accidental flatulence during a prayer-service, exiles himself for years; returning finally to his village in hopes that his embarrassing *faux pas* has long since been forgotten, he happens to overhear a lad ask his mother how old he is, to which she replies that he's ten years old, he having been born "on the very night that Abu Hasan farted"); no lascivious sultanas cuckolding their royal spouses with ape-like "slobbering blackamoors" who swing down from the trees to service them and their handmaidens while hubby is out of town; no sad but dutiful Grand Vizier showing up at the king's court every morning, shroud over his arm, expecting royal orders to lead his daughter off to execution as he has led her thousand deflowered predecessors—but there were Aladdin and his magical lantern, Ali Baba and the forty thieves, Sinbad the Seaman and Sinbad the Landman; there were the mighty wish-granting genies/jinnees/djinns in bottles and other innocent-looking containers (even as a kid, I wondered why it never occurs to Aladdin and other wish-grantees to cover their bets by wishing for *more wishes*!); there were the mermaids and dragons, the Open Sesames and other charms. . . . I was hooked.

And re-hooked for keeps years later, when—as an undergraduate book-filer in the Classics stacks of my university's library, re-shelving cartful after cartful of tomes to help defray my tuition and eagerly perusing as I re-shelved, while at the same time feeling the first stirrings of writerly Vocation—in the alcoves of what was called the "Oriental Seminary" I discovered among other marvels the ten folio volumes of Somadeva's enormous *Katha Sarit Sagara*: the 11th-century Sanskrit *Ocean of the Streams of Story* spun out by the god Shiva to his consort Parvati in reward for a particularly divine session of lovemaking. It contains not just tales within tales, but such entire *cycles* of tales-within-tales as the *Panchatantra* ("Five Principles") and the *Vetalapanchavimsati* ("25 Tales Told by a Vampire"), and is assumed to be among the antecedents of the Persian *Hazar Afsaneh* ("Book of a Thousand Tales") later translated and transmuted into the Arabic *Book of a Thousand Nights and a Night*. That too was there to be re-filed, in Burton's version and others, as were (in neighboring alcoves) such frame-taled European spin-offs as Boccaccio's ten-night *Decameron*, Marguerite of Navarre's seven-night *Heptameron*, Giambattista Basile's five-night *Pentameron* (or *Tale of Tales*), and other more or less racy delights, none of which were included in my otherwise excellent world-lit undergrad survey courses. What wannabe fictionist wouldn't lay into such a narrative smorgasbord?

I did, for sure, and Scheherazade in particular became an important navigation star in my own writerly adventures over the succeeding decades. While not presuming to her narrative achievement, I've found myself returning from time to time both to the Vizier's daughter herself, who shows up in several of my novels and stories, and to her appalling but endlessly fascinating situation. How can she expect to succeed where her thousand predecessors failed? Not by erotic expertise alone, for sure, although she's probably no slouch in that department: while properly virginal, she has, we're told in the frame-story, "read the books, annals, and legends of former kings, and the stories, lessons, and adventures of famous men. Indeed, it was said that she had collected a thousand history books [note the number] about ancient peoples and rulers. She had perused the works of the poets and knew them by heart. She had studied philosophy and the sciences, arts, and practical things. And she was pleasant and polite, wise and witty, well read and well bred." One bets that her library included the classic Sanskrit sex manual *Kama Sutra*, and one notes that at her and Dunyazade's double wedding at her stories' end, the kid sister "paced forward like the rising sun, and swayed to and fro in insolent beauty," while Scheherazade herself "came forward swaying from side to side," "shook her head and swayed her haunches," and "moved so coquettishly that she ravished the minds and hearts of all present and bewitched their eyes." So she can belly-dance too! Long live the Queen!

But as I've noted elsewhere,[1] she has a few other things going for her as well. We're told specifically that as word of Shahryar's homi-cidal virgin-a-night policy spreads, so many parents flee the country with their daughters that by the time of our story there's not a maid-enhead remaining for the Vizier to produce (on pain of death if he fails to) except those of his own daughters, whom Shahryar has been sparing as a political courtesy. Deranged though he is, one suspects that the King too is aware of that circumstance, and that if he kills Scheherazade the jig is up in any case. Moreover (as Scheherazade's dad will doubtless also have told her), back when the King first learned of his brother Shah Zaman's habitual cuckolding but was as yet unaware of his own, he'd vowed that if he himself were ever thus disgraced he would kill "a thousand women in revenge," despite the fact that "that way madness lies"—and now he's done so, and thus the time is ripe to re-think his *modus operandi*.

But hey, this is a Monarch we're dealing with, and a nut-case one at that, and so the royal Face must be saved even though the situation is staring him in it. Like, maybe, give him a little more time to come to terms with the obvious? Some sort of face-and-butt-saving interlude? How about an unobtrusively pointed *story*—or better yet, a whole *string* of stories and stories-within-stories, their delivery artfully timed to break off daily at sunrise just when the plot is really revving up, the way TV drama-serials will do a thousand years later?

And so on Night One, what will become a ritual is established: Against her rueful father's wishes (whom she disarms with a couple of also-pointed stories), Scheherazade "goes in unto the King," and as he prepares to go in unto her, she pleads with him to let her sister (whom she has prepped for the role) be with her on this "last night of my life." The King consents. Dunyazade takes up her position at the foot of the royal bed, witnesses her sister's defloration and the couple's post-coital nap, and at midnight, on cue from Scheherazade, begs for a story to entertain all hands till dawn. Big Sis secures permission from the King (who, not surprisingly, "happened to be sleepless and restless") and obliges with the intricated "Tale of the Merchant and the Jinee," itself involving three tales-within-the-tale, all having to do with the tellers' lives being spared by their stories, and the last winding up exactly at *their* teller's appointed doom-time, the crack of dawn. Dunyazade praises her sister's narrative performance; Scheherazade pooh-poohs it, declaring it to be nothing compared to what she could come up with *tomorrow* night, if only. . . . The King says okay ("By Allah, I won't slay her until I hear more of her wondrous stories!"), rises to go about his kingly business of "bidding and forbidding between man and man" (but neither bids the Vizier to go execute his daughter nor explains the reprieve), then returns for a second night of sex/sleep/storytelling—and the pattern is established for 999 nights thereafter, Dunyazade maintaining her rather kinky foot-of-the-royal-bed position as Primer of the Narrative Pump, Scheherazade turning out story after story (always, as each ends, immediately beginning another and then interrupting it at dawn's early light) and—so we learn on Night 1001—turning out baby after baby as well, for whose sakes she pleads on that fateful morn for her life to be thenceforth spared.

WHY THEN, RATHER than on Night 666, say, or 777, or 1111? Why indeed *are* there 1001 nights instead of some other number? Mainly, no doubt, because just as "a thousand" is traditional short-hand for "a *lot*" (as in the *Hazar Afsaneh*'s "thousand tales" and Scheherazade's "thousand books about ancient peoples and rulers"), so 1001 is "plenty and then some," like Simon Bond's popular *101 Uses for a Dead Cat*. But think again: three sons conceived, brought to term, and delivered over the same span of time that Shahryar previously took to fulfill his threat to "kill a thousand women" in revenge for his cuckolding. The moment is doubly auspicious, especially if it happens to coincide with Scheherazade's having . . . exhausted her narrative repertory, perhaps?

Maybe, maybe not. But while numerical appropriateness is sufficient cause, and narrative exhaustion a not-impossible extra reason for Scheherazade's choosing Night 1001 to plead for the reprieve that she no doubt understands (and Shahyrar promptly acknowledges) to have been long since tacitly granted her, my imagination was piqued some decades ago to come up with yet a third possibility, an additional coincidence suggested by her sons' approximate ages: "one walking, one crawling, one suckling." For the messy details, see the aforenoted essay "Don't Count On It," which half-seriously imagines that by way of additional life insurance the Vizier's cunning daughter will have timed her volunteered devirginization to coincide as closely as possible with one of her monthly ovulations, in hopes of a prompt impregnation (with her life hanging in the balance, she would most assuredly *not* want her menses to arrive early in the game!). Assuming for gee-whiz story-purposes a successful conception on Night 1 (Why not? It's an Arabian Night) and working then from the arithmetical average number of days from human conception to birth (266), then the average time from delivery to first subsequent menstruation (49 days), and from then to earliest *next* ovulation and possible *second* conception (14 days), et cetera, one arrives at the fascinating possibility that on that fateful 1002nd morning, when Scheherazade orders the nurses to fetch in the kids and pleads for permanent absolution on their behalf, not only will her three boys have been at the right ages for "walking" (two years + four days), "crawling" (thirteen months + ten days), and "suckling" (two and a half months), but their mom—having resumed post-partum menstruation 49 days after her third delivery (Night 974)—might to her own dismay on Morning 1002 have found herself, after only a normal lunar month, for the first time re-menstruating instead of having been re-impregnated per usual by the King! It's a circumstance of which Shahryar would have to be apprised immediately, since by Muslim law he cannot "go in unto" his wife that night, as their whole past history will have led him to anticipate doing. Having just concluded the Tale of Ma-aruf the Cobbler and Fatimah the Turd (her final narrative performance in the complete 10-volume Burton edition), this most resourceful of storytellers must either launch into some new one—surpassing it and Sinbad and Ali Baba combined—or else surprise her lord and master with something no less extraordinary than, so to speak, her first-ever Second Menstruation in their 1001-night history. Like, say, trotting in their offspring and saying, in effect, "Enough of this Let-Me-Entertain-You thing already: Why not come off it, marry me, and make our kids legit?"

It's a rather far-fetched bit of biological arithmetic, I'll grant, though quite within the salty parameters of the *Nights*. For details, see essay—which it was my privilege to deliver as an open-air lecture on a warm June night in 1983 at the American School in Tangier, Morocco, under a crescent moon signaling the end of the holy month of Ramadan, while muezzins called to the faithful from the lighted minarets of nearby mosques in the city that inspired Rimsky-Korsakov's *Scheherazade Suite*: a moving experience indeed for this long-time admirer of Ms. S.

Better yet, read the book: *her* book, the one called *The Arabian Nights* or *Book of a Thousand Nights and a Night*, which this Signet Classics version (and Burton's and all the others) are books *about*.

You'll be enchanted.

It Can Be Arranged:
A Novelist Recalls His
Jazz-Drumming Youth

A mini-memoir of sorts, published here for the first time.

Q: MUSIC, ESPECIALLY jazz, has played a significant role in your life and your writing, has it not?

A: Yes and no. My years as an ardent amateur and semiprofessional jazz drummer were certainly an important part of my life from my teens into my forties. But except for passages in the novel/memoir *Once Upon a Time* (1994) and the novella *Tell Me* (2005), I've seldom written directly about that experience in either my fiction or my non-fiction. More relevant to me as a writer, I believe, was my early ambition to be, not primarily a composer or a performer of music, but an *orchestrator*—an "arranger," as it was called back in those swing-band decades.

Q: Shall we "take it from the edge," as musicians say (or used to say)? A-*one*, a-*two* . . .

A: Well: As kids in a family of modest means on Maryland's Eastern Shore during the Great Depression, my twin sister and I had the privilege (though we didn't always see it that way) of weekly piano lessons and daily practice sessions from our elementary-school years through junior high. Because of our twinship, at our teacher's annual student recitals we were usually assigned duets, my sister playing the *primo*, or upper-octave melody part, and I the lower-octave *secondo*. And the recitals would climax, as I remember, with Miss Hubbard herself at the piano and her students providing a scored percussion accompaniment of tambourines, triangles, and such—more to my taste, actually, than the keyboard, although in my later dance-band-drumming days I still did a couple of "specialty" piano solos from time to time: self-arranged versions of "Bumble Boogie" (Rimsky-Korsakov's *Flight of the Bumblebee* with an eight-to-the-bar left hand) and the like.

As soon as we were allowed, at age thirteen or so, Sister Jill and I quit our piano lessons—and once released from the drudgery of obligatory practice, we found ourselves seriously attracted to music: not the classical piano-exercise books that we'd been drilled in, but pop tunes of the sort sold as "sheet music" in our father's lunchroom/soda-fountain in Cambridge along with magazines, comic books, and, when they were invented, paperback books (in those days virtually every house had a piano, and sheet music was sold wherever magazines were)—also the swing-band music we heard on the radio and on 78rpm recordings: Tommy Dorsey, Benny Goodman, Count Basie, Duke Ellington, Harry James. Through the Depression and then World War II years, our Dorchester County's public school system had neither a high-school band nor instrumental instruction of any sort (nor even a twelfth grade), but I pieced together a rudimentary drum set, and with Jill on piano and a couple of friends on trombone and alto saxophone, by age fifteen or sixteen we'd cobbled up a successful jazz "combo" called the Swingtette. Through our junior and senior high-school years we played regular Saturday-night dances at the Cambridge Country Club and the Salisbury Town Club in a neighboring county. We even made a recording that was played on the local radio station, and the band was featured onstage in a "Teen-Age Revue" at Schine's Arcade, the local movie theater.

In 1947, at age seventeen, after graduating from our eleven-year public school system, I enrolled in Juilliard's six-week summer program with money saved from those country-club gigs (I could never have qualified for admission to the Institute's regular curriculum). The placement test obliged me to take Elementary Theory, but oddly qualified me for a course in Advanced Orchestration, and I managed to do well in both. The instructor in that latter course was Ted Royal Dewar, orchestrator of *Brigadoon* and other Broadway musicals and a disciple of the then-fashionable Schillinger System, an avant-garde math-to-music method of composition with which one could, e.g., transfer a photo of the Manhattan skyline onto graph paper and convert the numerical values into a musical score. The technique didn't particularly interest me (though George Gershwin reportedly used it), but I quite enjoyed that summer in upper Manhattan—my first away from home, except for earlier Boy Scout summer-camping— from which I learned that while some of my classmates were quite likely to become bona fide professional musicians, I was not of that number. During that instructive six-week absence from home I also lost my high-school girlfriend to a no doubt more advanced rival, and so in mid-August returned to Maryland without the foggiest notion of what to do next.

Whereupon, to my happy surprise, I learned that I had won a one-year state-senatorial scholarship to Johns Hopkins University. It was either that or go to work in my father's store, and so *faute de mieux* off I went—solo, by bus—from my native Cambridge across

Chesapeake Bay to the city of Baltimore and a rigorous research
university that I'd never even visited, but from whose College of
Engineering my no-less-able older brother, after a similar scholarship
year, had dropped out and enlisted in the Army, so ill-prepared were
we eleventh-grade redneck high-school grads for serious university
work. One had to choose a college within the university: Engineering
being of no interest to me, and Business being none of my business,
I chose Arts and Sciences. And my major? Well: not the sciences or
mathematics, for sure; not history, not economics, not philosophy, not
languages. That left . . . well . . . literature, maybe? But the Hopkins
English Department was much heavier on English than American lit
back then, and taught mainly the famous dead Brits. If one wanted to
study Hemingway and Faulkner, say—and I sort of did, having read
a couple of their paperbacks from Dad's store—one could do it only
in a brand-new department called Writing, Speech, and Drama (later
renamed the Writing Seminars). Moreover, come to think of it, I'd
written a regular humor/gossip column called "Ashcan Pete" for our
high-school newspaper back in the day, so maybe . . . Journalism?

   I gave it a try: hung on by my fingernails through a difficult
freshman year during which two fellow Eastern Shoremen whom I'd
met and befriended on the bus to Baltimore dropped out, just as my
brother (who after the war completed his B.A. elsewhere with high
grades and went on to law school and a successful career in D.C.) had
felt obliged to do. I flunked Political Economy, but survived my other
courses; actually managed an A in the department's one Journalism
course (taught by a visiting lecturer from the Baltimore *Sun*'s senior
editorial staff, and having more to do with the history and "philosophy" of journalism than with hands-on newspaper work); did
well enough in my other required courses, such as Classics in the

History of Western Literature and Classics in the History of Western
Thought; and learned the valuable lesson that journalism wasn't really my thing. Importantly too, among my new friends was another
Eastern Shoreman—"Buzz" Mallonee from Centreville, across the
Chesapeake from Baltimore—a trumpet-playing engineering major,
several of whose prep-school pals were also Hopkins freshmen and
musicians. He organized a dance-band, recruited me as drummer,
and scored us dance-jobs in the city and over on the Shore as well as
regular Sunday-afternoon "tea dances" at the Naval Academy down
in Annapolis. Being non-union "scabs," we charged less than the
local professionals, but got more jobs: a Saturday-night frat-house
or other gig followed by the Sunday tea-dance earned me almost as
much in 24 hours as some classmates were making in a week's part-
time work. Better yet, Buzz found us a summer-long job at Betterton
Beach, a popular bayside resort on the upper Chesapeake: Five of
us—trumpet, sax, piano, guitar, and drums—played daily afternoon
sessions in the old Betterton Casino's dance hall when the Baltimore
excursion boat *Bay Belle* docked at the casino's pier with its load
of day-trippers, then an hour of dinner music at the nearby Rigbie
Hotel (for which our payment was three free meals a day) and another two-hour dance in the evening back at the Casino, in whose
ample storage-room we also lodged for free. On Saturdays the rest
of the band joined us from Baltimore and elsewhere for a three-hour
evening dance: four saxes altogether, two trumpets, trombone, piano,
guitar, drums, and occasionally a female vocalist, we played four-
number "sets" (three ballads and an up-beat "jump" tune, a few of
which I arranged) with a small break between and a half-time inter-
mission. I don't recall what we were paid over and above our free
room and board, but we sharpened our skills from all those daily

performance-hours, enjoyed ourselves on the beach in our free time—and I met a young state-college co-ed, waitressing at the Rigbie, whom two years later I would wed.

Meanwhile, if journalism wasn't to be my major, what was? Well: It being after all a Creative Writing program, and knowing myself to be no poet, in my sophomore year (scholarship expired, but I managed to cobble up tuition money from the band-gigs, parental dispensations, and assorted part-time work—including, importantly, a partial-tuition-defraying job filing books in the classics stacks of the university library) I signed up for an introductory fiction-writing course presided over by a gentle ex-Marine from Georgia named Robert Durene Jacobs, himself an English Department doctoral candidate completing his dissertation on William Faulkner. So immersed did I become in Southern Lit under his guidance, my maiden efforts at "Cree-aytive Rotting" (as the art sounded in his deep-south accent) were an Eastern Shore marsh-country mash-up of Faulkner and elements borrowed from Joyce's *Ulysses* and *Finnegans Wake*, which I was also imbibing. But Bob was gentle and encouraging; I persisted through my sophomore and junior years, doing better in my academic courses as well, and still playing dances and arranging a few scores for whatever band (I forget its name) succeeded Buzz Mallonee's.

Q: Arranging: That's where we came in, I believe.

A: I'm getting there. In my senior year I was bumped up into the department's graduate-level fiction-writing seminar, presided over by Louis Rubin—another young Southerner (writing his doctoral thesis on Thomas Wolfe) and a first-rate writing coach as well as, subsequently, a much-published non-fiction writer himself and the founder of Algonquin Books of Chapel Hill. At the same time, my library-book-filing adventures led me to discover such treasures as Rabelais'

Gargantua and Pantagruel, Sterne's *Tristram Shandy*, Burton's unexpurgated *Arabian Nights*, Boccaccio's *Decameron*, and the great
Sanskrit tale-cycles *Panchatantra* and *The Ocean of the Streams of
Story*, all of which would become important to me when I finally
got my authorial act together. Meanwhile, I married my Eastern
Shore girlfriend, who'd finished her associate degree and shifted to
Baltimore to work and share a modest student apartment with me
(we'd planned to wed after my undergrad degree, but her parents—
conservative Methodist minister and wife—intercepted and read a
letter I'd written to her while she was visiting home, saw what was
what, and insisted on immediate matrimony). Lots of married WWII
veterans on campus back then, thanks to the G.I. Bill of Rights, some
with children already, and so a 20-year-old married college senior
with first child in the works was a less anomalous phenomenon than
it would be now. We skimped, scraped, worked various part-time
jobs, and somehow managed.

Q: Things "in the works" . . . How about musewise?

A: Well: The department's policy was to urge its B.A.'s to move
elsewhere for advanced degrees, but when I graduated in 1951 I persuaded them to let me stay on with a teaching assistantship in their
one-year M.A. program—luckily, because with a first child about to
be born and two others soon to follow (those were the Baby-Boomer
days!), I depended on my dance-band jobs and additional summer
work to support us. My M.A. thesis was more faux-Faulkner: a
novel entitled *The Shirt of Nessus*, the memory of which I've happily suppressed except that its title was borrowed from my explora-
tions into Greek mythology.[1] Luckily again, after the M.A. I was
able to enter a new interdepartmental doctoral program in Literary
Aesthetics cobbled up between Hopkins's Writing and Philosophy

departments to provide a rigorous Ph.D. to wannabe writers inclined to pay the rent by teaching until they scored with a trade publisher. I survived for a year in that program, trying vainly to devise a scholarly dissertation-subject while also launching a new fiction project called *The Dorchester Tales*. A never-to-be completed reorchestration of the great tale-cycles that I'd discovered in my book-filing semesters, it aspired to be 100 tales of my marshy home county at all periods of its history; I set it aside a year or two later, but managed to weave several of its yarns into my later novel *The Sot-Weed Factor* before tossing the manuscript.

Just as I'd learned in my freshman year that I wasn't cut out for serious journalism, one year in that Hopkins doctoral program taught me that I wasn't meant to be a professional scholar/critic either. I quite enjoyed the seminar sessions, presided over by such distinguished scholars as the historian of ideas George Boas, the Romance philologist Leo Spitzer, and the eminent Spanish poet Pedro Salinas (in exile from Franco's Spain), and did well enough in my courses while still playing occasional dance-band gigs, turning out a second child, and working a summer night-shift job as a timekeeper in Baltimore's Chevrolet factory. But I had to find something that I could truly do for a living, and so in 1953 I applied for and was accepted at an entry-level instructorship in English Composition at the Pennsylvania State College (later University) in State College, PA. I bought my first car (second-hand Buick sedan, from an uncle in Cambridge who dealt in used cars) and shifted my growing young family (kid #3 already on the way) from urban Baltimore up to the pleasant land-grant campus known to its joking undergraduates as "Dead Center," it having been built in Centre County—the geographical center of the state—after passage of President Lincoln's Land-Grant Act.

It was a great job: My courses were Remedial English ("English Zip")—where I met a few Nittany Lion football stars and learned the actual rules of grammar, syntax, and punctuation that I'd been applying more or less correctly without formally knowing them—and Freshman Composition (basic theme-writing), and would eventually include Advanced Composition and a course in "Humanities" (literature and philosophy) as well. And I implemented my very low starting salary by playing drums in a not-bad local dance band with regular gigs in a nearby American Legion hall and occasional frat-house dances. But the rule for us entry-level instructors was "three years and then up or out": I.e., either finish a doctorate, publish a book, or find another job. And so in 1955, after two years of full-time teaching, I managed to complete a new and very different sort of novel from that faux-Faulkner M.A. thesis: *The Floating Opera*, inspired by memories of a Chesapeake showboat called *The James Adams Floating Theatre* that I'd seen tied up at the Cambridge municipal wharf in my childhood.

It worked—in the nick of time. In the spring of 1956, after its rejection by several publishers who found it too unconventional for their taste, and just as I was obliged to consider reapplying to Hopkins to attempt completion of that abandoned Ph.D., my agent called to inform me that *The Floating Opera*—still happily afloat in trade-paperback print 55 years later, as I write this—had been accepted for fall publication by Appleton-Century-Crofts with a princely advance of $750 ($675 after deduction of agent's well-earned commission). No matter the tiny sum, even by mid-20th-century standards: My academic butt was saved, I already had a second novel brewing (*The End of the Road*), and the *Opera*'s publication earned me a promotion from Instructor to Assistant

Professor. I stayed on at Penn State for eight more years and discovered in its Pattee Library the complete *Archives of Maryland* (documents of the colony's history from its founding by Lord Baltimore in 1634 to its statehood in 1776) and a late-17th-century poem by one Ebenezer Cooke called *The Sot-Weed Factor, or, A Voyage to Maryland: A Satyr,* said to be the first satire on life in the American colonies. Cooke's poem—together with another important library-discovery, Joseph Campbell's *The Hero With a Thousand Faces,* about the ubiquitous pattern of wandering-hero myths in various cultures throughout history—inspired my *Sot-Weed Factor* novel, and I reorchestrated Campbell in my next one as well, *Giles Goat-Boy* (its wandering hero somehow spawned by intercourse between a computer and a goat), meanwhile ascending the academic ladder from Instructor through Assistant to Associate Professor and still playing occasional dance-jobs with Bob Shea's band.

In 1965, the critic Leslie Fiedler, whom I'd met when he visited Penn State, persuaded me to join him in the English Department of the newly-upgraded State University of New York at Buffalo. I accepted—among other reasons because a full professorship with considerable salary increase, lighter teaching load, and other amenities, plus the shift from rural Pennsylvania to a more urban environ, we hoped might salvage what had become an unfortunately ever-more-strained and distanced marital connection.

It didn't, but my seven years on the shores of Lake Erie were otherwise fruitful indeed. In the lively, rather avant-garde atmosphere of "High Sixties" Buffalo, I published *Lost in the Funhouse* (subtitled *Fiction for Print, Tape, Live Voice*: fourteen previously-published pieces rearranged into a "series") in 1968, and in 1972 the novella-triad *Chimera,* a reorchestration of the myths of Perseus (*Perseid*),

Bellerophon (*Bellerophoniad*—a pun on his being, in my version, not a bona fide mythic hero but rather a "perfect imitation" of one), and Scheherazade's kid sister Dunyazade (*Dunyazadiad*). In Buffalo too I found among my new colleagues the ablest musician-friends I'd ever played jazz with: Ira Cohen, the Provost of Social Sciences, had played tenor sax with Glenn Miller's Army band and after Miller's death with his successor, Tex Beneke, and after VJ-Day had put his horn away and switched to chamber-music clarinet, but with the encouragement of pianist, bassist, trumpeter, trombonist, and drummer, in one semester he moved with us from 1940s big-band swing to the late-'60s "cool jazz" style of our current favorites: Stan Getz, Paul Desmond, Gerry Mulligan, and Dave Brubeck.

But while Author's work was going well (*Chimera* won that year's National Book Award, and I was rewarded with an endowed professorship whose perks included every third semester off with pay—a blessing for us scribblers), his marriage wasn't: It ended in divorce in 1969, just as the last of our children was preparing for college. To help with alimony and child-support expenses (including three college tuitions) I took as many speaking/reading engagements as I could manage and launched into a large and complex new writing-project, the novel *LETTERS*: a 20th-century reorchestration of the 18th-century epistolary novel genre that would take me seven years to complete.

One of those reading-gigs fetched me in February 1969 from an all-but-snowed-in Buffalo to a ditto New England, to do a reading at Boston College. The flight was delayed, the reading late, but intrepid Bostonians turned out in gratifying number—including (so I learned at the post-reading audience reception, when she came up to say hello) a former star student in my Penn State Humanities class:

in fact, that university's official 100,000th graduate, a distinction earned by her having achieved the highest academic average in the school's 100-plus-year history. Sharp, lively, and lovely, she was currently teaching in a local junior high school, she informed me, having known since elementary-school days that teaching was her destined vocation; after Penn State she'd done graduate work at the University of Chicago, and now here she was, having got word of my reading in the local press and trudged through the snow to say hi to her former prof. Our eager reminiscences about PSU days being properly constrained by my obligation to chat with other attendees, when my host informed me that it was time for him and me to step into a nearby elevator to attend a faculty reception upstairs, I reluctantly bade her *au revoir*—and was delighted when she asked, "May I come along?"

For details of what followed, see my essay "Teacher" in *Further Fridays:*[2] Enough here to report that by the end of that spring semester she and I had reconnected sufficiently for her to visit me at Lake Chautauqua (my post-marital residence, near Buffalo) and I her in Boston, spend the next summer together at the lake cottage, and marry in her Philadelphia hometown in December of 1970. The following semester, on leave from SUNY/Buffalo, I took a visiting professorship at Boston U.; we then returned to Chautauqua and Buffalo, where she tried teaching at an independent girls' school (Buffalo Seminary), which she expected not to like—all of her previous experience having been in good public schools—but discovered that she loved. She had a chance to hear her hubby play jazz with his SUNY/Buff colleagues and enjoyed that, too—but we both felt that this new chapter in our life deserved a new venue (I was weary of those heroic lake-effect upstate-New-York winters, and for all its pluses, Buffalo was no Boston), and so when an offer came to return to my alma mater in Baltimore on even more attractive terms than my current ones, we checked out the job possibilities for her down there. Though a bit wary of life below the Mason-Dixon line, she discovered St. Timothy's, another independent girls' high school just north of town, and was so taken with it—and the fact that Baltimore was, after all, just South enough for tennis nets to be left up all winter—that we happily shifted thereto at summer's end, bought our first house together, and began what after forty years remains a much-blessed union indeed: my moral compass, my editor of first resort, hiking/biking/sailing/snorkeling/kayaking partner, planner of all our meals, travels, and activities, and dedicatee of every Barth-book published since—*my* "arranger," my *sine qua non* Shelly.

The downside of that move, if any, was that among my new colleagues I found no replacement for my Buffalo jazz-pals. After a year or so I sold my drum-set and, encouraged by my new sister-in-law, began playing baroque and Elizabethan recorder duets with her, a pleasure that we still enjoy. As a wordsmith, I take a special satisfaction both in the differences between the two media—the feelings and ideas that music can express more eloquently than words, and vice-versa—and the pleasures both of solo performance with pen and word-processor and of ensemble (anyhow duet) performance on the recorder. As for "arranging," I feel blessed to have enjoyed it for so many years and to be doing it still, changes changed, at my desk: My forthcoming novel, for example—*Every Third Thought*—is among other things a reorchestration both of Shakespeare's *Tempest* and of characters from my 2008 story-series *The Development*.

Q: Shall we take it from the edge? Page *one*, page *two*. . . .

The End? On Writing No
Further Fiction, Probably

First published in the British journal *Granta*, February 2012.

I N 2011 AND 2012, two new products of this pen—a novel entitled
Every Third Thought and this *Final Fridays* essay-collection—are
scheduled for publication by Counterpoint Press, a non-"trade" publisher in California. Both were completed in 2009, my 80th year of
life and 53rd as a publishing writer. At the time of their composition, I didn't think of them as my *last* books, only as the latest: my
seventeenth volume of fiction and third of non-fiction, respectively.
But in the year-and-then-some since, although I've still gone to my
workroom every weekday morning for the hours between breakfast
and lunch, as I've done for decades, and re-enacted my muse-inviting
ritual, I find that I've written . . . nothing.

That room is divided into three distinct areas: Composition (one
side of a large work-table, reserved for longhand first drafts of fiction on Mondays through Thursdays and nonfiction on Fridays, with
supply drawers and adjacent reference-book shelves), Production
(computer hutch with desktop word processor and printer for subsequent drafts and revision), and Business (other side of worktable,
with desk calendar and office files). As for the ritual: Prep-Step One is

to seat myself at the Composition table, set down my refilled thermal mug of breakfast coffee, and insert the wax earplugs that I got in the habit of using back in the 1950s, when my three children (now in *their* fifties) were rambunctious toddlers, and that became so associated with my sentence-making that even as an empty-nester in a quiet house I continue to feel the need for them. Step Two is to open the stained and battered three-ring loose-leaf binder, now 63 years old and held precariously together with strapping tape, that I bought during my freshman orientation-week at Johns Hopkins in 1947 and in which I penned all my undergraduate and grad-school class notes, professorial lecture-drafts during my decades in academia, and first drafts of the entire corpus of my fiction and non-fiction. Step Three is to unclip from that binder's middle ring the British Parker 51 fountain pen bought during my maiden tour of Europe in 1963/64 (in a Volkswagen camper with those same three then-small children and their mother) at a Rochester stationer's alleged to be the original of Mister Pumblechook's Premises in Dickens's *Great Expectations*: the pen with which I have penned every subsequent sentence, including this one. (Its predecessor, an also much-valued Schaeffer that saw me through college and my first three published novels, was inadvertently cracked in my shirt pocket a few weeks earlier when I leaned against a battlement in "Hamlet's castle" in Elsinore—Danish Helsingor, near Copenhagen, the northernmost stop of that makeshift Grand Tour—in order to get a better view of Sweden across the water.) I recharge the venerable Parker with jet-black Quink, wipe its well-worn tip with a bit of tissue, fix its cap onto its butt, and proceed to Step Four. . . .

Which in happier days meant reviewing and editing either the print-outs of yesterday's first-draft pages (left off when the going was good and thus more readily resumed) or work-notes toward some project in gestation, to be followed by Step Five: re-inspiration and the composition of new sentences, paragraphs, and pages. Of late, however, Step Four has consisted of staring vainly, pen in hand, at blank ruled pages, or exchanging fountain pen for note-taking ballpoint and perusing for possible suggestions either my spiral-bound Work Notebook #5 (2008–) or my little black six-ring loose-leaf personal notebook/diary, to little avail. That latter—*The Black Book of not so bright (or sunny) observations & reflections*, its title page declares, on which also are the rubber-stamped addresses of its serial residences over the past forty years—has only a few blank leaves remaining, and no room for more. And the workroom's bookshelves, reserved for one copy of each edition and translation of every book, magazine article, and anthology contribution that I've published, are already crowded beyond their capacity, with new editions lying horizontally across older ones and jammed into crannies between bookcase and wall.

That almost-exhausted notebook-space; those overflowing shelves—are they trying to tell me something? I plug my ears; strain not to listen. Like most fiction-writers of my acquaintance (perhaps especially those who mainly write novels rather than short stories), I'm accustomed to a well-filling interval of some weeks or even months between book-length projects: an interval not to be confused with "Writer's Block." Indeed, I've learned to look forward to that bit of a respite from sentence-making after a new book has left the shop—bulky typescript both snail-mailed and e-mailed to agent and thence to publisher—and to busily making notes toward the Next One while final-copyediting and galley-proofing its predecessor. This time, however . . .

Well.

Well? A writer-friend from Kansas who knows about water-wells informs me of the important distinction between dry wells and "gurglers," which may cease producing for a time but eventually resume; he encourages me to believe that I'm still a Gurgler. I hope that's the case—but if in fact my well turns out to be dry, I remind myself that as we've aged, my wife and I have been obliged to put other much-enjoyed pleasures behind us: snow- and water-skiing, tennis, sailboat-cruising on the Chesapeake, and yes, even vigorous youthful sex (but certainly not love and intimacy, and as someone once wisely observed, "Sex goes, memory goes, but the memory of sex—that never goes"). If my vocation—my "calling"!—has joined that sigh-and-smile list of Once Upon a Times, its memory will be a fond one indeed.

Time will tell.

Meanwhile, maybe write a little piece about . . . not writing?

II.
TRIBUTES
AND MEMORIA

Introduction to *Not-Knowing:*
The Essays and Interviews
of Donald Barthelme

Although it's neither my first memorial tribute to Donald Barthelme
(1931–1989) nor my last,[1] what follows—written at the request
of Donald's brother Frederick (himself an accomplished novelist,
editor of *The Mississippi Review*, and alumnus of the Hopkins
Writing Seminars) to introduce a posthumously published collection of Don's nonfiction[2]—is the one I think best suited to open this
"Tributes and Memoria" section of *Final Fridays*.

" **H**OW COME YOU write the way you do?" an apprentice
writer in my Johns Hopkins workshop once disingenu-
ously asked Donald Barthelme, who was visiting. Without missing a
beat, Don replied, "Because Samuel Beckett was already writing the
way *he* does."

Asked another, smiling but serious, "How can we become better
writers than we are?"

"Well," DB advised, "for starters, read through the whole history of philosophy, from the pre-Socratics up through last semester.
That might help."

"But Coach Barth has already advised us to read all of *literature*, from Gilgamesh up through last semester. . . ."

"That, too," Donald affirmed, and twinkled that shrewd Amish-farmer-from-West-11th-Street twinkle of his. "You're probably wasting time on things like eating and sleeping: Cease that, and read all of philosophy and all of literature. Also art. Plus politics and a few other things. The history of everything."

Although I count myself among my late comrade's most appreciative fans—invariably delighted, over the too-few decades of his career, by his short stories, his novels, his infrequent but soundly-argued essays into aesthetics, and his miscellaneous nonfiction pieces (not to mention his live conversation, as above)—I normally see *The New Yorker*, in which so much of his writing was first published, only in the waiting rooms of doctors and dentists. I have therefore grown used to DB-ing in happy binges once every few years, when a new collection of the wondrous stuff appears (originally from Farrar, Straus, & Giroux; anon from Putnam; later from Harper and Row; finally from Random House) and I set other reading aside to go straight through it, savoring the wit, the bite, the exactitude and flair, inspired whimsy, aw-shucks urbanity, irreal realism and real irreality, wired tersitude, and suchlike Barthelmanic pleasures.

Finally, it says up in that parenthetical list of his publishers. The adverb constricts my spirit; I feel again what I felt when word came of Donald's illness and death in 1989, at age merely-58, in the fullness of his life and happy artistry: my maiden experience of survivor-guilt, for we were virtual coevals often assigned to the same team (or angel-choir or Hell-pit) by critics friendly and not, who require such categories—Fabulist, Postmodernist, what have they. We ourselves, and the shifting roster of our team-/choir-/pit-mates,[3] were perhaps more impressed by our *differences* than by any similarities, but there was most certainly fellow-feeling among us—and was I to go on breathing air, enjoying health and wine and food, work and play and love and language, and Donald not? Go on spinning out my sometimes hefty fabrications (which, alphabetically cheek-by-jowl to his on bookshelves, he professed to fear might topple onto and crush their stage-right neighbor), and Donald not his sparer ones, that we both knew to be in no such danger?

Well. One adds the next sentence to its predecessors, and over the ensuing years, as bound volumes of mine have continued to forth-come together with those of his other team-/choir-/pit-mates, it has been some balm to see (impossibly posthumous!) Donald's appearing as before, right along with them, as if by some benign necromancy: first his comic-elegaic Arthurian novel *The King* (1990); then *The Teachings of Don B.* (1992), a rich miscellany eloquently foreworded by T-/C-/P-mate Thomas Pynchon; now *Not-Knowing*; and still to come, a collection of hitherto unpublished and/or uncollected short stories.

Benign it is, but no necromancy. We owe these last fruits not only to Donald's far-ranging muse, but to the dedication of his liter-ary executors and the editorial enterprise of Professor Kim Herzinger of the University of Southern Mississippi. Thanks to that dedication and enterprise, we shall have the print-part of our fellow whole, or all but whole. Never enough, and too soon cut off—like Carver, like Calvino, all at their peak—but what a feast it is!

ITS COURSE IN hand displays most directly the high intelligence be-hind the author's audacious, irrepressible fancy. The complementary opening essays, "After Joyce" and "Not-Knowing" (that title-piece was for years required reading in the aforementioned graduate fiction-writing seminar at Johns Hopkins); the assorted reviews and pungent "comments" on literature, film, and politics; the pieces "On Art," never far from the center of Donald's concerns; the seven flat-out interviews (edited after the fact by the interviewee)—again and again I find myself once again nodding *yes, yes* to their insights, obiter dicta, and mini-manifestoes, delivered with unfailing tact and zing. See, e.g., "Not-Knowing"'s jim-dandy cadenza upon the rendering of "Melancholy Baby" on jazz "banjolele": as astute (and hilarious) a statement as I know of about the place of "aboutness" in art.[4] Bravo, maestro banjolelist: Encore!

Here is a booksworth of encores, to be followed by one more: the story-volume yet to come, a final serving of the high literary art for which that high intelligence existed.

And then?

Then there it is, alas, and for encores we will go back and back again to the feast whereof these are end-courses: back to *Come Back, Dr. Caligari*, to *Unspeakable Practices, Unnatural Acts*, to *Snow White* and *City Life* and the rest. Permanent pleasures of American "Postmodernist" writing, they are. Permanent literary pleasures period.

The Passion Artist
(tribute to John Hawkes)

Shortly after the author's death on May 15, 1998, this tribute to John
Hawkes was first published in *The New York Times Book Review*.[1]

THE DAY AFTER Frank ("The Voice") Sinatra died in California
at age 82, a no less distinctive American voice—in certain
quarters even more prized, though in the nature of things less widely
known—was stilled in Providence, Rhode Island. With the death at
age 72 of John Hawkes—fiction writer, fiction mentor, and fiction
live-reader *extraordinaire*—we lost one of the steadily brightest (and
paradoxically darkest) lights of American fiction through our century's second half: a navigation star for scores of apprentice writers
however different their own literary course, and as spellbinding a
public reader of his own work as I have ever heard, who have heard
many. *Passion* was this writer's subject, even when manifested by
non-human characters (the narrator/protagonist of his novel *Sweet
William* is a horse; the deuteragonist of *The Frog* is a very French am-
phibian); *impassioned* was his manner as author, teacher, reader, and
friend. He was, to echo another of his titles, truly a Passion Artist:
for five decades one of our most original literary imaginations and
masterful prose stylists.

THE WRITER:

Hawkes's books number nearly a score, from *The Cannibal* in 1949 (actually from a privately printed verse-collection in 1943, but the author never returned to poetry except in his prose, which never left it) through *An Irish Eye* in 1997. Mostly novels, all of modest heft, plus a scarifying story-and-novella collection and a volume of short plays, they have in common a preoccupation with the horrific, suffused with the erotic and redeemed by the comic. One sees affinities with Faulkner, Djuna Barnes, Carson McCullers, and Flannery O'Connor; to mention such affinities, however, is to be reminded of Hawkes's difference from those compatriots, all of whom he admired. Like theirs, his fiction is in the American-gothic grain, but his material is more cosmopolitan—closer in this respect to that of his bookshelf-neighbor Hawthorne, or to Poe. A Hawkes novel may be set in England, Germany, Maine, Alaska, the Caribbean, "Illyria," or some Transylvania of the soul; literal places are less important to him than the geographies of passion and language. His imagination, like Kafka's, is powerfully metaphorical. And dark. And comic.

It has been also one of the most consistent among our contemporaries', both in quality and in voice. One never knew what Hawkes would write of next—Nepal? Patagonia? The Moon?—but one recognized at once that narrative voice: the sensuous cadences refracting comic-horrific scenes (a boy plays Brahms outside the door of the lavatory where his father is committing suicide; an earnest but hapless male teacher is set upon and all but castrated by his murderous Maenad students in St. Dunster's Training School for Girls—and comes back for more); the fearsome, unexpected details (a sexually voltaged foursome retrieve from a dark pit in a ruined medieval fortress a rusted, toothed iron chastity belt; a dead horse's

ears are "as unlikely to twitch as two pointed fern leaves etched
on glass"); the ubiquitous sensuality and trademark rhetorical questions ("[Did she not] note Seigneur's unsmiling countenance and his
silence and the way he stood at a distance with his feet apart and
that strange mechanical staff gripped in a firm hand, its butt in the
sand and its small iron beak towering above his head on the end
of the staff? Wouldn't this sight be quite enough to instill in most
grown women . . . the first unpleasant taste of apprehension? But it
was not so . . .").

Hawkes-lovers recognize at once that such passages as the above
(from *Virginie, Her Two Lives*) are, among other things, disquiet-
ingly *comic*: neither de Sade played straight nor de Sade played for
laughs, but de Sade (and the artist) compassionately, *impassionedly*
satirized. "I deplore . . . nightmare," Hawkes declared in an interview
with Robert Scholes; "I deplore terror. [But] I happen to believe that
it is only by traveling those dark tunnels, perhaps not literally but
psychically, that one can learn . . . what it means to be compassion-
ate." What nightmare? Which terror? "My fiction," he goes on to
say, "is generally an evocation of the nightmare or terroristic universe
in which sexuality is destroyed by law, by dictum, by human perver-
sity, by contraption, and it is this destruction [that] I have attempted
to portray and confront in order to be true to human fear and . . .
ruthlessness, but also in part to evoke its opposite, the moment of
freedom from constriction, restraint, death."

Yes, well: also, one might add, to provoke the cathartic *laughter*
at sexual and fictive "contraption" afforded by that hard but pleasurably won freedom. So charged with Eros is just about everything in a
typical Hawkes fiction that my private ground-rule for him was *No
literal sex ever to be described, Jack*—a rule that I neglected to inform

him of until after its brief infraction in a couple of the later novels, but to which he gratifyingly returns in the last ones.

The last ones—that's not easily said. Hawkes's fiction has been widely admired from the start by literary critics and his fellow writers: His book-jackets are garlanded with enthusiastic testimonials from the likes of Flannery O'Connor, Robert Penn Warren, Saul Bellow, Anthony Burgess, Donald Barthelme, Leslie Fiedler. But his standing, alas, has ever surpassed his following, and that's a pity, for he's no more for connoisseurs only than is an excellent wine. For those unfamiliar with his fiction, a fine first taste is *Humors of the Blood & Skin, A John Hawkes Reader*: a self-assembled degustation with autobiographical notes by the author and a beautiful introduction by William H. Gass.[2] But really, one can begin anywhere: The voice is all of a piece.

THE TEACHER:

Whatever one thinks of the post-World-War-Two American phenomenon of poets and novelists as professors in creative writing programs, it has most certainly afforded a generation of aspiring writers and students of literature close access to practitioners of the art; in the best cases, to *masters* of the art, impassioned (that word again) about their coaching and their coachees as well as about their own congress with the muse. By all accounts, John Hawkes was among the chiefest of these. After a stint driving ambulances in Italy and Germany in the closing months of World War II, he married his indispensable, *sine qua non* Sophie (who with their four grown children survives him), graduated from Harvard and published his first novel in 1949, worked for six years at his alma mater's university press, began teaching there as an instructor in English, and in 1958 shifted to Brown, where he anchored the graduate writing program until succeeded upon his retirement by his close friend and distinguished writer-comrade Robert Coover. I too am a beneficiary of that post-war phenomenon, and inasmuch as a certain number of apprentice writers have gypsied between Brown and Johns Hopkins, we have over the decades had a number of alumni in common, every one of whom revered Hawkes as an intense, convivial, time-generous, *impassioned* mentor/coach as well as an inspired, inspiring artist. "Plus," the writer Mary Robison once said, concluding her introduction of him to an audience in Baltimore, "he wears the most adorable clothes, and anybody who doesn't think so can go straight to hell!"

Jack inspired that kind of fierce admiration. The least pedagogical of pedagogues, for a time in the latter 1960s he nevertheless involved himself—*passionately*, of course—with an innovative program called the Voice Project, meant to reform the teaching of writing in American schools as the New Math was meant to reform that discipline. Federal start-up funding forthcame, and at Hawkes's urging a considerable number of us writer-teachers convened at Sarah Lawrence College to learn about and perhaps help launch the project. We sat through a day of presentations by not-always-inspiring educationists; during one particularly sententious holding-forth, Susan Sontag asked me *sotto voce*, "Doesn't the guy realize that we're all here only for Jack Hawkes's sake?" Toward the end of that long day, I confessed to Donald Barthelme that I, for one, still didn't quite grasp what exactly the project-organizers meant by "Voice." "Neither do I," admitted Donald; "but Jack does, so it's probably all right."

Jack did—enough to devote a trial year to the project at Stanford while serving on a federal Panel on Educational Innovation. What

became of the Voice Project I have no idea; but as one of my own
undergraduate professors once observed, "a fine teacher is likely to
teach well regardless of what educational theories he or she may suf-
fer from." Hawkes's teaching voice—discerning, engaged, compas-
sionate, *impassioned*—was pedagogy more eloquent and effective
than any educative theory.

THE VOICE:

I heard him read publicly from his fiction many times: as a visiting
writer at my home campus, at literary festivals round about our republic, on shared platforms at such venues as New York's 92nd St.
Poetry Center, and most memorably through an extended reading-
tour of Germany in 1979 with William Gass and myself and our
spouses—a sort of American Postmodernist road show sponsored by
the USIA and local universities. None of us three, I venture, was an
inept speaker of our fiction, though we all understood that print-
prose is not theater, but an essentially silent transaction between its
author and individual readers. One need not have heard Jack read
his stuff in order to savor its distinctive, compelling "voice"—but in
his readings above all, the intensity, dark humor, and passion were
unforgettably on display. Indeed, his fiction, his letters, his telephone
and table-talk were all of a register; I hear that voice as I write these
lines, as stirringly as I heard it in Tübingen, Berlin, Providence, Palo
Alto, Buffalo, Baltimore. Unimaginable, that in the terabyte twilight
of the terrible Twentieth one will hear it now only in memory!

WELL: THAT OTHER Voice, Sinatra's, will endure in its recorded
performances for as long as his presently living fans remain interested, and perhaps even somewhat beyond their lifetimes; recorded

music is itself so young a medium that we have no way of knowing whether pop singers of the longer past—P. T. Barnum's "Swedish Nightingale" Jenny Lind, for example—would still be listened to with pleasure today. In the venerable and more stable medium of the printed word, it is another matter: For any who had the privilege of hearing him, the so-memorable living voice of John Hawkes rings out in stereophonic high fidelity from every line of his fiction; his *written* voice, however, is there for the much longer haul—perhaps, in Archibald MacLeish's words, for "as long . . . as the iron of English rings from a tongue";[3] most certainly for as long as the passionate few still read printed literature.

The Accidental Mentor
(homage to Leslie Fiedler)

This tribute to Leslie Fiedler was written early in 1997 for a Festschrift intended to celebrate the distinguished critic/professor's upcoming 80th birthday in March of that year. Alas, however, by the time of the volume's much-delayed publication in 2003,[1] the tributee had "changed tenses" (as Samuel Beckett was fond of putting it) at age 85. Adieu, colleague, friend, and accidental mentor.

I N 1956, A certain American first novel was blessed by a prevailingly favorable review from a certain noted American critic, who characterized it as a specimen of "provincial American existentialism" that committed its author to nothing and left him free to do whatever next thing he might choose. At the time, fresh out of graduate school, this interested reader of that review had no very expert notion of what Existentialism was. Intrigued by that critic's remark, like a good provincial American Johns Hopkins alumnus I set about re-reading Sartre and Camus (Heidegger was beyond me) and soon decided that all parts of the proposition applied: The book *was* provincial, American, and Existentialist, and its author was free to sing whatever next tunes his muse might call.

Which I did. 40 years later, I'm gratified to report, that novel, that novelist, and that noted critic are all still actively with us,[2] and Leslie Fiedler's instructive characterization of my *Floating Opera* still strikes me as altogether valid.

Not long after writing that review, the author of *Love and Death in the American Novel* and other notorious iconoclasms made a lecture-visit to Penn State, where I was then employed, and there began an acquaintanceship that over the years ripened into friendship and colleaguehood; that affected in large and small ways my professional trajectory; and that I remain the ongoing beneficiary of. I have counted those ways elsewhere and will gratefully here recount just a few of them:

IN THE MID-1960S, Fiedler recruited me to join Albert Cook's bustling new English department at the State University of New York at Buffalo, whereto he himself had lately shifted after his long tenure in Montana. More than any other single factor, it was Leslie's presence there that tipped my scales Buffaloward, and for the seven years following we were near neighbors. In retrospect, the lively intellectual/artistic/political atmosphere of that place in that turbulent time seems to me as much centered at the *Fiedlerhaus* as at the rambunctious university campus and the pop-artful Albright-Knox Museum, both nearby. A Buffalo book-reviewer recently opined, in the course of noticing a new book of mine, that its author had done "his most lasting work at Penn State, his most interesting work at Buffalo, and his most fatuous work since returning to Johns Hopkins." While I don't necessarily agree with any of those three propositions and would heatedly contest the last of them, I know what the chap means by that second one. It's the High-Sixties Buffalo *Zeitgeist* that

I associate with the story-series *Lost in the Funhouse* (1968), the novella-triad *Chimera* (1972), and the intricated ground-plan of the novel *LETTERS* (finally completed and published in 1979); and it is Leslie Fiedler, more than any other single figure, who for me embodies that so-spirited place and time.

From whom if not him did I learn, back then, that the USA had changed "from a whiskey culture into a drug culture"—just when I was learning to appreciate good wine? Who first alarmed me with the prophecy[3] that "if narrative has any future at all, it's up there on the big screen, not down here on the page"? In those pioneer days of Black Studies and Women's Studies, who puckishly (and illuminatingly, as always) offered counter-courses in White Studies and Male Studies? Whose prevailingly apocalyptic prognoses for literature (expanded to book-length in *What Was Literature?*)[4] would one take only half seriously, had one not seen heresy after heresy of Fiedler's turn into prescience?

The list goes on: He is a mentor from whom this incidental, often skeptical, sometimes reluctant mentee has never failed to learn, most frequently in that period of our closest association.

TOWARD THE END whereof—while I was visiting-professoring in Boston and deciding to return to Baltimore (though not, I trust, to blissful literary fatuity)—the fellow did me another significant service, a sort of bookend to his having recruited me to Buffalo in the first place. One would prefer to imagine that whatever official recognition one's writings earn, they earn purely on their literary merits. The world, however, is what it is, and so it did not escape my notice that the five National Book Award jurors in fiction for 1972 included two (Leslie Fiedler and William H. Gass) who had not only spoken favorably of my fiction, but had become personal friends of mine as well, together with one (Jonathan Yardley of the Washington *Post*) who had consistently trashed me, and two with whose literary-critical opinions I was unacquainted (the novelists Evan Connell and Walker Percy). I readily and thankfully assumed that it was owing to Fiedler and/or Gass that my *Chimera*-book was among that year's nominees; with equal readiness I assumed that that would be that: victory enough to have been a finalist, as had been my bridesmaid fortune twice before. Leslie even telephoned me in Boston from New York to assure me that I hadn't a prayer, inasmuch as "the other three" judges had favorite candidates of their own. Not long after, news came that *Chimera* had won the thing after all (more precisely, a divided jury divided the prize).

How so?

"You had two for you and two against you," Leslie cheerfully confided to me later, "and I drank the swing-vote under the table."

Owe you one there, pal. Owe you, rather, yet another.

"As Sinuous and Tough as Ivy" (80th birthday salute to William H. Gass)

Another birthday-Festschrift tribute,[1] this one to the eminent fictionist, critic, scholar, and teacher William H. Gass, who turned 80 in July 2004. Until his academic retirement in 1999, Gass was Distinguished Professor of Humanities at Washington University in St. Louis, where he also founded and directed the International Writers Center (now renamed the Center for Humanities). Unlike the preceding tributee, Leslie Fiedler, he is as of this writing still very much alive and busy at his art. Two of his essay collections have won National Book Critics Circle awards; the most recent, *A Temple of Texts*, won the 2007 Truman Capote Award for literary criticism.

N EARLY 40 YEARS ago, in 1966, his then-publisher sent me bound galleys of his first novel, as publishers will, in hopes of testimonial: *Omensetter's Luck*, by one William H. Gass.

Never heard of the chap, although I should have: His fiction had already been included in *The Best American Short Stories* in 1959, 1961, and 1962. Anyhow, my vows to the muse prohibit, among other things, the blurbing of blurbs except for first books by my former students. All the same, I opened the thing (in the middle, un-fairly), scanned a page or two in each direction, and found—in a passage describing a midwestern country picnic—these images: "All kinds of containers sat about the table in sullen disconnection. Some steamed despite the hot day; others enclosed pools of green brine where pickles drowsed like crocodiles."

Well, now, I thought: Imagine a professor of philosophy (so the jacket-note identified the author) who can write *pickles drowsed like crocodiles.* I was impressed enough to rebegin at the beginning and read the novel right through, more and more wowed as I went along. Wrote the author a fan letter, even, in lieu of blurb. Turned out he liked *my* stuff, too—some of it, anyhow—and there ensued a decades-long cordial comradeship-in-literary-arms. Membership in the dimly-defined ranks of our peaceable platoon was a matter less of voluntary enlistment than of assignment by reviewers and critics praising, blaming, or merely tabulating the Usual Suspects of "Postmodernism," "Metafiction," or whatever, and having thus been called to one another's attention, we-all most often enjoyed and ad-mired one another's writings.

Enjoyed too our professional path-crossings through the remain-der of the century: at one another's universities (most though not all of us were professors, typically though not necessarily of literature and/or its writing), at conferences and other literary functions here and there in our republic and abroad. As *Omensetter* was followed by the story-collection *In the Heart of the Heart of the Country* (which I liked even more than its so-impressive predecessor) and that by *Willie Masters' Lonesome Wife* (which if possible I enjoyed more yet: the most formally sportive item in Gass's oeuvre) and the several splendid essay-collections, I came to know their author a bit, sharing reading/

lecture platforms with him in Buffalo, St. Louis, and Baltimore, in New York and North Dakota, in Germany and in Spain. Admired his presence, onstage and off. Admired his formidable intelligence and learning, his commitment to teaching ("I'll probably keep at it till I drop," he remarked to me upon my own academic retirement in 1995, "and then I'll have myself stuffed and go on teaching"), his *obiter dicta* ("I'll never do a fiction-writing workshop," he once vowed to me: "When I'm reading a bad student paper on Plato, at least I'm thinking about Plato; but when I'm reading a bad student short story about trout fishing, I'm not thinking about *anything.*").

Admired and admire most of all, of course, the writing: in the fiction, those inhospitable landscapes and typically pathetic-when-not-monstrous characters, marvelously rendered into language; in the essays, the play of mind and wide-ranging erudition lightly deployed. And in both, the prose, the prose—in particular (if I were obliged to single out one element or aspect for special commendation, which I am not but nevertheless will) the *similes*: those homely yet show-stopping similes, still the Gass trademark for this admiring reader, which stick in my memory long after I've forgotten which work they're from and what subtle additional relevances they no doubt have to their context. A character's hands "quick as cats," drafts of air that "cruise like fish through the hollow rooms," a feeling "like the loneliness of overshoes or someone else's cough," a face "like a mail-order ax," "wires where sparrows sit like fists," an argument "as sinuous and tough as ivy"—and those drowsing pickles. . . .

One can sieve troves of such gems from Gass's pages. Indeed, the narrator of "In the Heart of the Heart of the Country" self-deprecatingly remarks, "Similes dangle like baubles from me." Not so: A Bill Gass simile does not dangle; it is of a piece with the cadence of its sentence, the stuff of its speaker, the situational moment. And it is no bauble, but an unostentatious gemstone: a diamond not really in the rough, but cunningly polished to *look* rough, if you follow me. A Bill Gass simile is like . . . is like . . .

TO THE RESCUE, *maestro*!

The Last Introduction
(memorial tribute to Joseph Heller)

Three times, at approximate 10-year intervals, it was my pleasure to introduce Joseph Heller to university audiences: first in the tempestuous High 1960s at the State University of New York at Buffalo, and twice later—in the post-Nixon 1970s and again in the twilight of the Reagan '80s—at Johns Hopkins. These professional path-crossings, along with our having each taught earlier at Penn State in our apprentice days and been often subsequently categorized together as "Black Humorists" back when that label was in fashion, added an extra fillip of literary comradeship to our cordial acquaintance, despite whatever differences between Joe's muse and mine. What follows is adapted from the last of those three introductions, delivered on October 4, 1988, when Joe and his wife Valerie were book-touring for his just-published "Rembrandt" novel, *Picture This*. Upon Joe's death 11 years later (in December 1999, at age 76), Valerie Heller projected a volume of memorial tributes to her husband from sundry of his friends and associates, and in keeping with our established pattern of one Heller-intro per decade, I contributed this one. If introductions had titles, I would call it

APPLAUDING JOE

Joseph Heller has done at least three literary things that I believe any of his fellow novelists would applaud. *I* certainly do.

To begin with, his first novel (*Catch-22*, published in 1961 and never out of print since) managed to be at one and the same time artistically serious, enormously funny (the correct adverb, I think, since its humor addresses such enormities as war, military bureaucracy, grisly chance, and ubiquitous death), blackly cynical (the novel is part of the canon of what came to be called Black Humor), and yet tremendously popular and influential. How gratifying it must be, for a serious American novelist at the close of the 20th century, to be read by millions of people who don't happen to be what Thomas Mann called "early Christians": devoted worshippers of literature. I would envy Joe that, were I the envying sort; in any case, I vigorously applaud.

Second, as anybody who lived through the American 1960s knows, that same novel played a certain role in the history of that decade, when Heller's Yossarian became a tutelary saint of the anti-Vietnam-war movement. I suspect that even those of us who have no *a priori* ambition to change the world with our art would be secretly pleased to see reality give way a little bit in the face of our fiction—particularly if the effect is benign, as it certainly was in this instance. Enviable: I applaud.

And third, who among us would not be gratified, even if our writing has no effect whatever on the course of history, to live to see it have at least a small effect on language? Perhaps what I most nearly envy Joe Heller is that his term "Catch-22" has come to be used so often, by so many people of all sorts, whether they've read the novel or not, to describe a not-uncommon phenomenon that we didn't have a ready name for until Joe gave us one. We hear it used in the press, by government leaders here and abroad, by anybody caught in such a catch. Not many authors manage to put their trademark on items of our common vocabulary: I think of Charles Dickens, Lewis Carroll, George Orwell, Anne Tyler, Joseph Heller—and I applaud.

BUT OF COURSE *Catch-22* is only the *first* book in Heller's oeuvre. Five-and-a-half others have followed it[1] (*No Laughing Matter*, the non-fictional account of his struggle with Guillain-Barré Syndrome, was coauthored with his friend Speed Vogel): books with characters ranging from Henry Kissinger to God. All are comic, even the remorseless *Something Happened* and the harrowing *No Laughing Matter*. None is cheering. Heller truly *is* a Black Humorist, and his new novel, *Picture This*, may be the darkest of the lot: entertaining indeed; profoundly skeptical if not flat-out cynical in its views of history, art, and classical philosophy; extraordinary in its subject matter; and (like all of Heller's books) cunning in its architecture. Its author is passing through Baltimore just now on its behalf, and very generously agreed to stop by Johns Hopkins, which he hasn't visited for a number of years, and to say hello again to our Writing Seminars.

Welcome back, Joe.

(And au revoir, much-missed comrade.)

Remembering John Updike

Written in 2010 for the John Updike Society's memorial volume *Remembrances of John Updike*, edited by Professor Jack De Bellis of Lehigh University.

A LTHOUGH IT WAS not my privilege to be among John Updike's many close friends, he and I were amiable and mutually respectful literary acquaintances for decades. I enjoyed his so-abundant and eloquent publications, from the earliest fiction, verse, and critical essays right through the touching final items written in his life's last weeks. We regularly sent each other copies of our books as they appeared, and our several path-crossings were invariably pleasant, often memorable occasions.

Unlike his friend John Cheever, for example, who had no use for the likes of Barth, Barthelme, and other "innovative" fictioneers, Updike was able to admire writing very different from his own finely-honed suburban-American realism (from which he himself ventured boldly from time to time, as in the novel *Gertrude and Claudius* and his several books for children): He supported my election in 1974 to the American Academy of Arts and Letters, and later seconded my nomination of the brilliant (and quite innovative) novelist Richard Powers to membership in that august body. In the early 1970s, when

I was professoring for a year at Boston University, my wife and I visited John in Ipswich: We strolled the nearby beach with him (New England waters too chilly for us tidewater Marylanders!), and—he having learned that I shared his fondness for playing early recorder music—his friend Peter Davison (poetry editor of *The Atlantic Monthly*) joined us for an evening of Elizabethan trios. That same year, John visited our temporary lodgings near Radcliffe College in Cambridge for dinner with Shelly and me and the poets George and Kathy Starbuck, followed by a spirited but friendly four-against-one argument about the Vietnam war (John granted our objections to it, but supported the administration's position anyhow). And not long thereafter, when he was living in Boston between marriages, I urged him to have another go at teaching: the same visiting-professorship in fiction-writing at Boston U. that I was currently enjoying and that Donald Barthelme would take an initiatory crack at after the Barths had shifted from Boston back to Buffalo and thence to Baltimore for the remainder of our academic careers. Perhaps to his own surprise, Barthelme found the experience agreeable, and taught regularly there-after in Houston until his all-too-early death. John, however, recoiled from Academia as had I from the chilly waters of New England: In the early 1960s he'd taught one course at the Harvard Summer School, quite disliked the experience, and (except to fill in for the temporarily indisposed Cheever one day in that same B.U. visiting professorship) never taught another class.

Our relations, however, remained warm, and once I was estab-lished in the Johns Hopkins Writing Seminars I persuaded him to have a go at something else to which he'd been habitually disinclined: John resisted public readings, but when he mentioned in a letter that he was seriously hooked up with a new woman, at my invitation he brought Martha down to Baltimore for what he happily declared to be their first public outing together. He gave a delightful reading at Hopkins that included, at Shelly's and my request, his story "Lifeguard" (one of our favorites), and we guided the new couple through such standard Baltimore sight-sees as the Inner Harbor area and the haunts of Edgar Allan Poe.

Over the ensuing decades, our connection was limited mainly to holiday greetings (we always relished his Christmas-card verses), first-edition swaps (more from that so-prolific John than from this less-prolific one), and occasional Academy-nomination business. Like many another of his admirers, Shelly and I were annually chagrined at his being passed over for the Nobel Prize in Literature: an award to which he would have done as much honor as it to him. In December 2008 we were dismayed to learn of his illness in what—incredibly!—turned out to be his final Christmas-note, and were much moved some months thereafter to receive from his publisher John's final three volumes*—the new edition of his *Maples* stories, the all-new story-collection *My Father's Tears*, and his fine last verse-collection *Endpoint*, with its so-touching final poem "To Martha, on Her Birthday, After Her Cataract Operation"—together with a note from his editor, Kenneth Schneider, addressed to both of us and saying *John would have wanted you to have these.*

We thank you for that, Mr. Schneider. And even more we thank *you*, John Updike, for being the miracle that you were—and will remain.

---

*Not really 'final' after all: In 2011 we were delighted to receive a just-published copy of Updike's essay-collection called *Higher Gossip*—not least of its pleasures the sprightly cover photo of the author by Irving Penn.

The Judge's Jokes:
Souvenirs of My Father,
the After-Banquet Speaker[1]

—cornflakes in washing machine / coon hound

—"Living Bra"? What'll you feed it?

—"I never kissed the Blarney Stone; I only sat on it."

MY FATHER, WHOSE first and last names I share—John Jacob "Whitey" Barth (1894–1980), late of Cambridge, on Maryland's lower Eastern Shore—was himself the fifth of six children: four girls and two boys born in the 19th century's closing decades to a German immigrant stone-worker and his wife. Having crossed from Bremerhaven to Baltimore and found both employment and a bride in that city's populous German-immigrant community, Herman Wilhelm Barth then crossed Chesapeake Bay with her to Cambridge and established himself there in the tombstone trade. His older son and namesake, evidently the favorite, aspired beyond his father's craft: Re-crossing the Bay after high school to study sculpting at the Maryland Institute of Art, young Herman (his middle name Englished from "Wilhelm" to "William") filled his parents' East Cambridge house with plaster replicas of classical and Beaux Arts statuary, just when International Modernism was hitting the

American scene in the 1913 Armory Show. Whether he would have been influenced by that radical new aesthetic, we'll never know: In World War I he went to France with the AEF to fight his father's fatherland and died there in the great flu pandemic of 1918, two months before the Armistice.

In contrast to Herman's ambition (and parental support, presumably: the Maryland Institute is not tuition-free, and few youngsters in that place, time, and class went off to higher education), his kid brother's was less lofty. As a small boy helping out in the stone-shop, my dad was put to work polishing a flat slab of marble with a piece of railroad iron; as he would tell the story later, chuckling, to his own children, he managed to mash a finger, was sent home crying, and never went back, at least not to apprentice himself to his father's and elder brother's trade. At age 16, for reasons never explained to us (but I don't recall our ever asking for explanation), he dropped out of high school and went to work in a little candy-and-soda shop a few blocks from home, near the bustling crab-and-oyster processing plants on the creek that divided East Cambridge from the town's business section and other residential wards. In 1917 he too enlisted, and spent the war years as a ground-crewman in the Army's fledgling "Aviation Section"—but he got no farther from his home town than Langley Field in nearby Virginia, and upon his discharge was content to come back to the bereft family homestead (where he was now the Only Son) and his former employment.

In which, unglamorous as it was compared to Art, he did well—and who knows whether his sadly short-lived brother would have scored as a sculptor or wound up carving tombstones like his dad? Having mastered as a teenager the ins and outs of the candy and soda-fountain business, in his and the century's twenties my father set up shop for himself, first as a wholesaler (his earliest printed stationery, now browned and crisped with age, is headed JOHN J. BARTH, *Wholesale High Grade Chocolates and Specialties, Cambridge, Md*) and soon after as a retail shopkeeper in his own soda-fountain/lunchroom/candy-store "uptown" on Race Street, the town's main business section. His later letterheads read WHITEY'S, *John J. Barth, Cambridge, Md*, and in time JOHN J. BARTH, *Fine Candy Since 1922, Cambridge, Md*. In addition to Whitman's Chocolates and assorted other candies, the store featured Dolley Madison ice cream, sundaes and sodas (no bottled drinks), cold sandwiches made at the counter (he didn't like cooking-odors on the premises), and soups made at home by our mom and reheated at the store on a small backroom stove. But the showcases of candy (mainly chocolate) were his chief interest: The business's name was Whitey's Candyland, but everybody called it simply Whitey's.

Whitey's? On *Race* Street? In the then totally segregated South?

Race Street, Cambridge MD, 1936, with Whitey's sign near center.

We'll get to that—though I don't recall our ever asking whence the nickname, either, which he carried from boyhood. Meanwhile it's 1922: The young shopkeeper meets and marries a local young milliner working in a hat-shop a few doors down from the Candyland; they move into a two-story white clapboard house next door to his parents, one block from the broad Choptank River and the hospital where over the next several years their children will be born, and where nearly 60 years later, still a resident of that house, at age 85 he'll breathe his last. Through the intervening half-dozen decades, despite a youthful sinus infection that in those pre-antibiotic days left him severely hearing-impaired for the rest of his life, he thrived in the small town and marsh-rich rural county that he had no interest in leaving (told by his doctor that the only hope for relief from his chronic sinusitis was a less humid climate, Dad replied that he'd rather be sick on the Eastern Shore than healthy anywhere else). He was gregarious, outgoing, and community-spirited: In addition to storekeeping from morning till night six days a week every week of the year, he served as an elected judge of the Dorchester County Orphans Court every Tuesday afternoon for a record-breaking 44 years, was a devoted member of the town's volunteer fire company as well as an organizer of similar companies in the county's smaller towns, and an American Legionnaire who not only marched with his fellow veterans in Cambridge's annual Armistice Day parade but became the chief organizer of those elaborate events. By comparison to his life, mine (literary and academic) seems almost reclusively detached, its radius much wider but its roots—in serial dwelling-places from Pennsylvania and upstate New York to Maryland and southwest Florida—less deep.

Because those volunteer fire companies, understandably, are tightly bonded social clubs as well as indispensable community-service outfits, in addition to their weekly meetings they have members-only banquets and fund-raising public barbecues and ham-and-oyster suppers. It was as the jocular after-dinner speaker at those banquets, in a dozen-plus venues around the county—his own beloved Rescue Fire Company and those others he'd helped organize—that Judge Whitey came into his own as an entertainer, in demand year after year: never a clown, but a humorist locally renowned for his joke-telling from at least the early 1940s until his death in February 1980, just a month before his scheduled appearance at the RFC's 37th Annual Memorial Banquet.

Rescue Fire Company, Cambridge, MD, 1938.

—*Doctor to patient: Your check came back. Patient: So did my arthritis.*

—*honeybee & horsefly / turnip in mouth / chicken with legs crossed / shad roe*

My siblings and I, alas, never got to see our father do his number. Nor did he often tell jokes at home, where our conversation was typically good-humored but, owing at least in part to his deafness, seldom extended or really "personal": witness those unasked questions about his nickname and his dropping out of high school. It was only as we went through his effects post mortem, in our middle age, that I found two small notebooks of handwritten joke-cues and 14 age-browned Whitey's Candyland envelopes containing more of the same on notepad-sized separate sheets and bearing the month and day, but seldom the year, of an upcoming gig and its location: *C'bge RFC, Taylors Island, Hoopers Island, Church Creek, Lakes & Straits, Neck District.* Some held a single sheet of perhaps nine cues; others five or six sheets with as many as 45 cues, occasionally annotated with a check, an X, or the word *used.* At times, evidently, he would "go around the table," naming his firehouse comrades and addressing a joke to each (name followed by cue). In all, more than 200 jokes, fewer than half of them written out in full. While free of profanity, about three-quarters of them by my rough count are more or less ribald teasings of romance, courtship, marriage, infidelity, divorce, male and female anatomy, or some other aspect of sex (though a man of impeccable virtue, the Judge was not strait-laced):

—*"Am I the first man to sleep with you?" "If you doze off, you will be."*

—*Mouse gets pregnant in A&P; didn't know about Safeway.*

—*Girdle: keeps stomach in, boys out.*

—*2 old maids: 1 trying to diet, 1 dying to try it.*

About one in 10 is "ethnic" or otherwise minority-directed, their targets most often African-American (always by cue only, for some reason)

—*cats on fence; colored woman*

—*baptize darkie; last thing remembered*

—*canning house; sleep with darkie*

but also including Native Americans (*Indian says, "Chance." Woman: "I thought all Indians said 'How.'" Indian: "I know how; just want chance."*), Chinese (*Chinaman, food, flowers*)[?], Scots (*Scotsman comes to U.S.; has 1st baby; wants to tell folks back home. Cablegram = 4 words for $8; he writes "Mother's features, father's fixtures."*), Jews (*Jewish couple, Abe & Becky, married 50 years, in bed*), and gays (*homosexuals & hemorrhoids = queers & rears = odds & ends*). The rest tease more "neutral" targets: doctors, judges, mechanics, farmers, animals, kids and parents, mothers-in-law. Offensive as one may find those "darkie" jokes in particular— told, one presumes, prior to the Cambridge civil rights riots of the late 1960s, with its attendant sit-ins of Whitey's Candyland (an obvious target) and other segregated businesses—it's worth remembering that they're an extension of the blackface minstrel, *Amos 'n' Andy* tradition popular among many blacks as well as whites from the 19th century to the mid-20th, and that unlike most other Southern eateries, Whitey's risked offending its white customers by serving blacks at least at the candy showcases and the soda fountain, as long as they didn't presume to sit down: the aptly named "Vertical Negro" policy, easy to tsk at from this remove, but considered liberal in that place and time.

Where did all those jokes come from? Nowadays one's e-mail is awash with them, forwarded by friends from friends of their friends: a high-speed electronic Oral Tradition. Back then, my guess is that they came from bantering exchanges with friends and customers, from vaudeville acts (even small towns like Cambridge had live vaudeville into the 1930s: touring road companies and the celebrated Adams Floating Theatre), from radio shows like the aforementioned *Amos 'n' Andy*, and perhaps from the odd joke book in the Candyland's magazine rack or paperback bookshelf. Not impossibly Dad made up a few of them himself; if so, it's a talent that his son (like him, the younger of two) didn't inherit. (While I'm sometimes described as a comic novelist, the only joke that I can recall ever having invented I literally dreamed up, and was surprised not only to remember upon waking but to find not unamusing: *Restaurant waiter serves wine in glass with stem but no base. "How'm I supposed to set this glass down while I eat?" "Sorry, sir: We don't serve customers who can't hold their liquor."*)

More to the point, what *about* all these jokes and joke-cues? Their most-often-fragmentary nature—*prodigal son / fish heads /*

rabbit sausage—reminds me not only that I never got to see and hear the fellow do this particular one of the numerous things that he evidently did well indeed, but that in this as in who knows how many other ways I never got to *know* him: that to a greater or lesser extent our knowledge even of close kin is often fragmentary, inferred like a fossil skeleton or an ancient vase from whatever always-limited experience and shards of memory we have of them. For better as well as worse, perhaps: Just as well *not* to know all those "darkie" jokes, although in the context of that time and place they'd have been as inoffensively entertaining, at least to his all-white audience, as a burnt-corked Al Jolson singing "Mammy." All the same, leafing through those time-browned, age-crisped cue sheets, like looking at his and Mother's photographs on my bookshelves (younger then than their son is now) or his Orphans Court name plaque on the shelf above my word processor—*John J. Barth, Chief Judge*—inevitably makes me think, as the old Irish song laments, "Johnny, we hardly knew ye!"

Nor you me, Dad, really; nor most of us one another, finally, beyond what souvenirs we've been given to imagine from, and what imagination we can bring to them:

—*nude sunbather on skylight over dining room*

—*birth control; shower / ice: 400 lbs*

—*Better try a different speaker next time: Even a rooster gets tired of chicken every night.*

Judge John J. "Whitey" Barth, circa 1950.

Eulogy For Jill

A final farewell—this one for Joan Derr Barth Corkran (May 27, 1930–August 7, 2009): my twin sibling Jill. Her German middle name was the maiden surname of our paternal grandmother, Anna Derr; my own Scotch-Irish middle name (Simmons) was our maternal grandma's married name (we kids never knew "Mommy Nora's" husband, nor to this day do I know what her maiden name was). Our nicknames—see below—were laid on us before our official given names, John and Joan. Given the circumstance of being a twin born under the zodiacal sign of Gemini and named after a nursery rhyme, it's to be expected that the motif of twins, doubles, alter egos, and the like may be found here and there in my fiction.

F OR THE FIRST nine months of our joint existence, my twin sister and I were womb-mates. Conceived just before the Stock Market Crash of 1929 and waiting to be born in the first dark spring of the Great Depression of the 1930s, we were blissfully unaware of everything except, I suppose, each other's presence in that warm dark comfortable space. Even that double presence was somewhat more than our mother and her doctor were aware of in those days before ultrasound scans: Having delivered her of a healthy baby girl and thinking both his and her labors done, the doc checked out—and to

all hands' surprise, an hour and twenty minutes later an also-healthy
baby boy followed, delivered by whoever happened to be on call.

Sister first, brother second: I'll come back to that.

When the news was announced to our three-year-older brother
Bill that he was no longer the family's only child, he gamely replied,
"Now we have a Jack and Jill!"—and much followed from that.
Having been *womb*-mates, for the next ten or twelve years my twin
sister and I were *room*mates (in twin beds, appropriately) and though
less genetically close than identical twins—indeed, no closer genetically than any other pair of siblings—I'd say we were otherwise about
as close as non-Siamese twins can be. From kindergarten through elementary school in Cambridge, on Maryland's Eastern Shore, we attended the same classes, had the same friends, and were each other's
best friend. We endured plenty of teasing from classmates about the
"Jack and Jill" thing (including some memorably naughty versions
of the nursery rhyme), but got used to it. When we took piano lessons, our teacher inevitably assigned us duets, wherein Jill always
played the upper-keyboard melody part (*Primo*, considered appropriate for the girl, I guess), and Jack played *Secondo*, the lower-octave
harmony-and-counterpoint part. Fine by me: It felt more manly down
there in the bass clef.

By high school, of course, our hormones had kicked in and we'd
begun to go our ever-more-separate ways: separate bedrooms, friends,
and high-school curricula. But we remained in close harmony both
literal and figurative. We organized a successful little jazz group, for
example, called the Swingtette—Ms. Primo on piano, Mr. Secondo
on drums, and a couple of our friends on sax and trombone—and
played regular Saturday-night dances at the Cambridge Country Club
through our junior and senior years. After graduation, however, our

paths diverged indeed: Jack crossed the Bay to university, and for the next forty years returned to Cambridge and the Eastern Shore only to visit; Jill went to business school in Wilmington, returned to work in a bank in Cambridge, met and married one of her customers (Bob Corkran of nearby Hurlock), and happily went into the accounting business with him there.

Over the ensuing decades, Jack's life had the wider radius, but Jill's had much deeper roots: The Corkrans seldom left the Eastern Shore even on vacation, but they maintained warm connections with old friends, enjoyed golf games, crab feasts, weekend evenings at the American Legion hall, and raising their daughter Jo. Jill went from being named the Delmarva Poultry Festival's "Chicken of Tomorrow" back in her teens to becoming Hurlock's First Lady when her husband was elected mayor of that small town. And when Bob was sadly and prematurely taken from her by cancer while only in his fifties, Jill soldiered on: She taught my non-Maryland wife Shelly how to cook a softcrab and roast a goose; she presided over her daughter's wedding and spoke fondly of her son-in-law; she oversaw end-of-life care and funeral arrangements for our parents and other elderly relatives (with a little help from her far-flung brothers and their wives, but Jill carried most of the load, and carried it ably indeed); she enjoyed her granddaughter's talents and triumphs—and then bravely and cheerfully, when the time came, she made her own move from her house in Preston (not far from Hurlock and Cambridge) to a "continuing care" establishment in also-nearby Easton, where she lived out her final life-chapters, her accountant daughter presiding over her as Jill had done for *her* parents.

My closing, warmest memory of my twin is from not long after she made that move. In the summer of 2002, the Cambridge High

School Class of 1947 celebrated its 55th reunion with a sunset cruise aboard a paddlewheel tour-boat from Suicide Bridge (yup, that's its name), up near Preston, down the Choptank River to Cambridge and back, with dinner and dancing to live music. Much as my wife and my sister enjoyed each other's company, Shelly had other commitments that day, and so I picked up Jill at her assisted-living place and we two enjoyed a lovely evening together with old school chums, reminiscing about (among other things) our long-ago Swingtette jazz combo. The high point of that evening, for me, was when one of those good buddies, whom I'd reminded that our group's theme-song had been the smooth old 1930s ballad called *Moonglow*, passed that info along to the band without telling us. Next thing we knew, they were playing it for us—first time I'd heard it in maybe half a century! My old womb-mate and I set down our wineglasses and danced—not for the first time, certainly, but for the first time in too long a time, and for the last time, alas.

I can hear it now:

It must have been moonglow,
Way up in the blue. . . .

Moonglow it was, Jill, on that moonlit river, our tidal birth-water—and moonglow it remains. Your old ex-wombmate and ex-roommate is in no hurry to become your *tomb*mate; but it's poetically appropriate, I suppose, for Ms. Primo to lead the way in our tale's last chapter, as she did in its first.

Rest in peace, dear Sis.

Notes

Foreword

1. New York: Putnam, 1984.

2. Boston: Little, Brown, 1995.

3. See "Keats's Fears, Etc.", the lead-off piece in this collection.

4. *The Development: 9 Stories* (Boston: Houghton Mifflin Harcourt, 2008).

5. Literally (which is to say, figuratively) "being breathed into again": the CPR of artists in any medium.

Keats's Fears, Etc.

1. As of 1997; another thousand-plus over the decade since. Scribble scribble scribble!

2. As of the date of this essay: Miller died in 2005.

State of the Art

1. xx:2, Spring 1996

2. Now defunct, alas.

3. See the essay "The Inkstained Thumb," to follow.

4. Indeed, novelists such as Richard Powers and my former Hopkins coachee Vickram Chandra use everything from Microsoft Excel spreadsheets and Project logistics programs to voice-recognition software for organizing and composing their novels: See Rachel Donadio's essay "Get With the Program," *New York Times Book Review*, June 10, 2007.

5. See "The Accidental Mentor," my 80th-birthday tribute to him, in the latter section of this volume.

6. For more on "Serial," see the essay "'In the Beginning, Once Upon a Time, It Was a Dark and Stormy Night'" farther on in this collection.

7. Coover himself, though a professor of e-lit, inclines to the p-variety for his own abundant and lively productions.

Two More Forewords

1. The five novels were *The Floating Opera* and *The End of the Road* (first published in 1956 and 1958, respectively, but reprinted in a single volume), *The Sot-Weed Factor* (1960), *Giles Goat-Boy* (1965), and *Lost in the Funhouse* (1968).

2. *Thor Tool Company v. Commissioner of Internal Revenue, 439 U.S. 522.*

3. In his knowledgeable and perceptive *Reader's Guide to Barthbooks* (Westport, CT: Greenwood, 1993).

4. The War of 1812, which to us children of the Chesapeake ranks as high as the Revolutionary War because so much of it was fought in our home waters, was even at the time often called the Second American Revolution. It is this second, more than the first, that figures in the historical portions of *LETTERS*. And those who lived through the American High Sixties will remember the apocalyptic air of "Revolution now!" that hung like tear gas over our university campuses especially.

"In the Beginning"

1. New York: Anchor, 1996.

2. Subsequently published as *Genesis: A Living Conversation* (New York: Doubleday, 1996).

3. More precisely, I'm told, it means "In the beginning *of*." Its deployment sans object in Genesis 1:1 is linguistically odd enough so that disagreement among Biblical commentators begins, appropriately, with this initial word of scripture. See, e.g., Robert D. Sacks, *A Commentary on the Book of Genesis* (Lewiston/Queenston/Lampeter: Mellen Press, 1990), pp. 2–3.

4. In fact, some such English adverb as *Beginningly* or *Originally* would be the formal-metaphoric equivalent of *Bereshith*. But *beginningly*, alas, is an over-selfconscious coinage, and *originally* is both forceless and inexact, implying some subsequent re-creation, as in "Originally the story began here, but later . . ." et cetera. An analogous problem faces English translators of Marcel Proust's *À la recherche du temps perdu*: That monumental novel about time opens with the word *Longtemps*, famously rendered and vitiated by C. K. Scott Moncrieff as "For a long time," which moves the key word to fourth place. The poet Richard Howard's version makes an ingenious restoration: "Time was . . ." (in the sense "There was a time when . . ."). See

the essay "'In the Beginning, Once Upon a Time, It Was a Dark and Stormy Night,'" farther on in this volume.

5. E.g., separation of the four elemental forces, prodigious inflation, reciprocal but not quite equal annihilation of subatomic particles and antiparticles, "quark confinement," and the commencement of nucleosynthesis, all within the initial second of Planck Time.

6. Some commentators judiciously prefer "the *sky* and the earth," inasmuch as the theological connotations of *heaven* play no part in this part of the creation-story. See Sacks, p. 4.

7. A history which itself rebegins in Chapter Five—"This is the book of the generations of Man," et cetera—with its recapitulation of Man's creation on Day Six of Chapter One and again in Verse Seven of Chapter Three.

8. Act Three—when, as Chekhov reminds us, all the pistols hung on the wall in Act One must be duly fired—will not be addressed in this essay: Armageddon, Judgment Day, the end of the created world in the Big Crunch of Apocalypse.

9. Notably the Weak, the Strong, and the Participatory, more or less advocated by such distinguished physicists as, respectively, Brandon Carter, Stephen Hawking, and John A. Wheeler.

10. Joseph Heller declares that he begins his novels by writing their last chapter first, after which he invents a sequence of events that necessitates that ending. (See the essay "'All Trees Are Oak Trees . . . ,'" farther on in this collection.)

11. Concerning biological evolution, for example, as well as human history, Stephen Jay Gould remarks, "History can be explained, with satisfying rigor if evidence be adequate, after a sequence of events unfolds, but it cannot be predicted with any precision beforehand" ("The Evolution of Life on Earth," *Scientific American*, October 1994).

12. E.g. Dante's out-Virgiling of Virgil in Canto IV of the *Inferno*, where he writes of himself being saluted in Limbo by the shades of *both* Homer and Virgil (not to mention Horace, Ovid, and Lucan), who welcome him as their peer.

13. Aeneas sometimes strays from destiny's path, as in his Carthaginian interlude with Queen Dido (Virgil's dutiful remake of Odysseus's long tryst with Calypso), but Mother Venus soon enough corrects his course.

14. A passage that never fails to remind me, profanely but respectfully, of Yeats's awed question in *Leda and the Swan*: "A shudder in the loins engenders there / The broken wall, the burning roof and tower / And Agamemnon

dead. . . . / Did she put on his knowledge with his power . . . ?" On
Matthew's evidence, the son, if not the mother, did.

15. As instanced by Virgil and Dante, the vocation of artisthood bears some
    analogy to those of mythic-herohood and messiahship—conspicuously so
    for the Romantics and the great early Modernists, with their characteristic
    conception of the artist as hero (one recalls James Joyce's Stephen Dedalus,
    originally named Stephen Hero, vowing to "forge, in the smithy of my
    soul, the uncreated conscience of my race"), more modestly so even for
    Postmoderns. In at least some cases, the present author's included, one's
    apprentice sense of calling may be far from clear even to oneself, and the
    "Jesus Paradox" may take on difficult additional dimensions, though sel-
    dom with such high stakes as attend the callings of mythic heroes and mes-
    siahs. One may be uncertain of both one's vocation and one's talent for it,
    or confident of one of those but not the other, or confident of both but mis-
    taken, or *doubtful* of both but mistaken, or correct on one or both counts.
    In the happiest case, one comes to have reasonable faith in both calling and
    gift and at least some "objective" confirmation that that faith is not alto-
    gether misplaced. But "real, non-scripted life" is slippery terrain, in which
    templates and prophecies are ill-defined, elastic, arguable, and verdicts are
    forever subject to reversal. One crosses one's fingers, invokes one's muse,
    and does one's best.

How it Was, Maybe

1. It's the genre's notorious tendency to substitute period color, historical information, and melodrama for other novelistic values.

2. A totally fabricated account of the doughty Captain's defloration of that
   thitherto impregnable maiden. But many scholars question Smith's own account of his rescue by Pocahontas.

3. In fact, Powhatan's people stream-bathed almost daily, and found the
   English to be foul-smelling.

4. Indeed, in a second edition of the satire, published in Annapolis in 1731,
   Cooke quite de-fangs the sot-weed factor's closing curse:

   . . . may that Land where Hospitality
   Is every Planter's darling Quality,
   Be by each Trader kindly us'd,
   And may no Trader be abus'd;
   Thus each of them will deal with Pleasure,
   And each increase the other's Treasure.
   I confess my preference for the original ending.

Further Questions?

1. Ann Arbor: University of Michigan Press, 2000.

2. See the memoir "The Judge's Jokes," farther on in this volume.

3. A decade later, it exceeds 500.

4. Both figures proportionately higher a decade later, like the number of degree-granting creative writing programs in American colleges.

5. See my essay "It's a Long Story," in *The Friday Book*.

6. For more on these tools, see "The Inkstained Thumb," farther on in this collection.

7. Enrique García Diez, late of the University of Valencia.

8. "Night-Sea Journey," in *Lost in the Funhouse*.

9. Itself now a dated question in the age of DVDs, themselves perhaps out-dated in turn by technologies that more with-it folk than my wife and I are acquainted with.

10. See "The State of the Art," earlier in this volume.

11. See "Eulogy for Jill," at this volume's close.

12. Or to the essay following this one: "Incremental Perturbation."

13. Further elaborated in "Incremental Perturbation."

14. Boston: Little, Brown, 1991.

Incremental Perturbation

1. *Creating Fiction,* ed. Checkoway (Cincinnati: Story Press, 1999).

2. More typically, however, the productions of these two writers, unconventional as may be their material and manner, are rigorously conventional in their dramaturgy. Kafka's "Memoirs of the Kalda Railroad" and Barthelme's "Bone Bubbles" are examples of non-dramatic extended metaphors; "A Hunger Artist," "The Country Doctor," "The Indian Rising," "Me and Miss Mandible," and most of the rest are classically constructed stories.

3. E.g., Samuel Beckett's 35-second drama *Breath*: Curtain opens on stage empty except for scattered rubbish. Voice-off sound of single human cry. Voice-off sound of single long inhalation and exhalation of breath, ac-companied by brightening and then dimming of stage-lights. Again the cry. Curtain closes.

"The Parallels!"

1. I pause immediately here to insert a footnoted but emphatically grateful hurrah to Mr. Weaver for bringing so many excellent modern Italian writers to us language-challenged Americans. There was a time, back in the 1950s and '60s, when I suspected that the French New Novel might have been invented in New York City by the poet Richard Howard, inasmuch as most of what I knew of Alain Robbe-Grillet and company was in Mr. Howard's translations. Similarly, most of what I know of such splendid writers as Elsa Morante, Carlo Emilio Gadda, Italo Calvino, and Umberto Eco I know in William Weaver's English. If I hadn't had the good fortune to interrogate a couple of these authors personally in the matter, I might well suspect Mr. Weaver of having invented Italian Postmodernist fiction—not that his having Englished it isn't a sufficiently admirable achievement. *Molto grazie*, William Weaver!

2. Collected in *The Friday Book*.

3. The unwritten sixth, to be called "Consistency," was to have dealt with Samuel Beckett and with Melville's Bartleby the Scrivener. Esther Calvino's foreword reports her husband's remark that he had material enough for *eight* Norton lectures, of which the last was to have been on Beginnings and Endings (*"Sul cominciare e sul finire"*). There is no mention of what the seventh lecture might have addressed.

4. "Don't Count on It: A Note on the Number of *The 1001 Nights*," in *The Friday Book*; see also "The Morning After" in this volume.

5. Included in his posthumously published *The Road to San Giovanni* (New York: Pantheon, 1993).

6. Indeed, in the "Autobiographical Essay" he declares, "In the course of a life devoted chiefly to books, I have read but few novels, and in most cases only a sense of duty enabled me to find my way to their last page."

7. More knowledgeable participants than myself in the University of California at Davis Calvinofest subsequently assured me that they did in fact meet, at least once, in Rome, near the end of Borges's life, and supplied me with a handsome photograph of the pair chatting over parallel cups of coffee in the Hotel Excelsior di Roma.

My Faulkner

1. Ed. Duvall and Abadie (Jackson: University Press of Mississippi, 1999).

2. The novel *Coming Soon!!!* (Boston: Houghton Mifflin, 2001).

3. See the essay "Ad Lib Libraries and the Coastline Measurement Problem," in *Further Fridays*.

4. E.g., in the aforementioned "Ad Lib Libraries" and the essay "*The Ocean of Story*" in *Further Fridays*; likewise in "The Morning After," farther on in this volume.

5. In the Foreword to the Doubleday Anchor edition of *The Floating Opera* and *The End of the Road*, reprinted in *Further Fridays*.

¿Cien Años de Qué?

1. *Literatura de las Américas 1898–1998* (León: Universidad de León, Secretariado de Publicaciones, 2000).

2. The influential Spanish "Generation of [18]98" included, among other notable literary figures, Pio Baroja, Antonio Machado, and Miguel de Unamuno.

3. The late-20th-century efflorescence of Latin-American literature, of which more presently.

4. Alas, the question is now moot: Federman died in 2009.

5. New York: HarperFlamingo, 1998.

6. Already quoted in the preceding essay, "My Faulkner."

A Window at the Pratt

1. And alas, died in 2009 without ever receiving: See my tribute to Updike farther along in this volume.

2. Indeed, in the years since, a couple of the Kerr Prize winners have placed items for publication—and the value of the award has increased to more than $60,000.

On Readings

1. See the preceding Friday-piece, "A Window at the Pratt."

2. The afore-referred-to *Coming Soon!!!*, which came too late (2001) for the turn of the millennium.

3. See "The Passion Artist," in the *Tributes and Memoria* section of this volume; likewise my tributes to Heller and Updike.

The End of the Word As We've Known It?

1. *When Prophecy Fails*, by Leon Festinger, Henry Riechen, and Stanley Schachter (Minneapolis: U. Minnesota Press, 1956).

2. "Largely," but by no means entirely—as witness the international public health alarm in 2007 over an Atlanta lawyer's managing to evade quarantine and make transatlantic flights despite having been diagnosed with drug-resistant TB.

3. The most elegant example of the quasi-electronic that I've seen to date is the admirable novel *Love in a Dead Language*, by Lee Siegel (University of Chicago Press, 1999), with its elaborately simulated "windows" and other computerish trappings.

4. See the essay "Incremental Perturbation."

5. Also from "The State of the Art."

6. Michael Korda, in "Out of Print," *Harper's*, April 2001.

"I've Lost My Place!"

1. Quoted in Thomas Flanagan's review-essay "Western Star," in *The New York Review of Books*, November 29, 2001.

The Place of "Place" in Fiction

1. Subsequently published in the *Hartford Courant* under the title "An Author's Sense of Place."

2. In his essay "The Argentine Writer and Tradition."

Liberal Education

1. Not mentioned in what follows (because I judged it inappropriate to the occasion) is my *chief* reservation about the admirable St. John's curriculum: its deployment of "tutors" in seminar-size discussion groups instead of (as at most good universities) eminent professorial authorities in a lecture-hall setting. The usual objection to the latter is that the students do more listening and note-taking than discussing; but we Hopkins undergrads did plenty of arguing and discussing in post-lecture Q&As as well as among ourselves and in follow-up seminars with Graduate Assistants—and our wrestlings with the texts were immeasurably illuminated by what we'd heard from those distinguished professors.

The Relevance of Irrelevance

1. *"La rilevanza dell'irrilevanza: Scribere da americani."* And the State Department's diplomatic phrase "explicit commentary on the events of September 11" can itself be translated into "explicit criticism of the George W. Bush presidency."

2. In 2003, Coetzee was quite deservedly awarded the Nobel Prize for Literature, perhaps in part because of his work's political as well as literary merits—whereas the at least equally deserving Borges and Nabokov (like Kafka, Joyce, Proust, and many another first-magnitude literary star) were never laurelled with that prize, to which they would have done more honor than it could imaginably do them.

3. For more on Scheherazade, see "The Morning After," later in this collection.

4. Whose trespasses against the civil liberties of U.S. citizens were much further empowered by the ill-named and hastily passed "Patriot Act" of October 2001, on the heels of the 9/11 bombings.

"All Trees Are Oak Trees . . ."

1. First delivered in 2003 at my alma mater, this talk was published the following year in *Poets & Writers Magazine.*

2. Already quoted in the preceding essay, "The Relevance of Irrelevance."

The Inkstained Thumb

1. Cincinnati: Writers Digest Press, 2006.

I.

1. Ed. Molly McQuade (Louisville, KY: Sarabande Books, 2009).

2. "We *are* the stories that we tell ourselves and others about who we are," declares Dennett in his treatise *Consciousness Explained* (Boston: Little, Brown & Co., 1991).

"In the Beginning, Once Upon a Time, It Was a Dark and Stormy Night"

1. More on Ms. Scheherazade in the following essay, "The Morning After."

2. For more on Genesis, see "'In The Beginning,'" *supra.*

3. And for more on this famous dictum of Horace's, see "Incremental Perturbation," also *supra*.

The Morning After

1. See the essay "Don't Count On It: A Note on the Number of *The 1001 Nights*," in *The Friday Book*.

It Can Be Arranged

1. Some decades later, when I returned to Hopkins as a professor and checked my old library-stack haunts, I was relieved to find that some scoundrel had stolen that thesis: Its title refers to the poisoned garment that killed Heracles.

2. Boston: Little, Brown & Co, 1995.

Introduction to *Not-Knowing*

1. The first, "The Thinking Man's Minimalist: Honoring Barthelme," appeared in *The New York Times Book Review* of September 3, 1989, just a few weeks after his death; the latest—"By Barthelme Beguiled," introducing two previously unpublished DB stories—in the October 2007 inaugural issue of the new *Hopkins Review*.

2. *Not-Knowing*, ed. Kim Herzinger (New York: Random House, 1997).

3. Some other Usual Suspects were Robert Coover, William Gaddis, William H. Gass, John Hawkes, and Thomas Pynchon.

4. For my own take on this subject, see the essay "Historical Fiction, Fictitious History, and Chesapeake Bay Blue Crabs, or, About Aboutness," in *The Friday Book*.

The Passion Artist

1. *NYTBR*, June 21, 1998.

2. New York: New Directions, 1984.

3. From MacLeish's poem "Not Marble Nor the Gilded Monuments":

   . . . men shall remember your name as long

   As lips move or breath is spent or the iron of English

   Rings from a tongue. . . .

The Accidental Mentor

1. *Leslie Fiedler and American Culture,* ed. Kellman & Malin (U. Delaware Press, 2003).

2. True at the time: Fiedler died in Buffalo, NY, on January 29, 2003.

3. Cited earlier in this volume, in "The State of the Art," and happily still an overstatement. See my essay "Inconclusion: The Novel in the Next Century," in *Further Fridays.*

4. Subtitled *Class Culture and Mass Society* (New York: Simon & Schuster, 1982).

"As Sinuous and Tough as Ivy"

1. First published in *Review of Contemporary Fiction*, Fall 2004.

The Last Introduction

1. As of 10/04/88, when this introduction was first delivered. Two more volumes were to come: the novel *Closing Time* in 1994 and the memoir *Now and Then* in 1998.

The Judge's Jokes

1. First published in *The American Scholar* 76:2, Spring 2007.